THE DECEIVED

INGANNATI COMEDIA

DE GLI INTRONATI RECI
TATA NE GIVOCHI PV
BLICI DEL CARNO=
VALE IN SIENA.

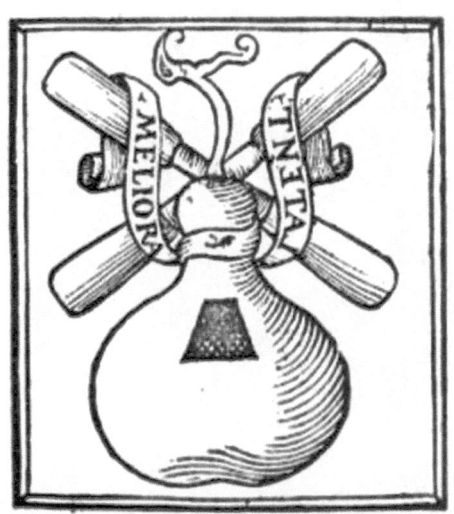

THE DECEIVED

by
The Intronati of Siena

A New English Translation of *Gl'Ingannati*
in a Dual-Language Edition
by
Donald Beecher
and
Massimo Ciavolella

Italica Press
New York
2018

Copyright © 2017 Donald Beecher
and Massimo Ciavolella

ITALICA PRESS RENAISSANCE AND MODERN PLAYS SERIES

ITALICA PRESS, INC.
595 MAIN STREET
NEW YORK, NEW YORK 10044

All rights reserved. No part of this publication may be reproduced, stored in a retrieval system, or transmitted, in any form or by any means, electronic, mechanical, photocopying, recording, or otherwise, without prior permission of Italica Press. For permission to reproduce selected portions for courses, please contact the Press at
inquiries@italicapress.com.

LIBRARY OF CONGRESS CATALOGING-IN-PUBLICATION DATA
Names: Beecher, Donald, translator. | Ciavolella, Massimo, 1942- translator. | Accademia senese degli intronati.
Title: The deceived : a new English translation of Gl'Ingannati in a dual-language edition / The Accademia degli Intronati of Siena ; translated with introduction and notes by Donald Beecher and Massimo Ciavolella.
Other titles: Ingannati. English
Description: New York : Italica Press, 2018. | Series: Italica Press Renaissance and modern plays series | Includes bibliographical references.
Identifiers: LCCN 2017038124 (print) | LCCN 2017046645 (ebook) | ISBN 9781599103310 (E-Book) | ISBN 9781599103297 (hardcover : alk. paper) | ISBN 9781599103303 (pbk. : alk. paper)
Subjects: LCSH: Ingannati. | Italian drama--To 1700. | Italian drama--Italy--Siena.
Classification: LCC PQ4561.A1 (ebook) | LCC PQ4561.A1 I616 2018 (print) | DDC
852/.3--dc23
LC record available at https://lccn.loc.gov/2017038124

Cover art: Pier Antonio degli Abbati or da Modena, wood intarsia, Padova, c.1475.

FOR A COMPLETE LIST OF TITLES IN
RENAISSANCE AND MODERN PLAYS
VISIT OUR WEB SITE AT
HTTP://WWW.ITALICAPRESS.COM/INDEX130.HTML

About the Translators

DONALD BEECHER is the Chancellor's Professor in the Department of English at Carleton University in Canada, where he specializes in the literature of the sixteenth and seventeenth centuries. His research and teaching have taken him in many directions, from the history of medicine to the cognitive sciences, with salient adventures along the way into Ben Jonson studies, early English prose fiction, tricksters, folklore, early music, Italian theater, exploration and pharmacology, witchcraft, and the history of collecting. This is his eighth book-collaboration with Massimo Ciavolella, including their work on the English and French editions of Ferrand's *Treatise on Lovesickness*. Their future projects together include a new translation of tales from Boccaccio's *Decameron* for Broadview Press.

MASSIMO CIAVOLELLA studied at the Universities of Bologna, Rome, and British Columbia, where he received his Ph.D. in Classical, Medieval and Renaissance Studies. He taught at Carleton University and at the University of Toronto before becoming Director of the UCLA Centre for Medieval and Renaissance Studies. He was the co-founder and co-editor (1970–91) of *Quaderni d'italianistica*, and he is currently co-editor of the Carleton Renaissance Plays in Translation Series and of the University of Toronto Press's Lorenzo Da Ponte Italian Library. In addition to many articles, he has written and co-edited several books, including *Saturn from Antiquity to the Renaissance; Scrittori, tendenze letterarie e conflitto delle poetiche in Italia (1960–1990); Ariosto Today: Contemporary Perspectives; Culture and Authority in the Baroque;* and, among the eight co-publications he shares with Donald Beecher, two critical editions of Jacques Ferrand's *A Treatise on Lovesickness*, one in English, the other in French.

Contents

About the Translators	v
Introduction	ix
The Historical Times and Events Reflected in the Play	ix
The Intronati, Their Preoccupations and Cultural Activities	xiii
Authorship, Setting, and Plot Sources	xviii
Genre Interpretation: Deception and Representation	xxviii
Game Theory	xxxiii
Satire, Carnival, and Laughter	xxxiv
Sequels to *The Deceived*	xli
Lelia Types, Beloved, Admired, and Distrusted	xlix
Final Thoughts	li
Select Bibliography	liii
Plot Summary	lvii
The Deceived	1
Dramatis Personae & Prologue	3
Act 1	13
Act 2	51
Act 3	91
Act 4	129
Act 5	169
Notes	196

Introduction[1]

The Historical Times and Events Reflected in the Play

The small city-state of Siena in the heart of Tuscany, a day's ride on horseback to the south of Florence, had established its independence as early as the twelfth century. Until 1520, it had remained a proud and productive university city of 19,000 with its noble families, traditions of art, architecture, and civic festivities. But that political independence by then was on the verge of collapse. Florentine political aspirations had been encroaching upon Sienese territory for some time, and the political life of the entire peninsula had been much affected by the military invasions of the trained national armies of the Valois and the Hapsburgs for which the local mercenary armies of the Italian city states were no match. The Hapsburgs had been particularly active in and around Siena, and the local population itself vacillated for years between loyalty to one outside protector or another, until, in 1530, the city fell into the receivership of the Hapsburgs as a puppet state.

Alfonso Piccolomini was driven out of office and replaced by a foreigner, Lopes de Soria, who in turn brought to the city a garrison of 300 Spanish soldiers. As quasi-conquerors, they roamed the city and joined with the ranks of the common rabble in terrifying merchants, householders, and women. Such men, billeted at citizens' expense, were not easily rebuffed. Giglio, the Spanish mercenary in the play, is menacing proof as he threatens to torch Pasquella's house if she does not return his rosary (5.5).[2] In all of these events, the

---

1. Although the authors are well aware of the issues raised by this play concerning gender and father-daughter relationships, they have chosen to eliminate three chapters originally planned for this introduction: "Cross-Dressing and the Production of Gender," "Gender Anxiety and Renaissance Medicine," and "The Problem with Fathers." They refer readers to the Bibliography, below, p. LIII.
2. As in all such matters, however, closer inspection does reveal ironies, as Laurie Shepherd points out in "Siena 1531: Genesis of

Introduction

Sienese had to accept some responsibility for their ineffective and uncoordinated diplomacy and their inability to cooperate for their own protection. Giglio is created in the spirit of the erudite theater, which brought forward plot motifs and character types from the comedy of ancient Rome. His type was pioneered by Plautus in his play *Miles gloriosus* or the Braggart Soldier. This vainglorious coward is thus a stock comic character with a theatrical tradition behind him, and yet, given the political circumstances in Italy in the sixteenth century, he simultaneously profiles a contemporary pest and parasite upon the locals, no doubt contained more readily through the wish-fulfilling humiliation imposed upon him in the play than in reality.

This work is equally mindful of the social challenges of the times in the back story of Lelia, the female protagonist, who, unprotected, was captured and confined by the victorious Spanish troops following the Sack of Rome in 1527. That alone was enough to sully her reputation for life as a fallen or compromised young girl, whether she was or not. Since then, her entire life had been an exercise in dodging malicious gossip. As a victim of war, she was debased in the eyes of the world. Those harsh realities of Italian history linger quite tellingly throughout the play. When Clemenzia, her nursemaid, asks Lelia outright whether she had lost her virginity, she replies evasively that if Clemenzia wants to know, Clemenzia will have to ask the Spanish soldiers who imprisoned her (1.3). Perhaps for no other reason was her father, Virginio, willing to marry her to old Gherardo, his neighbor, who was sufficiently infatuated with the girl to take her off Virginio's hands

---

a European Heroine," *Quaderni d'italianistica*, 26.1 (2005): 3–19; 13. The entry of the Spanish was actually welcomed by the highest social echelons of the city, and the Academy of the Intronati, responsible for the creation and production of the *Gl'Ingannati* in 1531, were also commissioned for the production of a grand triumphal entertainment for the entry of Charles V into the city. Moreover, as quickly as 1531, Don Lopes was replaced by another Piccolomini, and the garrison was reduced to 100 soldiers. The soldiers, as suggested, had dealings largely with the commoners, and not with the nobility and mercantile classes.

without a dowry. Laurie Shepard goes so far as to suggest that Virginio's name was derived from Lucius Virginius, who was unable to protect his maiden daughter from soul-destroying rape by the Roman magistrate, Appius Claudius.[3] Virginia found her shame intolerable and called for revenge against her aggressor, compelling family members to keep faith with her after her suicide. Similar thoughts may have come to Lelia who likewise felt despair before meeting Flamminio, whose love for her gave her new cause to live (1.3). To the degree the comparison with Virginia is apt, to that degree Lelia's back story is darkened; it makes her desperation to recover Flamminio's love all the more poignant.

As theater historians have long recognized, Lelia gave rise to a lasting legacy of energetic, loyal, imaginative, spirited, and persistent young heroines in the theaters of Italy, France, Spain, and England. Although wounded by experience, she remains, nevertheless, a charmingly witty and innovative girl; rejected in love, she never gives up on her first love to the point of proactively entering his service in the guise of a boy. None of her successors will equal her in terms of the emotional trauma produced by the rough handling of men, but they will all have her ingenious turn of mind and independence of spirit — representing for many of her sex a champion of emancipation. Yet her suppressed suffering and feelings of vulnerability are sometimes easy to miss in a play that otherwise abounds in scenes of buffoonery and badinage, particularly among the secondary characters, befitting the spirit of the Carnival season for which it was conceived — or at least that provided the context for its first production. Which ethos prevails — the scars of war or the escapist frivolity of Carnival? They move in parallel throughout the play. So, is this play a study in tragi-comic mode, psychologically delicate and nuanced in matters of gender, or a carnivalesque romp of playful inversions, phallic allusions, and harmless deceits down to a rousing romantic closure? Deciding on the prevailing ethos of the play is good critical work.

---

3. "Siena 1531," 11.

Introduction

That Sack was never far from Italian minds — a time when citizens were robbed, slain, raped, and abducted — a time when nothing was held sacred. Even the physical damage to the city of Rome was enormous. In this turmoil, families were separated and identities were temporarily lost while the capital was looted and violated for months on end by the unpaid Spanish and German soldiers. Those momentous events predate the action represented on stage by two years.

During that intervening period, Lelia escapes from Rome, enjoys Flamminio's love, suffers his abandonment, and is finally sent to live with nuns. The action of the play begins just after Lelia has escaped from the convent in male disguise and has managed to find a place in Flamminio's household as his page. For this role she takes the name Fabio and, under that identity, finds herself the beloved of Isabella, the woman she is sent to court on Flamminio's behalf. Such is the signature cross-imbroglio that defines the play's tradition down to Shakespeare's *Twelfth Night*. During the months following the Sack of 1527, not only had Lelia temporarily gone missing, but her brother Fabrizio had been lost sight of altogether — a grief that Virginio, their father, suffers on a daily basis. The entire family had been victimized. But ultimately, with Lelia on the brink of exposure in her double dealings as a page, the fortuitous timing of comic plotting brings her look-alike brother home to Modena just in time to resolve, unwittingly, his sister's dilemma.

As all readers of Shakespeare's *Twelfth Night* will know, the cross-dressed heroine has circumstantial constraints placed upon the working-span of her disguise — in Lelia's case, by tattle-tale servants who have witnessed the kisses enforced upon her by Isabella. Fabrizio's homecoming is critical. It follows that, for a time, we have two Fabios, each one "a boy-girl," until circumstances clarify their respective genders to everyone in their social set. Fabrizio frees Lelia from her entanglement, while her involvement with Isabella provides him with a wife. At the same time, a family is reunited after a period of separation and loss. The reunion includes Clemenzia, who was the wet nurse and maternal figure in the lives of both Lelia and Fabrizio. In this manner, a symphony of emotions

and feelings for siblings, lovers, and their community, are brought together in a rush of emblematic events leading to deliverance, union, and general flourishing.

The conclusion is all very festive, indeed, yet harbors a tear of joy after latent sorrow. This play defines its happy ending out of fragmented societies, the violence of invaders, alienation and wandering, and families divided, together with the double romances of brother and sister achieved through error and deception. Nevertheless, its blocking circumstances and restrictive mores remind us that deep issues pertaining to the human condition, those that create the crises in the play, are never resolved, thereby aligning this play more closely with Shakespeare's so-called "problem comedies" than with his *Twelfth Night*.[4]

THE INTRONATI, THEIR PREOCCUPATIONS AND
CULTURAL ACTIVITIES

Much or little might be said about the members of the Academy of the Intronati who, at some time, wrote and later produced

---

4. Several definitions of this group of Shakespearean comedies — such plays as *Troilus and Cressida*, *Measure for Measure*, *All's Well that Ends Well*, and *The Merchant of Venice* — have been proposed, but essentially there is a consensus that these plays with happy endings nevertheless remain ethically stained by the darker social issues incorporated into their actions, issues pertaining to war, justice, the corruption of human nature, racism, and more. Arguably, *Gl'Ingannati* has claimed a critical place for itself expressly because it vacillates in our imaginations between a play of deep and potentially troubling interrogation into the human condition and a play of innocent inversions in the pursuit of life-affirming values set against a background of unthreatening folly. That perspective is central to the thinking of Catherine Scott Burriss, who looks upon all the sexual "irregularity" alluded to in the play as a source of destabilization that troubles the disorder-to-order plotting of the neoclassical theater. The play ends in a pro forma romance yet fails to regularize the society out of which it is forged. "Performing Theory: Gendered and Erotic Complications in Cinquecento Comedies, and Some English Reverberations" (Ph.D. Diss., University of California, Santa Cruz, 2006), 55.

Introduction

this play for the Sienese Carnival of 1531/32. A moment's consideration of the circumstances of its performance, together with the playful postures and carefree attitudes of the men who created it, provide a unique understanding of the play as a mirror of their spirited activities, their waggish perception of their audiences, and the jocund ambience of their social gatherings. At the time of their first assembly in 1525, there were but five who had grouped themselves around the presiding figure of Antonio Vignali. Words fail to capture their humor in the aggregate, but wit, mirth, ingenuity, humanist understanding, and competitive play might provide clues. Moulton describes them as "hyper-intellectual, religiously skeptical [and] intensely masculine."[5]

The meaning of the name they chose for themselves has multiple resonances; the "Academy of the Intronati" signifies the "stunned," the "dazed" or "bewildered," but in relation to what? For a start they were stunned into silence over political matters, given the dangers of the era, and being so stunned, they styled themselves as little more than an assembly of intellectual buffoons and inoffensive clowns with funny names and inane activities.[6] Nevertheless, they had more serious endeavors in mind. They had also joined together to promote poetry and elegance in the vernacular, as well as in Latin and Greek, to write and to read on humanist topics as preludes to their debates and discussions, and to reiterate by their activities their total detachment from matters political or military. They would think only upon philosophy, music, love, games, and poetry.[7] The motto of their academy

---

5. Antonio Vignali, *La Cazzaria / The Book of the Prick*, trans. and ed. by Ian Frederick Moulton (New York: Routledge, 2003), 1.
6. Each member of the society adopted an enigmatic or self-effacing name, such as Il Bizarro (The Weird One), or Malevolti (Pain-in-the-Face), Sodo (Hard-Headed), Scaltrito (Sharp-Witted), Importuno (The Irksome One), Moscone (The Dull-Witted One, The Suitor).
7. Michele Maylander, *Storie delle accademie d'Italia*, 5 vols. (Bologna: Lincino Capelli, 1926), 3:355. His information on the Intronati is based largely on MS. V.I.I. in the Biblioteca Comunale di Siena.

translates approximately as: "Pray, study, celebrate, do harm to no one, believe no one, and give no concern to the world."

Wit was of the essence for them, and they had a salacious side to their play as well. Their founder, Antonio Vignali, wrote a book in those same years that discussed every aspect of sexuality and the private functions of the body in a richly humorous vein. The book was entitled *Cazzaria (The Book of the Prick)*. He makes the claim that academicians unable to talk about such things are no true students of learning for lack of an essential curiosity and intellectual polish. Whatever his intent — whether to indulge in smut and ribaldry, to parody academic treatises, or even to create a hidden political allegory — his work captures the earthier side of the cultural productions and activities of the Intronati. This play is true to form, for the speaker of the Prologue comes on stage sporting a huge boner, which he offers to exhibit to the ladies in the course of presenting the play as a bid for reconciliation and sex. In that regard, the play is one giant peacock's tail, a festival of the phallus, with allusions to randy nuns craving masculine service, to the shocking size of Fabrizio's masculine parts, and to the campanile in Modena that was so erotic that recommendations were made to put a sheath over it to calm the city's libido. These are inconvenient facts for those seeking to retype the play as a sober investigation into sexual ambiguity and androgynous sensitivity. Yet those overtones are likewise present, whether in earnest or in play.

Having "stunned" minds was the insurance offered to the authorities that sedition was beyond the interests or capacities of the Intronati. Such were the times. But the name might also be glossed as "thunderstruck" in relation to the frustrations of their collective erotic ambitions. Posing as lovelorn scholars scorned by the women became a part of their social posturing, based on a full acknowledgement of the imperial power held by women to reject unwanted lovers without much fear of reprisal. Male interests might then fall back on academic strategies of flattery and courtship to win them back, making wit their medium of supplication. Alternatively, they might consolidate their intellectual capacities to intimidate the

women through a unified front of disinterest and scorn. In that mode, their opening salvo for the festive season of 1532 was a masque of ritual dismissal that they called *Il Sacrificio (The Sacrifice)*. It was all strategically calculated, though, because the insult was followed by the present play, through which they sought to repeal their unkind theatrical affront. In other words, whatever else *Gl'Ingannati* may be in critical terms, it began as part of an elaborate social joke played out dialogically between the members of a club and their ladies in the audience.

Pretending they were not receiving their due allowance of sexual attention, the men first wrote a theatrical piece in which they turn against the women, renouncing their services. The women, implicitly, get even more standoffish, thereby bringing the men to their knees. So they alter course to write about things they think the women will relish — flattery, topsy-turvy humor, being in charge of their destinies, and getting the man they want.[8] Hence, the play begins with an elaborate

---

8. We are slipping past the question that has preoccupied some readers, whether this exchange with the women reported in the Prologue was based on social reality. It matters to them that it was, because the reality of it would give additional credence to the hypothesis that Intronati culture was an imitation of, and therefore a commentary on, court culture. Catherine Scott Burriss takes up the issue in detail in her Ph.D. dissertation, "Performing Theory," 48–49. Were the women actually playing their parts in this elaborate game, or were they taken by surprise when the Prologue in the *Gl'Ingannati* explains to them the gaming connection between the two plays? In explaining the matter to them, the Prologue was met with their silence. Moreover, the whole contrivance was in the making before the women had a chance to stage a sex strike between early January and early February 1532. See also Richard Andrews, *Scripts and Scenarios: The Performance of Comedy in Renaissance Italy* (Cambridge: Cambridge University Press, 1993), 91, where he talks about the exchanges at court based on sexual courtship relating to marriage and the management of power simultaneously reflected in the games of the Intronati and the play's framing story. According to Andrews, all of which is dismantled in the play, according to Andrews, by the erotic deviancy and sexual indeterminacy ensuing from Lelia's masculine mask. That would mean, of course, that the play failed to

The Deceived

Prologue that signals their regret and beseeches the women to have pity. What we are led to understand is that the women, in the manner of their counterparts in the *Lysistrata*,⁹ had gone on a sex strike. The speaker of the Prologue goes so far as to bemoan the flaccidity of the members' members as a result. This element of erotic humor suffuses the play.

Antonio Vignali was still a presiding spirit, and the Intronati's tolerance for ribaldry continued to run high. As a result, the "thunderstruck" are moved to a state of creative excitement, challenging us to integrate the elements of the play with the concerns of their framing tale. Clearly, these academicians were obsessed by the culture of love with its ceremonial acts of flirtation, rejection, and supplication. But what are we to make of all that ribaldry and bawdy about male sexual drives? Is it just Carnival humor or a topic exciting to the ladies as well? Lelia's nurse is concerned about what might happen to her ward, now disguised as a boy and sleeping in a room adjacent to her master's bedroom. What if her beloved Flamminio should try to assault her as a him? And what about the act of vigorous love-making (5.5) audibly witnessed by a child and reported to her mother in terms of astonishment and confusion? In those matters, the Intronati showed little reticence at all, keen as they were to extract all the smutty permutations of cross-dressing their wits could contrive as a foil to their resoundingly heterosexual finale.

Playwriting was a regular part of the Intronati's activities, along with evening games in which players were called upon, under the watchful guidance of a games-master, to pronounce tongue-twisters, recite stories, pose riddles, invent flirtatious speeches, or imitate each other's witticisms.¹⁰ Members were,

---

achieve the goals being sought according to the Prologue: renewed heterosexual flirtation and mating.
9. In this play by the ancient Greek comedian, Aristophanes, Lysistrata convinces all the women of the warring states to join with her in a universal withdrawal of their sexual favors until their bellicose husbands agree to lay down their arms.
10. The Intronati made their contribution to a social practice that was spreading throughout Italy, backed by a growing number of treatises, on evening gaming. These participatory activities

Introduction

in fact, expected to contribute a play as the price for their admission into the academy. But if that rule was followed, the number submitted must have been rather greater than the number actually produced, given that by 1532 the membership had grown to at least thirty, while only two plays are known to have been performed before *Gl'Ingannati*, namely *I prigioni* of 1529–30, and *Aurelia*, the performance of which is traditionally assigned to the summer of 1531.

AUTHORSHIP, SETTING, AND PLOT SOURCES

Just who wrote *Gl'Ingannati (The Deceived)* has provided good work for historians, but the results are inconclusive. That new members provided plays for admission might suggest solo creations were the norm, but the prevailing view is that *The Deceived* was not an initiation play but more likely a collaborative effort much in the spirit with which it was presented to the ladies in the audience. The scenes involving the stock comic characters, the *balia* or nursemaid, the pedant, the braggart soldier, and the competing innkeepers are easily imagined as inset contributions from sundry authors. Marcantonio Piccolomini was the "archintronato" at that time and might well have been the coordinator of the production. Others have looked to Alessandro Piccolomini, who revealed his gifts in such plays as his *Alessandro*. The Intronati were indeed rich in theatrical talent. Giovanni Aquilecchia proposed Francesco Maria Molza (mentioned in the play) and Claudio Tolomei.[11] Robert Melzi argued that the work was by Lodovico

---

of intellectual wit and flirtation are related to the groups who gathered to tell *novelle* in social settings, beginning with the *brigata* in Boccaccio's *Decameron*. By the sixteenth century, the kinds of games had become widely diversified and codified. The practices of the Intronati were written down some forty years later by Girolamo Bargagli in his *Dialogue on the Evening Games which the Sienese Used to Play*. The treatise was most recently published as *Dialogo de' giuochi che nelle vegghie sanesi si usano di fare*, ed. Patrizia D'Incalci Ermini (Siena: Accademia Senese degli Intronati, 1982).
11. "Per l'attribuzione della commedia *Gl'Ingannati*," *Giornale Storico della letteratura italiana* 154.487 (1977): 368–79.

Castelvetro, a neo-classical scholar residing in Modena, because clearly someone involved in the play's creation knew something about the city in which the action is set.[12] Douglas Radcliff-Umstead was inclined to concur.[13] But few others have followed them, if only because Castelvetro was hardly the type to write such a lighthearted piece. We have no surviving plays by his hand, and there is no record of his presence in Siena in 1532. Hence, the matter of authorship remains unresolved, especially in consideration of the testimony in the Prologue that the play was a hasty group effort.

In effect it comes down to the credence of their boast, or apology, that the play's composition took up "nearly all of the last three days." Read at face value, it had been a rush collaboration, and we are free to imagine just what modus operandi they might have followed to turn a clever and complex scenario, conceived by a committee, into an integrated and innovative representation of human desire and volition. By all accounts, it is a tour de force, a monument to distributed intelligences and disparate wits acting with synergistic efficiency. This prospect takes us back to the occasional factors in the production, so permit us to enlarge a bit more.

What was this disagreement with the women all about that led to this three-days' wonder of a play? A closer look reveals more about the genesis of the play. As mentioned above, on Twelfth Night, January 6, 1531/32,[14] the Intronati

---

12. Robert C. Melzi, "From Lelia to Viola," *Renaissance Drama* 9 (1966): 67–81 at 68.
13. Douglas Radcliff-Umstead, *The Birth of Modern Comedy in Renaissance Italy* (Chicago: University of Chicago Press, 1969), 196. See also Beatrice Corrigan, "Il Capriccio: An Unpublished Italian Renaissance Comedy and Its Analogues," *Studies in the Renaissance*, 5 (1958): 76, on plays addressed to female audiences in playful and flirtatious ways on behalf of a group of men.
14. There were two calendars in those years. By the old calendar year, ending March 31, the play would be dated to the end of the year, 1531, whereas for us, functioning by the new calendar, the January and February in question were at the beginning of 1532. Officially, in Catholic countries, the Gregorian (new) calendar did not replace the Julian (old) calendar until 1582 (and even later in Protestant countries). Henceforth, we will use new calendar dating.

treated their ladies to an insulting little masque *(Il Sacrificio)* in which all thirty members of the academy, despairing of their success with their women, made a solemn procession to the altar of Minerva to forswear their services and devotion under the leadership of their "sacerdote," the archintronato Il Sodo (Marcantonio Piccolomini).[15] Henceforth, they would consecrate themselves to their philosophical pursuits and humanist endeavors.

The ceremony began with the singing of an ode after which they consigned to the flames, one by one, all their tokens of love: among them a charm, a scarf, a pair of glasses, an image of Cupid, a ring, a gold chain, a tear-stained handkerchief, a lock of hair, a group of sonnets, a mirror, a glove, and some sort of time piece. Each then recited a poem as the object burned. In all this mock sobriety, built out of the conventions of Petrarchan poetry and courtly love, they were, of course, having a very good time berating their ladies for their hardheartedness. But in the Prologue to its sequel, *The Deceived,* they describe an ensuing stroke of conscience. Reputedly, the God of Love had become angry and reminded them that without love the world would collapse into chaos. Hence, the play becomes their token of remorse.

And yet, it could not have been the last minute cobble-together they describe. As the careful research of Nerida Newbigin has established, as early as January 8, only two days after the masque's production, the Intronati had already contacted the municipal leaders in search of the financial aid required to adapt the playing space inside the communal palace for their Carnival production of the present play.[16]

---

15. These two dramatic works, the masque and *The Deceived* were for a long time thereafter associated in print, beginning with the first publication in 1534. And curiously, in many of those editions, only the name of the masque appears, as in the following, published in 1575: *Il Sacrificio, comedia de gli Intronati celebrato ne i giuochi di uno carnovale in Siena, Di nuovo corretta e ristampata in Venezia, Presso Domenico Cavalcalupo, MDLXXV.* All told, there were some twenty editions of the play by the end of the century — a publishing success.
16. As the play specifies, the action took place on the last day of Carnival, February 12, 1532, new calendar.

Such a request at that early date suggests that they had more than a vague idea of what those performance requirements would be. With that perspective in mind, the drafting of the play as a three-days' wonder looks rather suspicious. The play, after all, was a public event for the Carnival season, hence a carefully planned affair. The city complied with an advance of 140 scudi, which, in itself, testifies to the importance of the Intronati's theatrical contributions to civic life. This was public money that was granted to them, the Palazzo Pubblico was the finest venue in the city (as anyone who knows Siena can confirm), and the patrician citizens were involved. The postures of pouting and renewed flirtation with a coterie of ladies may seem cozy and intimate, but the play itself was part of the official culture of the city.[17]

The Deceived was first performed in the Great Hall of the Council in Siena's central palazzo late in the Carnival festivities of 1532. And to demonstrate even further how public in conception the play may have been, further archival investigation suggests that it may well have predated the 1532 Carnival season, for which it was ostensibly written, by at least two years. Should that prove true, it is a sober reminder that nearly any social comedy featuring obstacles to love overcome and comic character types sporting their humors will have overtones of Carnival and license. Comedies of deception will always invite impressions of worlds turned upside down. Thus, the carnivalesque may actually be more generic than specific to this play.

What if it had been written to correspond to the *actual* moment at which Lelia made her escape from the Convent of San Crescenzio in boy's clothes borrowed from the nuns? According to the timeline of events, that would have been some thirty months earlier in the late summer of 1529. Then, what if the play was initially conceived to have the time of its action correspond to the occasion of its production, giving the illusion that the story was happening simultaneously in

---

17. Nerida Newbigin, in *Three Italian Renaissance Comedies*, ed. Christopher Cairns (Lewiston, NY: Edwin Mellen Press, 1996), 255–56.

the city of Modena? Ben Jonson sought to evoke that same illusion in conceptualizing *The Alchemist* as a concurrent action in the streets and houses just outside the theater. Fleshing out Lelia's story as history, she would have been quite young, barely thirteen, when she was abducted, and no more than fifteen in 1529 when she played the page to Flamminio. It was the perfect age for a girl to assume the part of a youthful boy, even though her father describes her as filled out like a young woman. And the most likely event anticipated for that year in need of spectacle and entertainment was the proposed visit to Siena by the Emperor Charles V. That visit never materialized, but *The Deceived* may well have been devised as a theatrical novelty fit for a royal visit. This is no more than speculation, but should it prove true, then the play was written earlier, ended up in a drawer, and was taken out later for adaptation. So could that three-day collaboration mentioned by the Prologue essentially boil down to the framing events involving the ladies in the audience following the *Masque of Sacrifices* appended to a pre-written play? It is more than possible that necessity was the mother of just such a refitting.

In keeping with contemporary practices, the adapted acting space in the Palazzo Pubblico, paid for in part by public money, would have required an elaborate backdrop or, alternatively, a modified version of the perspective stage constructed around a piazza. For performances of similar erudite plays in these same years in Mantua, Ferrara, Venice, and Rome, surviving accounts tell of vast cityscapes painted by artists as famous as Raphael — painters who expended their rare talents in creating massive panoramas used as luxurious displays of aristocratic or patrician wealth only to be discarded once the performances were over.

For *The Deceived,* presented as a spectacle in a known public place, it would seem reasonable to imagine an extensive backdrop or constructed setting representing Modena, its crossroads leading into the city, two inns from which their respective owners emerge and characters enter, as well as the urban dwellings of Gherardo, Flamminio, Clemenzia, and

The Deceived

Virginio, not forgetting the great cathedral of Modena with its statuary and bell tower, the Ghirlandina, remarked upon by characters in the play.[18] An even closer reading is bound to produce further hints of the scene, such as the arched doorway that frames the famous kiss.

The overall psychological effect of a cityscape around enclosed spaces, however, is claustrophobic, with characters bumping into or barely avoiding each other as they move about the stage in pursuit of conflicting desires. The play is, in a secondary way, the tale of a city whose close public spaces and architectural affordances shape and define the options of the characters.[19] An engaging challenge for the spectator is to keep track of where all the characters are, not only in terms of their respective parts within the emerging story, but in relation to the physical setting. After all, characters are always somewhere because they never leave the city. They are merely visible or invisible, and even when they are out of sight, we hold their circumstances in mind in anticipation of their subsequent appearances.

---

18. A caveat is worth mentioning, however, that the painting could not represent all that is alluded to in the play from any authentic historical or geographical point. It would have to be a pastiche cityscape of the kind woven into tapestries as early as the eighteenth century of, say, Venice, in which several disparate monuments and buildings are incorporated into a single scene from an imaginary point of view. Nerida Newbigin provides details in her notes, indicating that the locations of the Porta Bazohara or Bazzovara, the Duomo, the Rangoni Palace, and the unidentified inns, for a start, would make it impossible "to match the scene of the play to the real topography of Modena" (*Three Italian Renaissance Comedies*, 436).
19. The relation between the city and the characters is explored in greater symbolic and thematic depth by Jack D'Amico, who sees the city almost as a personality participating in the encouragement yet obstruction of the dreams and ambitions of the characters. The city, as their living space, he argues, becomes integrated into their lives, ultimately as a constant factor, too, in the whirligig of their existences. "The Treatment of Space in Italian and English Renaissance Theater: The Example of *Gl'Ingannati* and *Twelfth Night*." *Comparative Drama* 23.3 (Oct. 1989): 265–83.

Introduction

Modena is also constituted of its people as represented by the play's characters, denizens of a city that the Sienese considered mad or foolish. That point pops up in the play. Poor Bergamo bore the brunt of such a reputation in the minds of the Florentines, who thought the Bergamasques were mere brutes and laborers.[20] The choice of Modena was hence no accident. Fabio, taking Virginio for a madman in need of a straitjacket, states in an aside: "I've seen a lot of crazy people in Modena — too many to keep track of" (3.7). This simple aspersion is enough to establish an ethos of inversion, followed by ridicule and laughter. The city exists in Carnival mode and thereby symbolizes disorder, a place where anything can happen and where nothing is what it seems.

With those details in place, our own stereotyping faculties complete the associations. The rivalry between the two innkeepers, through their recitations about food and drink in contrasting milieux of elegant restraint and carousing copiousness, leads Stragualcia to pronounce that the kitchen of The Jester Inn has ample supplies "for the whole Roman court at Carnival, and still have stuff left over" (3.2). We do not see the evidence on stage; we only hear the report. But our sense of place grows with references not only to the houses and monuments of the city, but to the mentality of the people and the resources of festivity. How we select and blend these materials through analogy is work for neuroscientists. But that we do, hints at the ways in which we charge settings with meaning and bring to our imaginary worlds thematic overtones drawn from the salient features of place. Only our own reading experience will tell us whether Fabrizio's allusion to a city of mad folk links up with the putative madness that arises from identity confusion and the reign of the appetites in the play. But the option is surely present. The Intronati were consolidating their choices to form a thematic program,

---

20. Giovanni Francesco Straparola, in *The Pleasant Nights* (9.5) tells the story "Of the Bergamasques and the Florentines," with the reversal by trickery of their respective reputations. Ed. Donald Beecher, 2 vols. (Toronto: University Press, 2012), 318–29, including the commentary.

but not every provision need figure large in the reduction of events to the allegorized categories we call meaning.

Regarding the use of music in 1532, the record is silent. But if the production of this play in Naples in 1545 is any indication, there might have been a great deal of it, for in Naples the roster of actors contains the names of all the city's leading musicians, including Lo Zoppino, who was in charge of the entire production. Moreover, according to Maria Rika Maniates, theater music after 1530 "assumes definite characteristics according to the kind of drama in which it is used."[21] Had such music survived from the present production, or that of 1545, it could have told us much about the ethos of the play as perceived by its own performers.

The Prologue boasts that *The Deceived* is an entirely new play, and in remarkably telling ways, it is. But epitomizing the artistry of a play written according to erudite conventions, as this one was, by definition entails imitation of the plot motifs and character types of ancient comedy. Hence, erudite plays are performances in cultural memory, and as such, the familiar story elements, typologized personalities, and verbal echoes become part of the educated reader's experience. The practice relates to the cultural literacy of the sixteenth century and an implicit ability to read in relation to antecedent models and motifs, only parts of which can be shared with modern readers through commentary and textual annotations. More precisely, the ancient theater established practices involving restricted time periods, confined spaces, designed reversals, moments of discovery, and a unity of ethos that were honored through imitation by the playwrights of the sixteenth century. It also supplied such types as the pedant parasite, the clever or cantankerous servant, the crotchety father, the bully soldier, and the panicky lovers, all of whom find representation in the current play. Seeing such elements as part of an emergent exploitation of the literary past may be of little interest to modern readers. But it is well to know, nevertheless, that such

---

21. Maria Rika Maniates, *Mannerism in Italian Music and Culture, 1530–1630* (Chapel Hill: University of North Carolina Press, 1979), 455.

plays as *The Deceived* were built through such referentiality, and that they carry in their plots, characters, and conventions a cumulative legacy of playwriting going back to the ancients.

In terms of plot motifs, *The Deceived* offers a masterful tweaking of the plot of twins — twins who become separated, converge incognito, and confuse entire communities when each is repeatedly mistaken for the other. The design was first explored in Plautus' *Menaechmi* — arguably the master template for all such plays. It is famously reworked in Shakespeare's *Comedy of Errors*. Initially, the plot type was confined to male twins, but it took on wonderfully new possibilities when Cardinal Bibbiena, in his *Calandria*, reframed the twins as a lookalike brother and sister. Now gender confusion becomes an additional source of sport, deception, and anxiety. So what particular delight are we being offered when girls are taken for boys and pursued even down to kissing, or boys are taken for girls and locked up for safekeeping with other girls, who they are now free to seduce?[22] Is it indulged and exploited only for a good snigger? The Intronati may have intended it so, simply as a brio display of their wit. But where masks redefine characters and confuse observers with regard to gender, darker questions may arise.

A glance at Bibbiena's trend-setting play can help establish the chain. In the *Calandria*, he imagines the separation of the two siblings as his *antefatto* to the play's action. They then assume disguises not only of the opposite gender, but they adopt each other's names, before independently turning up in Rome: Lidio as Santilla, and Santilla as her brother. Remembering that each is always a self and another person at the same time makes for a stimulating bit of concentration. Lidio's intent is to court a married Roman matron twice

---

22. Giulio Ferroni investigates the six principal combinations of twin confusion, suggesting that "bisexual twinning" leads to the most compelling complications. Not only are such twins able to deceive many in their social set, but they are also, at times, able to deceive even each other, as in *The Calandria*. But that does not happen in *The Deceived*. See his *Il testo e la scena: Saggi sul teatro del Cinquecento* (Rome: Bulzoni, 1980), esp. 43–84.

his age by finding employment in her household as a girl named Santilla, while Santilla adopts a masculine disguise as Lidio to avoid captivity by the Turks as an unprotected girl. Sound familiar? Of course, the ensuing action will unfold as a fantastic exploitation of double cross-dressing (or double-cross dressing), with all the erotic substitutions, mistaken identities, and even groping to establish sexual identity, afforded by this situational "fact." Bibbiena was a prankster by predilection, cardinal though he was, and willing to extract from his witty plot every permutation of sexual confusion he could think of. There are even occasions on which both siblings, without recognizing each other, are present on stage at the same time either as two males or as two females, each claiming to be the real one.

The Deceived, through its heavy indebtedness to this play, perpetuates the *ars combinatoria* established by the conventions of erudite comedy and comes up with a new formula at the same time.[23] Bibbiena's siblings are rewarded with marriages, but in largely pro forma ways as a necessary gesture of closure. These couplings are entirely devoid of enacted bonding, trial, growing affections, or deliverance into happiness. By contrast, Lelia brings a genuine measure of sincerity to the action through her sad memories and desperate devotion to Flamminio. Bibbiena reputedly makes rather more of his siblings as a look-alike pair in every physical aspect than do the Intronati. In *The Deceived*, some readers are left with the impression that the siblings do not, and need not, look alike — that Lelia's disguise is effective only because she masters the enactment of masculinity and not because she looks like Fabrizio.[24]

---

[23]. For further references to plays displaying motifs likely borrowed from Bibbiena's seminal play, see Donald Beecher, "Introduction to *The Calandria*," in *Renaissance Comedy: The Italian Masters* (Toronto: University of Toronto Press, 2009), 2: 27–28.

[24]. Burriss (*Performing Theory*, 61), is among those espousing the absence of references to such physical resemblances in full contradistinction to the Bibbiena play.

Introduction

But the Intronati actually do state that Fabrizio and his sister were nearly indistinguishable on more than one occasion, thus accounting for much of the imbroglio. Not only is that implied when Gherardo mistakes Fabrizio for Fabio. But in Act 3.4, Frulla, the innkeeper, reports to the newly arrived Fabrizio that there is a page dressed in white, just as you are, and "resembles you so much he could almost be you." Clemenzia confirms the matter even further when she sees Fabrizio and states (5.6): "that's got to be him, he's Lelia's spitting image." And their resemblance is surely encouraged by the alacrity with which Isabella receives Fabrizio into her bedroom as Fabio based on appearance alone. Hence, the thesis that courting confusion arises in the play exclusively from the compelling performance of gender requires careful reconsideration. Regarding the siblings' physical similarities, *Gl'Ingannati* is still very much in the Bibbiena tradition of lookalikes baffling those involved with them in matters of desire and mating. A far more significant departure is the clever extension of the plot whereby the girl disguised as a page is chosen as a lover by the woman she had been sent to woo on behalf of her master. That is the signature novelty that distinguishes the *Ingannati* group. New social considerations will arise as the combinations are reconfigured, but within the erudite tradition of "theatregrams" and appropriation, the lookalike siblings were a vehicle for mannerist exploitation to generate deliciously ironic situations and titillating errors.[25] Nevertheless, assessments of the play will not stop there.

Genre Interpretation: Deception and Representation

When one moves from gender, scientific, and anthropological interpretation to form or genre criticism, there is little point, it would seem, in overstating the obvious concerning the

---

25. "Theatregrams" has become a most useful term for helping to explain the movement of cultural and plotting materials and conventions from play to play in the unique manner of the writers of "erudite" comedy. See "Theatregrams," in *Comparative Critical Approaches to Renaissance Comedy*, ed. Donald Beecher and Massimo Ciavolella (Ottawa: Dovehouse Editions Canada, 1986), 15–34.

The Deceived

play's title: that audiences may expect to encounter, as an organizational and thematic principle, a goodly number of deceptions or deceived people in the play. That point can be made simply by identifying as many episodes involving beguilement, duplicity, or disappointment as possible. Yet the value of even so self-evident an exercise could be misleading insofar as the plays of the era were, in general, built around genres with emplotted tactics whereby one party sought to take advantage of another for profit or for play.

Deception is so omnipresent in the erudite theater of the sixteenth century that no play in the genre would be misrepresented by bearing such a title. Moreover, audiences are all pretty well versed in seeing and enjoying acts of deception for what they are — unless, of course, the playwright goes out of the way to keep the comic ironies hidden from the spectators as well. Routinely, however, as in the case of *The Deceived*, spectators enjoy a privileged perspective, one that is far better informed than that of the characters induced into the shortfalls of knowledge that make them dupes.

Specifically, we are made party to the reasons and means of Lelia's disguise, which is, arguably, the single grand deception-maker of the play. According to the title, that is her principal mandate: fool people and let us enjoy the consequences. Yet for her, the imperative is love and a daring quest made possibly only through deception. Her tactical identity change held no more malice aforethought than was collaterally necessary to fulfill her life's calling. In that regard, her ploys are innocent; they differ categorically from those engineered by out-and-out tricksters, practical jokers, shamsters, con men, or self-appointed satiric legislators willing to plan and prepare the social terrain to the anticipated cost, discomfort, or humiliation of their victims. Modes of comedy are determined by these levels of intentionality, and the diversity to be found in *The Deceived* has largely been addressed already.

Regarding the stock comic characters, their defining traits identify them as targets of laughter, and the playwrights arrange the activities through which their tilted preoccupations are exposed to our indefatigable amusement. Thus, there

Introduction

are agents of deception both inside the play and designing the play, whereby the embarrassing or shocking shortfalls of knowledge are brought to the attention of the "unknowing" characters.

Virginio and Gherardo are two of the most benighted and contrive through their self-justified anger to prolong the discovery of the truths pertaining to their children. The Intronati make great and derisive sport of their refusal to acknowledge the facts. These are the reversals that define plots as they work systematically through states of blindness to final states of revelation: those that lead to mating and marriage, and those that lead to exposure and laughter. This, in turn, relates to the play's eternal challenge: whether the representations in the play are the product of social reflection and critique or merely mannerist exploitations of stock characters for purposes of pushing artifice to its limits. It is a perfect Neckar Cube, the one that opens pointing up or pointing down, depending on how the eye reads three-dimensionality into the bi-dimensional image of a box.

By default, the play is a representation of a social reality of some kind. These are human beings planning, desiring, acting to advance themselves, being fooled, getting angry or despondent, and ultimately winning or losing their goals. They engage our moral and social values on an as-if-real basis. But their behaviors are also set up by ironic and ambiguous situations dreamed up by the Intronati in relation to the ingenious plots of coincidence, inversion, and humor concocted by preceding playwrights in the erudite tradition. This procedure is tantamount to a collective quest to expand the genre by working its conventions into ever more ingenious exploitations of the human comedy through marginally probable, yet technically possible, scenarios. It is a contest in wit, in style and artifice, in blending comedic character types, and, for this play, in teasing out all the sexual innuendoes and identity confusion imaginable through a cross-gendered disguise. Hence, spectators are obliged to conduct their social adjudications in relation to mannerist play, and then to wonder how much social reality can contribute to invention

and laughter, and how much the desire for wit and amazement may impose upon the mirror held up to life.

The play taken for social realism based on carefully mirrored mores may be the greatest deception of all — a trick played by the Intronati on their readers and spectators. Hence, it is well not to forget their experimental motivations and to know, as well, that in pursuing these conventions to ever greater extremes, the playwrights will progressively undermine the integrity of the entire genre by the end of the century.[26] The genre does not fade out into the light of common-day realism or belabored social criticism, but into the artifice of forced conventions and baroque decadence. *Gl'Ingannati* is a production that figures into that historical continuum. Social realities so contrived require judicious interpretation.

The convention of the title, in naming a leading value in the play to represent the whole of its action, was a common practice of the period. Plays might be named "the rivals," or "the jealous ones," or "the faithful ones," or "friendship," or "constant love," each title anticipating a prominent social transaction coupled to a social value such as fidelity, jealousy, friendship, or rivalry. Closer to the idea of deception but more enigmatic was Ariosto's *I suppositi*, which implies "the substitutions," or "those who exchange places," again calling attention to a prominent plotting motif — one character standing in for another — that consolidates the ethos of the plot. The first English translator of the play, George Gascoigne, however, translated the title as *Supposes* and thereby added the notion of supposition, of formulating provisional ideas of the world, which may or may not prove true. He too was concerned with the gaps in knowledge that induce characters into error, leading to moments of recognition and reversal concerning truths the spectators have known all along. Ariosto's play is about exchanging one thing for another, the Intronati's about mistaking one thing for another. Hence, their titles. But how much these titles should tyrannize over the interpretations of plays is a moot matter. Caro named his

---

26. See Donald Beecher, "Introduction," *Renaissance Comedy:* 1: 28–30.

Introduction

play *The Scruffy Scoundrels* in reference to two old men who dressed in rags as an act of protest while pursuing litigation in Rome. It is an amusing motif, but far from the hermeneutic center of the play.

Further to the notion of deception as a thematic core, it can come about through stupidity, self-blindness, refusing to acknowledge things that are true but inconvenient, or through oversight due to hyperbolical desire. It might also have arisen through the ontological certainties about who Lelia was in the minds of those who encountered her — certainties that prompted them to misread the contradictory evidence provided by their own eyes. Satire will follow if gulls are made of those who should have known better. But in that regard, much depends, too, on the malice of knaves and the intentions behind their schemes to trick others through false promises, misrepresentations, or the exploitation of vulnerability.

More theoretically, we function in groups through expectations of trust, transparency, and sincerity. Yet we know that human nature is such that some will compute advantages for themselves while trimming their contributions to the common good, and they will do so by misrepresenting their activities, or they will seek indirect and blameless means to betray rivals and competitors. We have strong reactions to those practices because they violate our feelings of trust and reciprocity. Such feelings we bring to the reading of imaginary worlds as well. Finally, there are those who trick merely for the pleasure of realizing their little Gestalts by leading others into their traps. In that regard, readers are divided on their reading of Lelia's latent intentions, real or imagined. Is she experimenting on purpose at the cost of others, or merely stirring up unanticipated side-effects?

Deception is always about the liability of ignorance with greater and lesser consequences. *The Deceived* centers its dramatic ethos in the goodly number of misinformed or duped persons in the play by placing them under a common aegis. But they are not all of the same cloth. Giglio is deceived by Pasquella, who finds a weakness through which

The Deceived

she gains possession of his rosary before bantering him into retreat. Purely circumstantial deception comes to Virginio who mistakes Fabrizio for Lelia and thus obstructs the homecoming of his long-awaited son. Isabella pursues love with a girl in taking her for a boy.

The concept of deception thus takes on several roles, not the least of them in furnishing the audience with structural expectations and a unifying principle to the diverse actions of the play. But are these deceptions sporting cognitive jags or signs of deep social malaise? Deception is always about ethical performances, the rights and wrongs in the manipulation of information whereby parties gain benefits over others through withheld disclosures of the truth. Deception will always sharpen our wits with regard to such matters as the means employed in the pursuit of desire, the morality of expediency, responsibility for inadvertent effects, provisional planning with the intent to deceive, and so much more that pertains to the machinations behind self-advancement in a competitive world. In that regard, the play's title does, perhaps, announce the play's presiding theme. Love is Lelia's imperative and the principle by which we come to tolerate her means; such tactics applied to lesser goals will alter our moral reactions.

Game Theory

One way out of the confrontation between social reality and the representations of art is to apply the logic of gaming. If social imbroglios about very real concerns are managed on the model of a game through which a witty gamester compels all in her entourage to play according to the rules imposed by her disguise trickery, then social reality can be shaped in accordance with the manner in which games establish winners and losers. This is merely another frame of analysis for dealing with the meaning of the conventions imposed, implicitly, by disguise. Games are artificial worlds with arbitrary rules to which all subscribe in order to participate. At the same time, in psychological terms, there are the social games people play whereby they shape their worlds to their own advantage by inducing others to comply with the offered terms of play.

Introduction

Lelia has made herself vital to her world and therefore has power to impose her own conditions, making the removal of her disguise her means to a victory that all in the play's society are obliged to acknowledge. Games occupy this magic middle ground between imaginary worlds with their idiosyncratic rules and the play factor in very real human psychological negotiations. The game at this juncture becomes a metaphor for artifice in social negotiations. At the center of these transactions is the feint, the misrepresentation of the self to strategic ends, justified by the unfair conditions that make duplicity the only efficient choice for a deserving seeker. Deception is the presiding condition of Lelia's game and the reigning ethos of the play, telling us potentially how to read the play's representational reality in relation to the license requested by the cumulative traditions of comedy. But we would not say that is necessarily the final word.[27]

Satire, Carnival, and Laughter

The concentration on Lelia's psychology in terms of realism and clinical cogency results from the reputation she gained as a prototype to rather more interiorized versions of the suffering heroine, among whom Shakespeare's Viola, Rosalind, Helena, and Isabella prominently figure. Moreover, the heroine's salience is further enhanced in later recensions through the systemic deletion of the stock comic personalities of the learned theater — the pedants, recalcitrant servants, boasting soldiers, and randy old men — thereby giving far

---

27. Again, Laura Giannetti, who has investigated these plays as closely as anyone in recent years, noted this challenge posed by the ending. "On the Deceptions of *The Deceived*," 66–67. For Giannetti and Laurie Shepard, "Siena 1531," 10, the conditions of the game are invoked as a way of thinking about the conventions of erudite comic plotting and as an explanatory model for dealing with unsatisfactorily hasty reversals and closures. As Shepard states, Lelia has "the wit to transform self-pity and fear into a game that is ultimately productive."

more prominence to her role.[28] But as the Intronati initially conceived the play, there was also a crowded and potentially satirical cross-section of Modenese society reconstituted out of the stock fools and knaves of the Roman comedy. There were the donkey-minded servants, the combative hostlers, the importunate soldier, the pontificating pedant, the gerontian lover, and a pair of low-lifers who nearly spring Lelia's entire enterprise after witnessing the kisses between Isabella and Fabio.

The play, in sum, is a medley of eccentrics, fools, and babblers, with their contrasting jokes, slapstick, nattering, prating, and propositioning. The Giglio plot, the first to go in the play's afterlife, is prominent in the original as an attempted deception on the part of an unsavory social parasite whose stock reputation precedes him. He was fair game for humiliation by anyone clever enough to contain him. His greatest fault, paradoxically, was his cowardice, and audiences clearly took delight in seeing his displays of pusillanimity accompanied by his barrages of verbal rationalization. Meanwhile, he took himself for an irresistible lover even among women of the highest social echelons, yet would settle for sex with women like Pasquella, who used her chickens to pull off the theft of his precious rosary. Placing all these episodes together, we have a little essay on base human nature scrapping over food, lodging, material possessions, and sex, prating as connoisseurs, while exposing their lowly obsessions.

The sum effect of the play may be constituted by the community of spectators sharing in the common language of laughter as the play's highest good. Tricking soldiers and mocking schoolmarms lost in their Latinity is old stuff, yet by cultural prompting they might remain among the adequate

---

28. Charles Estienne translated this play quite faithfully into French as *Les Abusés* (1543), yet, even at that early date, he dropped the Giglio scenes. Lope de Rueda in *Los Engañados* (1567) took an altogether freer approach, concentrating on the love intrigue, as so many adapters of the plot would do. He showed no interest in farce or in the local color of Modena. His Lelia is also more timid and hesitant, reflecting the kind of girl the Spanish of the era could still accept as a heroine of marital romance.

stimuli to iterative laughter. Pasquella and Giglio are equally matched liars, each playing for the critical spot of weakness that will give one of them the advantage, with sex or a rosary as their respective prizes. Our sense of laughter can interpret what their gains and losses might mean in a raw game of courtship or simply relegate them to the realm of the playfully harmless. Laughter disempowers, smooths, and consolidates. These were stock routines in the theatrical vocabulary of the Intronati. But the degree to which these characters are also cyphers for the social enormities of the times and extend our collective scorn beyond the play as applied satire has constant potential, as well, and we are good at making the analogies that satire is based on. But at the least, the laughter raised by cognitive jags, or unexpected invention, or social ridicule, or pointed disapprobation express our limbic judgments of the social disorders represented in the play. So which ones? If the play makes us laugh, or feel the equivalent of laughter, then we are challenged to define just what we are laughing about. Satiric laughter can be powerful because it replicates that amusement or disapprobation in our viscera and throats. Such comedy remains one of the "unacknowledged legislators of the world" in some things. But *The Deceived* is a very particular play which, for all its frankness and wit, does not seem to be leveling a massive bolt of scorn at the world. Yet it is a play that is conducive to laughter, to building an urbane and secure perspective for those who enjoy the authors' confidence, and to tolerance even through acts of satiric judgment rendered benign once the machinations of mischief are exposed, excused by their wit, or contained by understanding.

By the time Thomas Love Peacock translated *The Deceived: A Comedy* in 1862,[29] nearly all that remained of the original was the romance intrigue with its cross-dressing and cross-wooing. English readers, by then, had every right to think of the play as a sentimental journey obstructed by old men

---

29. London: Chapman and Hall, 1862.

and the misaligned proclivities of the heart.[30] But as stated above, the complete original is far more diverse. Therein Lelia is, at times, the nearly absent middle of the play, for she has far less freedom to impose her presence under the social constraints by which she lives than do her subsequent counterparts. The play may be about her, principally, but she by no means dominates the stage. Rather, there is a medley of foolery, pedantry, mockery, prating, and courting on the part of the *ripieno* or background characters of the cast, essentially providing dramatic "stuffing" to swell out the spectacle with idle tricks, buffoonery, and bickering. It is their play too, and they cut capers in the mode of traditional Carnival entertainments.

So viewed, Lelia's quest is just a part of a dramatic spectacle deemed fit for the celebration of the winter festive season in Siena, and for the spirit of Carnival at any time. Fabrizio states as much, considering all the astonishing events he had confronted: "What a great story for Carnival or for telling at wakes" (3.7). In essence, the principal business of the play is a perfectly carnivalesque entertainment, to which the Intronati would most assuredly concur.

But the question remains concerning the degree to which such plays are merely fit for performance during Carnival, or actually reflect in their concerns the symbolic values of Carnival. The distinction is often overlooked. This annual event in the life of a city is what it is: a time for masks and disguises, hence courting in costume, feasting, drinking, laughter, stage productions and impromptu entertainments, boisterousness and bragging, even ritual defiance of authority. It was a time of permitted license, of trickery and tomfoolery when authorities turned a blind eye, all in anticipation of a period to follow of penance and fasting.

---

30. Bullough, in his translation of *Gl'Ingannati* for the *Narrative and Dramatic Sources of Shakespeare* (London: Routledge and Kegan Paul, 1958), likewise deleted most of these scenes. They had become irrelevant insofar as Shakespeare, in reworking the love plot, had also dropped them (following Barnabe Riche), before adding his own brand of buffoonery in the characters of Sir Andrew and Sir Toby, along with the trick put upon Malvolio. Hence, Bullough's translation is also a major misrepresentation of the original.

Introduction

The freedom of Carnival *sensu stricto* is defined exclusively by the time of self-mortification and devotion to follow; it is not a foil to God, law, the social contract, and the natural world order, but to Lent.

That alignment of contrasting activities and their accompanying states of mind represents something binary and symbolic that is difficult to quantify, although not for lack of trying, for Carnival is one of the most theorized sets of behavior patterns in Western culture. Nevertheless, through symbolic thinking, it has come to represent all that the human spirit can imagine concerning release, indulgence, resistance, insubordination, inversion, larking, or satisfying the appetites in opposition to obedience, legality, guilt, governing bodies, punishment, and even the natural and spiritual orders.

Loading up everything the erudite comedy may propose by way of disruptive behavior with the values of Carnival might appear to be an unproblematic extension of the play's meaning — indeed, a packaged way of declaring its meaning. What you see by way of resistance through pleasure is merely a carnivalesque expression of the yearning human spirit. But if the play is about rights to self-exploration, or the felt imperatives of nature, or the recovery of social order, or sanctimonious satire, the Carnival model will begin to disappoint, particularly if its holiday capers and low appetites trivialize the play's purposeful destabilization of patriarchal or tyrannical institutions. That symbolic alliance can only be allowed when Carnival itself has been promoted to the level of a profound assault upon those same institutions. Then the Carnival once permitted by authority becomes reconstituted as defiance against that order.

In a putatively common spirit, the play's buffoons, boasters, squabblers, and epicureans perform a kind of inverted world order in strutting the stuff of their respective masks. They assume permission, within the play world, to indulge appetites, spout nonsense, and prowl for food, sex, and occasions to prate. These things can be done in traditional holiday spirit in both venues without theorizing such actions through the Bakhtinian terms of protest, rebellion, or subversion. Even so,

the holiday structure through which restriction is contrasted to license carries a felt cultural significance. A relaxing of the laws and mores both sacred and secular that were in force during the rest of the year allows for dissimulated identities and indulged urges, all of which may serve as a matrix for comedic imitation within the permissive conventions of comedy. Thus, in broad descriptive terms, the play might be seen as a medley of interrelated episodes of expedient disguising, jockeying for resources, and pontificating over piffle. Most assuredly, it features the pursuit of fleshly cravings, petty one-upmanship, boasting, philandering, and getting around the authority figures — all in a Carnival spirit.

But the analogy may grow more tenuous in light of the ruses by which the sly win by deception, or disorder is resolved by the fulfillment of romance, or the participants in disorderly frolic are held up to the ridicule of laughter. What does it mean when mono-dimensional characters, "in their humors" as Ben Jonson would say, are displayed on stage as disruptive, underproductive, silly, and self-absorbed? Do these dramatized themes express the cultural values of Carnival? Critics have long thought that comedic treatments of these matters do align themselves in cogent ways with the "traditions of popular festive forms," and thereby produce commentary on "social and political structure[s]."[31] That is to assume that popular forms produce social and political protest and that comedy does so in the same way by appropriating the forms of those festivals. But that assumed coalescence continues to invite investigation and demonstration. Carnival is a time of permitted indulgence while satire treats folly as a violation of the common order at all times.

In *The Deceived,* an old man yearns for a young bride, Giglio negotiates for sex with a lowly but shrewd housekeeper, the pedant is humiliated by his irresistible proclivity for pederasty, and the two old fathers are beaten soundly in the game of patriarchal dictatorship. Are these acts of assertive resistance,

---

31. Michael Bristol, "The Festive Agon: The Politics of Carnival," in *Twelfth Night,* ed. R.S. White (New York: St. Martin's Press, 1996), 73.

laughable indulgence, or shame-worthiness? Such stuff may entertain Carnival-goers, but does it reflect the essence of the occasion? If social imbroglios in need of "unknotting" through comic plotting are enough to qualify, then *The Deceived* is a carnivalesque play through-and-through.

But Carnival activities do not constitute crises in need of disentanglement in order to bring the holiday to a meaningful close. Does the play's society constitute a symbolic world order posed in defiance of oppression in serious religious or political terms? Carnival as a foil to privation and penitence may thus be interpreted as a generic signifier that incorporates all that is impious, sub-legal, unspiritual, and disobedient. That signifier can then include things originating in the appetites as declarations of freedom from oppression that are in turn willing to make cause out of cultural artifacts that may share its patterns of disorder.

How then do we see the design of the play if only a single template can prevail? Is it a romance with buffoonish and satiric outriders, or a plenary arrangement of social inversions on every motif associated with the themes and ethos of Carnival? Luckily, we do not have to decide, and the variety of interpretative frames is worth recognition. In effect, all the characters who attempt to separate, imprison, tempt, rival, and otherwise torment true love are simultaneously the denizens of a world of comic excess. Moreover, just as Carnival ends itself in Lent, so comedic disorder eventuates in the restoration of social order, the passing of generations, the containment of sterile pursuits, and the instantiation of fertility and futurity on the basis of love and commitment. All comedy has a way of moving in those directions by way of reversal and denouement. Thus, the reversal in human fortunes pertaining to love coincides with the end of license simply because the play, itself, comes to an end. Hence, as some critics have observed, genre, theme, holiday, satire, romance, the indulgence of appetites, and laughter all collaborate through symbolic forms that we are able to imagine and conflate. Then Lelia, herself, may become the mistress of Carnival through the inversions caused by her disguise as well as the mistress of Nature's immutable laws.

The Deceived

Carnival and sexuality are easy to conflate at the level of craving and instincts. In that sense, the Intronati, with their notion of art as sexual solicitation, provide a banquet of proof and Carnival is the appropriate season. To the end that Carnival and this play serve as erotic feasts, they are one and the same in spirit and in meaning.

Sequels to *The Deceived*

As stated at the outset, the genre pioneered in this play by the Intronati was taken over through translation or imitation by dramatists and prose fiction writers in Italy, France, Spain, and England during the following seventy years. The Sienese writers had hit upon the formula by searching out further intrigue potential in plots involving a cross-dressed heroine and her look-alike brother. Their most novel contribution consisted of sending a girl disguised as a boy on a courting mission to the woman beloved by her master, only to become the object of that woman's affections. Just as the deception is about to be exposed, the heroine's male sibling makes his surprise appearance and thereby, in effect, turns Fabio into a real boy by assuming her role.

That combination of error and substitution served as a plot matrix that, despite modifications to detail, remained intact right down to Shakespeare's celebrated *Twelfth Night* (1602) in which Viola plays the ingénue page with brio and occasional bewilderment. It would be misleading, however, to treat Shakespeare's adaptation as perfection imposed upon a series of faulty prototypes. Geoffrey Bullough, even after translating the Lelia portions of the play, had only this to say about the creation of the Intronati: that it was "farcical, satiric, loosely constructed despite the Plautine framework, and entirely lacking in poetic feeling, although some of the characters and their motives have considerable vitality."[32] From a purely Shakespearean perspective, he was not entirely wrong, given that he chose to fault the original in light of

---

[32]. Geoffrey Bullough, *Narrative and Dramatic Sources of Shakespeare*, Vol. 2, "The Comedies, 1597–1603," 278.

what Shakespeare did well. But the Intronati did not write their play to rival Shakespeare, or even to provide him with a remote source. They wrote by their own criteria, for their own occasion, according to the production conventions, humors, and tastes of their own time, about a heroine more severely confined by her suffocating social conditions, with a cast of comic characters traditional upon their stage, and in that spirit produced a masterpiece. Point made.

Even so, the trajectory from Siena to London during the intervening seventy years has become an inevitable part of the story of the original play. We can only take a quick glance at it here. Given what followed, we can be certain that the idea of the play generated by the Intronati commanded attention and set dramatists and translators to work to appropriate a story type suited to changes in milieu, adjustments to character, and adaptation to alien societies and their tastes. Among those refittings were Niccolò Secchi's play *Gl'Inganni* (1547), Lope de Rueda's *Los Engañados* (1567) and Charles Estienne's *Les Abuséz* (1543) by whose efforts the signature formula became known not only in Italy, but in Spain and France.[33] And to complicate matters even more, Estienne's play was translated into Latin by an English schoolmaster.[34] Rueda's is a relatively

---

33. See Florindo Cerreta's "Introduction" to *La commedia degli Ingannati* (Florence: L. S. Olschki, 1980). *Gl'Inganni* was first performed in Milan in 1547 and published in Florence by Giunti in 1562. There is a second play by Secchi entitled *L'Interesse* on the same core design, which was translated as *Self-Interest* by William Reymes in 1660, ed. by Helen A. Kaufman (Seattle: University of Washington Press, 1953). The Italian text was published in Venice by Francesco Ziletti in 1581. This play was likewise imitated by Curzio Gonzaga in his *Gl'Inganni* of 1592, creating confusion by adopting the title of Secchi's first play on this plot; and by Domenico Carnacchini in his *Inganni* (Venice, 1605).

34. This play was dusted off in 1595 with a new prologue and epilogue composed for the visit of the Earl of Essex to Cambridge. As a school play, the pedant received even more Latin jokes, tags, and quips. Scholars have been motivated to sack this play for word echoes in Shakespeare, and their best reward is Lelia's line "O festus dies hominis" to which they trace the origin of the name Feste. In fact, the play was quite obscure and falls into the Shakespearean

free translation that does not hesitate to lop out nearly all of the farcical scenes as well as the social mores of Modena-cum-Siena, condense the plot, and change all the names. His heroine is less clever, independent, and perceptive than Lelia, presumably in accordance with what Spanish audiences expected from their charming women. And of course, there would be no interest in Spain in seeing Spanish soldiers acting like fools in foreign countries, propositioning the local women, and cringing like cowards. Estienne likewise saw fit to exclude the Giglio plot.

On the prose fiction side, Matteo Bandello published the story as "The Novella di Nicuola."[35] His retelling of the Sienese play is relatively faithful, including, for example, much of the back story pertaining to the horrors of the Sack of Rome. He, too, supports the view that the city had it coming to them for their sins — just not from fellow Christians, whose deplorable behavior exceeded that of the Turks and heathens. He lays blame at the same time at the doors of Rome's leaders who could have done far more to protect citizens from rape and pillage. Bandello makes clearer than in the play that Nicuola's Spanish wardens had spared the heroine from rape in order to propose a steeper ransom. Further interpretational alterations include his deletion of the scene in which Fabrizio is locked into Isabella's room. Rather, Isabella herself invites him into the house as Fabio, thinking, no doubt, to take up where they had left off their kissing. He preserves the wonderfully ironic speeches of Lelia, however, speaking to Flamminio about Lelia's love for him in the third person, thereby sharing her own feelings by imagining out loud how Lelia must be feeling. That motif passes through Riche to Shakespeare by

---

discomfort zone of "little Latin and less Greek." It was edited by G.C. Moore Smith as *Laelia: A Comedy Acted at Queens' College, Cambridge, Probably on March 1st, 1595* (Cambridge: Cambridge University Press, 1910).

35. Part II, No. 36 of his *Novelle* (1554).

way of Pierre de Belleforest's translation of Bandello into French in his *Histoires Tragiques*.³⁶

Routinely, editors of Shakespeare have sought to master these materials and decide which are more germane to the shaping of *Twelfth Night,* mixing and matching influences, allusions, character details, and echoes of language. Secchi's heroine in *Gl'Inganni* is particularly lively and vivacious, suggesting to some that Shakespeare needed this extra inspiration to invent his Viola and somehow had access to the play.³⁷ But ultimately, the sources of *Twelfth Night* come down to what Belleforest received from *Gl'Ingannati* through Bandello, and what Barnabe Riche took for his story "Of Apolonius and Silla" from the Belleforest translation of Bandello,³⁸ combined with cognate materials from "Cesare Gravina," in Giovan Battista Giraldi's *Hecatommithi*.³⁹ This is the actual line of descent that carries the story from Siena to London, insofar as Shakespeare derived his materials for *Twelfth Night* from Riche, with possibly a few details taken directly from the original play.⁴⁰ The matter of his first-hand

---

36. Depending on the edition either no. 59 or 61 in volume 4 (1579).
37. *Narrative and Dramatic Sources of Shakespeare,* 2: 274. See, also, the article by Helen Kaufman, "Secchi as a Source of *Twelfth Night*" in *Shakespeare Quarterly* 5.3 (Summer 1954): 271–80. The quandary about the Italian sources Shakespeare may have known is made even more perplexing by a comment in the 1602 diary entry by John Manningham, after attending the first production of *Twelfth Night,* that the play is "most like and neare to that in Italian called *Inganni*," suggesting that Shakespeare knew the Secchi play rather that the Intronati play, or that Manningham knew the Secchi play and caught the resemblance, signifying nothing more. *Diary of John Manningham,* ed. John Bruce (Westminster: J.B. Nichols & Son, 1868), 18.
38. Story 2 of *His Farewell.* This edition contains a discussion of the relationship between Riche's story and Shakespeare's stage adaptation, pp. 74-80.
39. Part 1, Decade 5, Story 8 of *Hecatommmithi overo Cento Novella* (Venice: Girolamo Scotto, 1566), 464.
40. There is also the matter of Emmanuel Forde's *Parismus* (1598), whose heroine is named Violetta. She too is hired as a page by the

knowledge of *Gl'Ingannati* is still debated by scholars, but the search for word echoes from the Italian, going all the way back to J.M. Lothian and T.W. Craik in their 1906 edition of *Twelfth Night,* has produced little incontrovertible evidence.[41] The Bard, in working essentially from Riche, made numerous changes in readapting the now formulaic plot for the stage, the first performance of which took place in the Middle Temple on February 2, 1602.

Riche, himself, had rewritten the inaugural circumstances behind Silla's quest (the Lelia–Viola of his story) by drawing upon the models of Greek romance. The setting is in Cyprus where Apolonius (Flamminio–Orsino), a duke from Constantinople, puts in for a visit to her father's court where Silla falls in love and sets her cap on him. The poor girl receives barely a nod of interest, yet her passions launch her on a voyage of discovery and a dangerous rite of passage. Accordingly, she ships out with a ruffian captain who seeks to rape her, bringing her to resolve upon her own death rather than to lose her virtue. In keeping with the genre, a storm provides escape from his clutches — leaving her the sole survivor in a strange land. Then, for her safety, she hits upon the idea of a cross-gender disguise, which includes adopting the name of her brother, Silvio, setting up all the confusion to follow when her brother comes looking for her. Shakespeare, for the sake of dramatic compression, drops the prelude in Cyprus and does not place Viola on a mission to recover a lost love in the manner of both Lelia and Silla.

Riche's rendition has likewise jettisoned all the farcical elements to concentrate on the imbroglio of cross-dressing in the pursuit of love. A telling motif in Riche that is laundered out by Shakespeare has to do with Silvio's relationship with Julina

---

man she loves, now named Parismus. She too sleeps essentially by his side, yet never reveals her sex. But while the play holds resemblances to *Twelfth Night,* including the similarity between the heroines' names, Violetta does not win her master, but settles for another man whose long-suffering love for her is revealed and, who in a sense, has earned her love through patience and the accumulation of credit.

41. See the Introduction to their edition most recently republished in 1975 by Methuen and Co. in London.

Introduction

(Isabella–Olivia). He not only makes love to her in replacing the Silvio feigned by his sister, but gets her pregnant too.[42] The situation becomes quite wonderful when Julina, in desperation, appears at the court of the man who loves her to report her condition in order to blame his servant Silvio (Fabio–Cesario).

Riche states to his women readers, "For God's love take heed, and let this be an example to you, when you be with child, how you swear who is the father before you have had good proof and knowledge of the party, for men be so subtle and full of sleight that, God knoweth, a woman may quickly be deceived."[43] (Precisely what happened to Isabella in *The Deceived*, without the pregnancy.) Riche's Silla, at that moment, knowing herself incapable of the act, makes a long speech about the misbehavior of women, which puts Julina into a lather, which she articulates in another great speech of protest and outrage. The duke, looking on, moved by the lady's words, draws his rapier to assault his innocent page, whereupon Silla falls on her knees to beg for a private audience with Julina. There she pulls down her shirt to expose her pretty bosom saying "Lo, madam, behold here the party whom you have challenged to be the father of your child."

Only under those circumstances does she identify herself as the daughter of a noble duke in love with the man who had abandoned her, suggesting that her own passions and torments were just as vehement as Julina's. Now it is Julina (the Isabella–Olivia figure), who breaks the news to Apolonius about Silla's disguise and her desperate love. Then Apolonius "perceived indeed that it was Silla the daughter of Duke Pontus," embraces her, and pronounces a long speech on her virtues, patience, wit, and suffering, followed by a grand marriage ceremony. Only then, as the news of this remarkable event begins to spread, does Silvio get word of it and return to the scene to make amends to Julina. "Take courage madam, for behold here a gentleman that will not stick both to father

---

42. That twist Riche may have found in the play by Secchi, but more likely it came from one of his favorite stories, "Cesare Gravina" from Giraldi's *Hecatommithi* 1.5.8.
43. Riche, *His Farewell*, 197.

your child and to take you for his wife."[44] How different in detail, yet how much the same it all remains. The Intronati plot was difficult to better.

Much the same kind of argument must be made on behalf of Riche as was made on behalf of the original play. Riche likewise wrote according to his own literary sensibilities, in prose, in the tradition of the *novella*, for his own particular readership, and not as a furnisher of theatrical plot material. Riche's largely stillborn mission was to translate the conventions of the *novelliere* into England, and in that endeavor he could take inspiration from as many as eight primary sources at a time and remix their parts and conventions into new creations. As stated, for "Of Apolonius and Silla," Riche relied upon Belleforest, with only a few details taken from Giraldi's "Cesare Gravina," and indirectly upon the legend of St. Eustace. From Giraldi he presumably borrowed the idea of the attempted rape of Silla by the ship's captain, and from the legend he took the idea of a sister imprisoned in her brother's stead for putatively having gotten a woman pregnant. But over these supplemental sources we need not linger, because neither has bearing on the *Gl'Ingannati* or *Twelfth Night*.

The comparatist is invited to think through the subtle ring of changes implicit in, say, turning the Intronati's Isabella into a widow in Riche or a virgin lamenting the death of her brother in Shakespeare. It could matter, too, that Shakespeare's Viola makes a sea voyage and is shipwrecked, but not in tracking down a former lover. There are differences, as well, in the representation of intimacy between the two cross-courting women, the one guarding her cover, the other deceived by the page's disguise. The Intronati are by far the naughtiest in ratcheting up the overtones of latent lesbianism in that error. They also focus more upon Lelia's prospects with Flamminio as the play closes, whereas Shakespeare concentrates upon the moment of recognition between brother and sister. Like Lelia and Viola, Silla as a page is careful in the presence of her beloved master to retune his mind in ways beneficial to her long-term desires. All of them, as girls in disguise, did

---

44. "Of Apolonius and Silla," p. 201.

Introduction

something to make an ambivalent male receptive to love and devotion; their tactics are likewise ripe for comparison.

There is reason, moreover, to think that Shakespeare found much in Apolonius upon which to base his melancholy Orsino. As Louise Schleiner states, through Silla's good offices, "Duke Apollonius [sic] learns that he can enjoy simple, day-to-day intimacy and affection with a woman too, when she is page-like, just as he always has with boys and men; the intimacy contrasts sharply with the stilted and bookish feelings he had earlier for the beloved of his conventional suit."[45] Julina, for him, was an object of literary passion, while the page taught him to relish simple domestic pleasures with a boy who changes little in becoming a girl. More generally, in all of these plots the denouement must correspond to a psychological time frame; the discovery of the heroine's feminine identity must wait for the essential moment when her master becomes receptive to her as a woman, even while that moment is constantly threatened by a premature discovery. The Sienese writers force that moment by the tattling of the servants about the kiss. That makes Clemenzia's part all the more critical in shaping Flamminio's receptiveness to Lelia through a story replicating her exact dilemma. Such psychological timing is critical to all recensions of the story.

For Leo Salingar, Shakespeare tops Riche in his creation of realism through greater individualization of his characters and through their dramatized encounters. Shakespeare likewise relies more upon thematic coincidence and the role of Fortuna in resolving events. He opines, moreover, that Riche's narrative operates only on one plane, while Shakespeare's operates on two through such characters as Feste, who, in his visions of long-ago, sets up the dimensions of festive comedy.[46] In that, Salingar favors the festive theme he finds in *Twelfth Night,* in which the nuanced and bittersweet stasis nevertheless elicits a

---

45. Louise Schleiner, "Ladies and Gentlemen in Two Genres of Elizabethan Fiction," *Studies in English Literature 1500–1900,* 29 (1989): 12.
46. Leo Salingar, "The Design of *Twelfth Night,*" *Shakespeare Quarterly,* 9 (1958): 117–39.

time of universal merriment and contentment. Comedy can do that through a temporary repression of all that troubles and divides. Right or wrong, his perspective challenges the comparatist to consider each cognate version of the story for its cathartic powers of closure. Riche, imposing the Greek mode upon the narrative design, aligns the story rather more openly with the psychology of romance. Silla, in her own right, is another study in female loyalty made proactive through desire, invention, and moxie in the pursuit of her future on her own terms. That story, too, has its limbic orchestra, signaling deliverance or well-being in relation to nature's imperatives regarding cooperation between the sexes.

Lelia Types, Beloved, Admired, and Distrusted

As stated at the outset, the agency acquired by the female protagonist of this play gave rise to a new kind of comic ingénue. The demands of the role called for an expansion of the heroine's personality, granting her the psychological sufficiency to "write" the action, define its terms, and actualize her desires with an intelligence that manages contingency to the best of her abilities. Arguably, she becomes the first self-instructed, independent female protagonist on the early modern stage. So much, even in the England of Shakespeare, would never have come to fruition without her lead.

In words to describe Viola in Shakespeare's *Twelfth Night*, Lelia "cuts through the subterfuges and disguises of the others with absolute clarity, and she provides us with a center for the movement, a standard or normality which is never dull."[47] This Lelia is not the agent of unresolved anxiety, but the agent of contentment — an archetype of flourishing womanhood through a mastery of her environment.

Louise George Clubb discusses the Lelia type as a moveable "theatregram," an idea that can be translated from play to play featuring "woman as wonder," secure in her identity and sure

---

47. Joseph H. Summers, "The Masks of *Twelfth Night*," in *Twentieth-Century Interpretations of* Twelfth Night, ed. Walter N. King (Engelwood Cliffs, NJ: Prentice Hall, 1968), 15–23 at 20.

Introduction

of her destiny. Clubb seeks to distinguish these heroines from the charmers of "ordinary life" who do not become agents of "transcendent truth." Rather, this "figure is distinguished by a remarkable intrinsic worth, established by her effect on other characters and by structurally disposed contrasts with them as foils."[48] Robert Melzi had already pioneered this thesis; it was he who first set up the chain of theatrical and novelistic texts that led not only from Lelia to Viola as seriatim sources, but that produced the cumulative portrait of an emerging heroine type.[49]

What matters in this celebration is the emergence of feminine agency in a confined social world that invites admiration and approbation, as well as resistance on the part of some because she isn't nasty and aggressive enough. In that regard, Lelia–Viola is a feminist touchstone, controversial because some of us love and admire such wonderfully inventive yet attractive personalities, while confirming for others that her adaptive rebellion is either a good start, or merely a measured sop to sentimentalists.

---

48. Louise George Clubb, *Italian Drama in Shakespeare's Time* (New Haven: Yale University Press, 1989), 67–68. Clubb cites other heroines in this category from the early Italian theater: Lucrezia in *L'amor costante* (1531) by Alessandro Piccolomini (another member of the Intronati and a most likely collaborator in the creation of *The Deceived*); Elfenice in Raffaello Borghini's *La donna costante* (1578), who also seeks her lover in male disguise and, like Juliet, allows herself to be buried for dead; Drusilla in Girolamo Bargagli's *La pellegrina* (1567-68), who follows her beloved in a pilgrim's disguise and delicately re-establishes his love for her; and Erminia in Sforza Oddi's *Prigione d'amore*, who takes her brother's place, submits to ducal law, and is putatively executed.

49. Melzi, "From Lelia to Viola," 67–81. Melzi recognized the "wonder woman" type and proposed that her history be assessed by examining all the interim works contributing to this evolutionary process. They do not, however, form a linear growth sequence, for Viola emerged out of Lelia, it would seem, as the story passed directly to Bandello, then on to Barnabe Riche (most probably through Belleforest), whose "Apolonius and Silla," in the *Farewell to Military Profession*, served Shakespeare as his principal, if not his only source for *Twelfth Night*.

The Deceived

FINAL THOUGHTS

With that, our work may be close to its end, not in imposing a definitive reading, but in opening potential readings through a reassessment of the traditional topics that have occupied readers of the erudite theater in general. Behind all of these options, there is a common intent to ground the experiences of art in the experiences of our culture and our own perceptions of human nature. It is what we do in reading and in rehearsing in our imaginations the experiences of characters on an "as if real" basis; in so doing, we are able to feel and perceive the merits of their actions and assess them in relation to verisimilitude.

All such evaluation begins with our own psychologies, the ways in which we deal with other persons, their intentions, beliefs, and desires in everyday life, through the assessments furnished by our innate social computations and social feelings. But there are leading — and often mutually contradictory — cultural suppositions, as well: that we are a species that understands symbolic play that we can use for political purposes; that we can fashion provisional identities and live through them to expedient ends; that our cultures shape our fundamental values as a destiny; that gender is plastic, malleable, and even fragile, or largely essentialist and genetically conditioned, and that we had better be careful with our self-representations; that humans can never ultimately escape their instincts and appetites and are doomed to mischievous first-person drives in their sometimes foolish pursuits of pleasure and well-being; that we are group oriented and strategize our futures through cooperation and avoidance; and that we are survival machines with mentalities designed by the pressures of ancestral environments to actualize our destinies through planning and emotional support.

Give priority to any one of these perspectives in particular and a reading of this play emerges, often posited in the name of social justice, holiday inversion, sexual drives and personal autonomy, libertarian reform and progress, or the default necessity of our natures. Those who pursue mates through high-risk activities demonstrate one set of values;

Introduction

those who lose track of their own sexual orientation reveal other conditions; those who cooperate in seeking collective fairness reflect yet other values; and those who risk censure through blindness to their own follies and appetites expose still another vision of the human condition.

This play touches upon all such matters, and yet there is the critical need, in the search for a unity of ethos, to make one prevail as the fuse that drives the entire play. It's how "interpretation" works. The Intronati claimed to have no agendas, but desired merely to entertain, and perhaps, by extension, to leave judgment to our laughter and let our subconscious minds determine the bases for community and goodness that matter the most to our species. That is why *The Deceived* is such a brilliant mirror of the values and properties of the human condition, and likewise why it is bound to continue to stir discussion and disagreement.

■ ■ ■

Select Bibliography

Andrews, Richard. "*Gl'Ingannati* as a Text for Performance." *Italian Studies* 37 (1982): 26–48.

——. *Scripts and Scenarios: The Performance of Comedy in Renaissance Italy.* Cambridge: Cambridge University Press, 1993.

Aquilecchia, Giovanni. "Per l'attribuzione della commedia *Gli Ingannati*." *Giornale Storico della Letteratura Italiana* 154.487 (1977): 368–79.

Bargagli, Girolamo. *Dialogo de' giuochi che nelle vegghie sanesi si usano di fare.* Ed. Patrizia D'Incalci Ermini. Siena: Accademia Senese degli Intronati, 1982.

Beecher, Donald. "Introduction to *The Calandria*." *Renaissance Comedy: The Italian Masters.* Toronto: University of Toronto Press, 2009, 2:23–33.

——. "Concerning Sex Changes: The Cultural Significance of a Renaissance Medical Polemic." *Sixteenth Century Journal* 36.4 (2005): 991–1016.

Brand, Peter. "Disguise and Recognition in Renaissance Comedy." *Journal of Anglo-Italian Studies* 1 (1991): 16–32.

Bristol, Michael. "The Festive Agon: The Politics of Carnival." *Carnival and Theater: Plebian Culture and the Structure of Authority in Renaissance England.* New York: Routledge, 1985, 199–213.

Bullough, Geoffrey. "The Comedies, 1597–1603." In *Narrative and Dramatic Sources of Shakespeare.* London: Routledge and Kegan Paul, 1958, 2:269–339.

Bullough, Vern L., and Bonnie Bullough. *Cross Dressing, Sex, and Gender.* Philadelphia, University of Pennsylvania Press, 1993.

Burriss, Catherine Scott. "The Economics and Anxieties of the Intronati's Legendary Comedy, *Gl'Ingannati*." In "Performing Theory: Gendered and Erotic Complications in Cinquecento Comedies, and Some English Reverberations." Ph.D Diss. University of California Santa Cruz, 2006, 44–85.

——. "Troubling Doubling, Exceptional Oeconomia, and Compensation." *Quaderni d'Italianistica* 34.1 (2013): 65–92.

Bibliography

Celse-Blanc, Mireille. "Du travesti a la folie simulée, ou les jeux du masque dans la comédie siennoise." *Visages de la folie (1500–1650)*. Ed. Augustin Redondo and André Rochon. Paris: Publications de la Sorbonne, 1981, 45–54.

Cerreta, Florindo. "A French Translation of *Gl'Ingannati*: C. Estienne's Les Abusez." *Italica* 54.1 (April, 1977): 12–34.

———, ed. "Introduction" to *La commedia degli Ingannati*. Florence: L.S. Olschki, 1980.

Clubb, Louise George. *Italian Drama in Shakespeare's Time*. New Haven and London: Yale University Press, 1989.

———. "Theatregrams." *Comparative Critical Approaches to Renaissance Comedy*. Ed. Donald Beecher and Massimo Ciavolella. Ottawa: Dovehouse Editions Canada, 1986, 15–33.

Coller, Alexandra. "Fathers, Daughters, Crossdressing, and Names: *L'Anconitana* and Angelo Beolco/Ruzante's Contribution to Commedia." *MLN* 127 (2012): 124–41.

Concolino Mancini, Bianca. "Travestimenti, inganni e scambi nella commedia del Cinquecento." *Atti dell'Istituo Veneto di Scienze. Lettere ed Arti* 5.147 (1988–89): 169–213.

Corrigan, Beatrice. "Il Capriccio: An Unpublished Italian Renaissance Comedy and Its Analogues." *Studies in the Renaissance* 5 (1958): 74–86.

D'Amico, Jack. "The Treatment of Space in Italian and English Renaissance Theater: The Example of *Gl'Ingannati* and *Twelfth Night*." *Comparative Drama* 23.3 (Oct. 1989): 265–83.

Ferroni, Giulio. *Il testo e la scena: Saggi sul teatro del Cinquecento*. Rome: Bulzoni, 1980.

Garber, Marjorie. *Vested Interests: Cross-Dressing and Cultural Anxiety*. New York: Routledge, 1992.

Giannetti, Laura. *Lelia's Kiss: Imaging Gender, Sex, and Marriage in Italian Renaissance Comedy*. Toronto: University of Toronto Press, 2009.

———. "On the Deceptions of the Deceived: Lelia and the Pleasures of Play." *MLN* 116.1 (2001): 54–73.

Giannetti Ruggiero, Laura. "When Male Characters Pass as Women: Theatrical Play and Social Practice in the Italian Renaissance." *Sixteenth Century Journal* 36.3 (2005): 746.

Giraldi, Giovanni Battista. *Hecatommithi overo Cento Novella.* Venice: Girolamo Scotto, 1566.

Greenblatt, Stephen. "Fiction and Friction." In *Shakespearean Negotiations: The Circulation of Social Energy in Renaissance England.* Berkeley: University of California Press, 1988, 66–93.

Herrick, Marvin T. *Italian Comedy in the Renaissance.* Urbana and London: University of Illinois Press, 1960.

[Intronati of Siena]. *Gl'Ingannati.* In *Il teatro italiano*, 2, "La commedia del Cinquecento." Ed. Guido Davico Bonino. Turin: Einaudi, 1977, 2: 87–183.

———. *Il Sacrificio, comedia de gli Intronati celebrato nei giuochi di uno carnovale in Siena, Di nuovo corretta e ristampata.* Venice: Presso Domenico Cavalcalupo, 1625.

Kaufman, Helen Nicole. "Secchi as a Source of *Twelfth Night.*" *Shakespeare Quarterly* 5.3 (Summer 1954): 271–80.

Laqueur, Thomas. *Making Sex: Body and Gender from the Greeks to Freud.* Cambridge, MA: Harvard University Press, 1990.

Lope de Rueda. *Los Engañados. Medora.* Ed. Fernando Gonzáles Ollé. Madrid: España-Calpe, 1973.

Marcono, Paolo. *La città come forma simbolico.* Rome: Bulzoni, 1973.

Maylander, Michele. *Storie delle accademie d'Italia.* 5 vols. Bologna: Lincino Capelli, 1926, 3:355.

Melzi, Robert C. "From Lelia to Viola." *Renaissance Drama* 9 (1966): 67–81.

Milligan, Gerry. "Behaving Like a Man: Performed Masculinities in *Gl'Ingannati.*" *Forum Italicum* 41.1 (March 2007): 23–42.

Newbigin, Nerida. "Introduction to *The Deceived.*" In *Three Italian Renaissance Comedies.* Ed. Christopher Cairns. Lewiston, NY: Edwin Mellen Press, 1996, 251–318.

———. "Politics and Comedy in the Early Years of the Academia degli Intronati of Siena." *Il teatro italiano del rinascimento.* Ed. Maristella Lorch. Milan: Edizioni Communità, 1980, 1:123–34.

Newman, Karen. "*Gl'Ingannati* and Shakespeare's Romantic Comedy." *Stanford Italian Review* 3.2 (1983): 201–11.

Peacock, Thomas Love. *Gl'Ingannati. The Deceived: A Comedy Performed at Siena in 1531 and Aelia Laelia Crispis.* London: Chapman and Hall, 1862.

Bibliography

Pettrachi Costantini, Lolita. *L'Accademia degli Intronati di Siena e una sua commedia (Gli Ingannati) etc.* Siena: Accademia degli Intronnati, 1928.

Pietropaolo, Domenico. "The Stage in the Text: A Theatrical Stratification of Italian Renaissance Comedy." In *Comparative Critical Approaches to Renaissance Comedy*. Ed. Donald Beecher and Massimo Ciavolella. Ottawa: Dovehouse Editions Canada, 1986, 35–51.

Pinker, Steven. *The Blank Slate: The Modern Denial of Human Nature*. London: Penguin Books, 2003.

Pruvost, Réné. "*The Two Gentlemen of Verona, Twelfth Night*, et *Gl'Ingannati*." Études *anglaises* 13 (1960): 1–9.

Radcliff-Umstead, Douglas. *The Birth of Modern Comedy in Renaissance Italy*. Chicago: University of Chicago Press, 1969.

Riehle, Wolfgang. *Shakespeare, Plautus and the Humanist Tradition*. Cambridge: D.S. Brewer, 1990.

Riche, Barnabe. *His Farewell to Military Profession*. Ed. Donald Beecher. Binghamton/Ottawa: Medieval & Renaissance Texts & Studies/Dovehouse Editions, 1992, 74–80, 180–201.

Salingar, Leo. "The Design of Twelfth Night." *Shakespeare Quarterly*, 9 (1958): 117–39.

———. *Shakespeare and the Traditions of Comedy*. New York: Cambridge University Press, 1974.

Secchi, Niccolò. *Gl'Inganni*. Florence: Giunti, 1562.

———. *Self-Interest*. Trans. William Reymes (in 1660). Ed. Helen A. Kaufman. Seattle: University of Washington Press, 1953.

Shakespeare, William. *Twelfth Night*. Ed. J.M. Lothian and T.W. Craik. London: Methuen and Co. (1906), 1975: esp. xxxvi–xlvii.

———. *Twelfth Night, Or What You Will*. Ed. Roger Warren and Stanley Wells. Oxford: Oxford University Press, 1994.

Shepherd, Laurie. "Siena 1531: Genesis of a European Heroine," *Quaderni d'italianistica*, 26.1 (2005): 3–19.

Stewart, Pamela. "A Play on Doubles: *The Calandria*." *Modern Language Studies* 14.1 (1984): 22–32.

Vignali, Antonio. *La Cazzaria /The Book of the Prick*. Trans. and ed. Ian Frederick Moulton. New York: Routledge, 2003.

Plot Summary

Act 1

Scene 1: The play opens with two old men arguing over wedding plans. Virginio, Lelia's father, has offered his daughter to his old friend Gherardo, and as they discuss money matters they fill in some of the complex historical facts that have shaped the present situation. Both Lelia and Fabrizio, her brother, were victims of the Sack of Rome in 1527. Virginio lost both of them for a time. Lelia was imprisoned and putatively abused by the Spanish soldiers before her release, while Fabrizio was lost until he makes his appearance midway through the play, some two years after the Sack. During the interim, Lelia had enjoyed the requited love of Flamminio before she was sent away to live with a relative, only to discover, upon her return to Modena, that he had forgotten her and was in passionate pursuit of Isabella, the daughter of Gherardo, the very man to whom she had been pledged by her father. More recently, Lelia had been placed in a local convent for her safety, but by the time of the play's opening scenes, she could no longer be found. As subsequent scenes will reveal, she had cross-dressed to make her escape and had already found employment as a page in the household of the man she loved to attempt to regain his affection. Soon, however, Lelia as Fabio the page is sent on love missions to Isabella on behalf of her master Flamminio. Eventually, Isabella finds herself in love, not with Flamminio, but with Lelia in her male disguise. The principle imbroglio of the play is taking shape: a girl in disguise has become the love object of the girl she has been sent to court for her master.

Scene 2: Lelia's father, Virginio, meets with her nursemaid, Clemenzia, who is mumbling about omens of amazing things to happen, which Virginio interprets as signs of matrimony. Clemenzia complains at the same time about the folly of marrying a fifteen-year-old girl to a man nearing old age.

Plot Summary

SCENE 3: Lelia in disguise is in search of her nursemaid to tell her about her arrangements with Flamminio. Clemenzia is dismayed to hear about her activities, but Lelia manipulates her nurse and eventually enlists her in the scheme. In the process, we get a full history of Lelia's past. Describing her sleeping arrangements in a room adjacent to her master, Lelia causes Clemenzia to imagine all sorts of compromising threats. Lelia reveals her plan to tilt Isabella and Flamminio against each other in hopes that Flamminio might rediscover his love for her.

SCENE 4: Clemenzia meets with old Gherardo, who is betrothed to Lelia by her father, already anticipating of his future joys. As Spela, his servant, makes fun of him, Clemenzia dresses him down for his misplaced passions.

SCENE 5: Spela now meets with Virginio's servant, Scatizza, and both of them provide servant-class perspectives on their bosses. Scatizza also reveals the hypocrisy of convent life after going there to find Lelia. He recounts how, once inside this closely cloistered community, he found himself confronted with sexual teasing and outright propositions.

ACT 2

SCENE 1: Flamminio talks to his page (Lelia as Fabio) about his progress with Isabella, and Fabio spins his prospects as hopeless, urging him to let her go and to look elsewhere. Flamminio expresses his deep concern and affection for his page, confessing how he was once in love with Lelia.

SCENE 2: Now Lelia/Fabio meets with Pasquella, Gherardo's housekeeper and Isabella's go-between with Fabio. Pasquella tells the "boy" how badly he has been behaving toward Isabella and how much he will one day regret his cocky disinterest. But of course, the more Lelia/Fabio plays along with this impossible affair to maintain her cover, the more she places her disguise in jeopardy, especially if Isabella becomes interested in more than kissing. Pasquella convinces Fabio to pay Isabella another visit, creating an encounter that will become a turning point in the plot both strategically and psychologically.

The Deceived

SCENE 3: This scene introduces a subplot in which Pasquella is visited by a Spanish soldier who is trying to seduce her. She makes clear that she never intends to embrace him, while he is even less serious. He is seeking only casual sex, as well as someone to wash his clothes and steal for him from her own boss.

SCENE 4: Flamminio questions his servant Crivello why he is unable to find Fabio who is visiting Isabella. Crivello reveals that he bears no good will toward the page who took the job he had sought for himself.

SCENE 5: Spela buys musk at the apothecary's shop for Gherardo after Clemenzia told him he looked like an old goat.

SCENE 6: This is the famous "lesbian" kissing scene that has teased many imaginations. Crivello and Scatizza, servants to Flamminio and Virginio, meet outside Isabella's house just as she is coming out with Fabio. They hide to spy on the two as Isabella flirts and ultimately draws Fabio into an archway to kiss him. The two servants whisper a smutty commentary, and Crivello sees his chance to get even with Fabio by reporting the kissing to his boss, Flamminio.

SCENE 7: A critical scene in which Lelia/Fabio meets with her master and urges him to abandon all interest in Isabella. Flamminio begins to worry that Isabella might believe his love for Lelia is not over, and he decides to make a public announcement of his for her, at which point Lelia collapses into a malaise that awakens Flamminio's deep concern for her as his page — a boy he esteems and never wants to lose.

SCENE 8: Crivello reports the kissing to Flamminio, who, after his initial incredulousness, vows revenge upon his page. Now Lelia, in triple flight, goes into hiding

ACT 3

SCENE 1: With Lelia's fortunes sinking, her brother Fabrizio reappears in Modena with a small entourage consisting of his tutor in the person of the comic Pedant, and a burlesque

servant, Stragualcia, a glutton. They tour the city pointing out some of Modena's famous landmarks.

SCENE 2: Fabrizio's party and two rival innkeepers negotiate arrangements with much talk of hospitality, food, and drink. The party is invited to inspect the kitchens of The Jester Inn and sample the offerings. The contest is between abundance and simpler fare versus refinement and smaller portions, but also provides a chance to showcase the stock antics of the Pedant and Glutton, types drawn from the ancient comic theater.

SCENE 3: Virginio confronts Clemenzia, claiming that because of Lelia's behavior, he has become the scandal of the city. Clemenzia's job is to rationalize for her ward, Lelia, whom she protects as a mother, while calming the old man down. By this time, one of the nun's with a name that means "gossipy tell-tale" has spread information that Lelia is disguised and in the service of a gentleman in the city. That convinces Virginio that his daughter has been debauched and ruined.

SCENE 4: Fabrizio searches for his father after being warned by Frulla that he has a look-alike in the city right down to the color of his clothes. A brother and his sister are soon to be confused to great dramatic effect.

SCENE 5: Fabrizio meets Pasquella, who takes him for Fabio and talks at cross purposes about his relationship to Isabella. Fabrizio imagines himself the beloved of a beautiful girl. A possible opportunity begins to emerge.

SCENE 6: By this time, the news Virginio has about Lelia in disguise has been passed along to Gherardo. He is now vacillating over whether to abandon her or try to win her over. Virginio tries to convince him that it's not as bad as it looks.

SCENE 7: Events in this scene follow inevitably. Virginio meets Fabrizio and takes him for the disguised Lelia. Fabrizio protests to no avail as his father treats him to harsh correction. Fabrizio identifies his family, and even his father by name, refusing to acknowledge this insane old man is his father. Gherardo likewise deceived, takes this young man for his

The Deceived

Lelia, and decides that "she" is still so beautiful that he will marry her despite her many ruses and indiscretions. A plan follows to capture "her" by force if necessary, and to lock "her" in with Isabella for safe keeping. In so doing, they place a male with the girl who will take him for Fabio/Leila and invite him to her bed.

ACT 4

SCENE 1: The Pedant and Glutton take their bickering to a new level of insult and name-calling. Ostensibly, it is about establishing the pecking order between them by bullying and intimidation, but it is also just a comic show of verbosity.

SCENE 2: The Pedant runs into Virginio, his old master, and establishes their former connection. While Virginio is certain his son is dead, the Pedant assures him that he is not only alive but in the city and that he has pursued his learning and has not been abused in the meantime. A quest is launching to find him, not realizing that the son is the same person sent to Isabella as Lelia.

SCENE 3: Once the Pedant discovers his old master, he makes up with Stragualcia so together they can look for ways to exploit their old patron. All three go off to the inn for a drink, only to see Lelia, whom they naturally assume has escaped from Isabella and Gherardo's house.

SCENE 4: Lelia is questioned about how she got free. She, in turn, sasses her father in denial of everything. She even denies being herself, while Clemenzia reports, truthfully, that Lelia has been at her house the entire day and accuses the accusers of being drunk. Meanwhile, critical pieces of information are systematically emerging. Lelia learns that her brother is still alive and back in town.

SCENE 5: Pasquella, after unlocking the door to see what the two girls might be up to, finds them kissing and rolling on the bed. She is now in a position to break the news to the audience that the person with Isabella is decidedly not a girl because she has seen all his male equipment ready for action.

Plot Summary

SCENE 6: This scene takes up the subplot about the rosary, which Pasquella now manages to take from Giglio by playing a trick with her chickens in order to prevent him from following her inside before she gets the door locked. The soldier, bamboozled, threatens violence until he sees the master arriving and scampers away.

SCENE 7: Pasquella's boss, Gherardo, accuses her of letting Lelia get away. Just who Pasquella now thinks is in the room is no longer clear, but she assures Gherardo that Lelia is still there, only to be forced to turn over the key so that the master can verify it on his own. He, of course, finds a man with his daughter, presumably in flagrante delicto, and assumes somehow that it is a trick by Virginio. The logic of that accusation will never be unpacked because the two old men will come to swords long before they come to sense over the matter.

SCENE 8: Flamminio asks Pasquella when she last saw Fabio. still intent on revenge against his page, even after Isabella has been seduced by someone else. He brandishes a knife to use for disfiguring Fabio's face. As Flamminio leaves, Gherardo comes back to proclaim that he intends to take the man to court whom he has found in sex play with his daughter.

SCENE 9: The Pedant laments their inability to find Fabrizio. Gherardo then accuses Virginio of sending a male into his daughter's room. Virginio thinks he is defaming Lelia to get out of the marriage. Their potentially comi-tragic miscommunication leads to an armed showdown in the next act.

ACT 5

SCENE 1: Virginio appears in a suit of armor, urging his "troops" to equip themselves amidst talk of honor and weaponry. The fight is forestalled when it is announced that Fabrizio has been found in Isabella's room, and that they have made vows to each other. At last, the father meets with his long-lost son, now as Fabrizio.

The Deceived

SCENE 2: Crivello reports to Flamminio that he has found Fabio at Clemenzia's house. Flamminio sets out for a confrontation, but Clemenzia denies having a boy in the house. Before "Fabio" comes down, Clemenzia tells Lelia's entire story — her disguise and her service to a beloved master as his page — all in fictive form, before asking what Flamminio would do if he had been that man. Suspecting no trick, and moved by the story, he swears he would reward her with unconditional love. Clemenzia promises to reveal both the girl and her lover, but then calls for Fabio to come down.

SCENE 3: Before Flamminio can turn violent, Clemenzia challenges him to look the "boy" closely in the face and tell what he sees. The light of understanding emerges; he had been royally deceived. Clemenzia then connects the two stories and challenges him to keep his oath or face a court judge. Conveniently, Pasquella appears and announces that Isabella is already married to Fabrizio and that preparations for the feast are underway. That shock to Flamminio is followed by the news that Lelia is promised to Gherardo, which angers him even more. So he claims Lelia for himself immediately, and they pledge their vows before a legal witness.

SCENE 4: Giglio, the braggart soldier, is treated to a last set of lies by Pasquella about how Isabella stole his rosary and that negotiations would be required to get it back. That is enough to consider the story settled.

SCENE 5: Clemenzia's little girl, overhearing Lelia and Flamminio in the next room making passionate love, comes out to recount her mystified shock and awe, while the rest of us are treated to bawdy assurance that this play, in the end, is all about mating, coupling, and reproducing the race, by making public Lelia and Flamminio's consummate heterosexuality.

SCENE 6: Fabrizio is reunited with his nursemaid Clemenzia. She, after all, had been everything to him that he would know of a mother. The Intronati reserved this little scene to signal the play's concern with the reunion of families separated by catastrophe and war.

Plot Summary

SCENE 7: Virginio and Clemenzia express their relief and happiness that everything has turned out so well, leaving the stage to the glutton, Stragualcia, to announce the coming feast and the play's end.

■   ■   ■

GL'INGANNATI

■   ■   ■

THE DECEIVED

THE INTRONATI OF SIENA

1531

The Intronati of Siena

Recitatori della Comedia

GHERARDO, vecchio
VIRGINIO, vecchio
CLEMENZIA, balia
LELIA, fanciulla
SPELA, servo di Gherardo
SCATIZZA, servo di Virginio
FLAMMINIO, innamorato
PASQUELLA, fante di Gherardo
ISABELLA, fanciulla
GIGLIO, spagnuolo
CRIVELLO, servo di Flamminio
MESSER PIERO, pedante
FABRIZIO, giovinetto figliuolo di Virginio
STRAGUALCIA, servo del Fabrizio
AGIATO, oste
FRULLA, oste
FANCIULLINA, figliola della balia

Prologo

Io vi veggio fin di qua, nobilissime donne, meravigliare di vedermivi cosí dinanzi in questo abito e, insieme, di questo apparecchio come se noi avessimo a farvi qualche comedia. Comedia non vi dovete pensare: ché, infin l'anno passato, voi poteste conoscere che l'Intronati avevano il capo ad altro che alle comedie; e poi vedeste, l'altro giorno, qual fusse intorno alle cose vostre l'animo loro e che non volevano piú vostra pratica né venirvi piú dietro, come quelli che non gli piaceva piú essere morsi, rimenati per bocca e tocchi fino al vivo da

The Deceived

DRAMATIS PERSONAE

GHERARDO FOIANI, the father of Isabella
VIRGINIO BELLENZINI, the father of Lelia and Fabrizio
CLEMENZIA, Lelia's nursemaid
LELIA, daughter of Virginio, often disguised as Fabio, the page
SPELA, the servant of Gherardo
SCATIZZA, the servant of Virginio
FLAMMINIO DE' CARANDINI, in love with Isabella
PASQUELLA, Gherardo's housekeeper
ISABELLA, the daughter of Gherardo
GIGLIO, a Spaniard
CRIVELLO, a servant of Flamminio
PIERO, a pedant, Fabrizio's tutor
FABRIZIO, the son of Virginio
STRAGUALCIA, a servant of Fabrizio
AGIATO, owner of the Mirror Inn
FRULLA, owner of the Jester Inn
CITTINA, the daughter of Clemenzia

The action is set in Modena.

PROLOGUE

Even from up here, my fine ladies, I can spot the surprise on your faces to see me standing in front of you decked out in these clothes and surrounded by all this scenery, as though some comedy's about to begin. Well, I guess that would astonish you given how, until last year, the members of the Intronati were preoccupied with other projects, as you all know, not to mention that you found out a few days ago just what they thought of you — how they don't want to chase after you or be around you, so they don't get snapped at, chewed out, and mauled by you anymore. You saw what

voi. E però abbruciarono, come voi vedeste, quelle cose che gli potevano far drizzare la fantasia e crescer l'appetito di voi e delle cose vostre. Ora vi voglio cacciar questa meraviglia del capo. Questi Intronati, a dirvi 'l vero (e crediatemi, ch'io gli ho sentiti), si dolgono strettamente d'essere entrati in questo farnetico ed hanno una gran paura che voi, come quelle che avete di che, non pigliate quella lor faccenda per la punta di modo che, per l'avvenire voi glie ne teniate la lingua e gli voltiate le spalle ogni volta che gli vedrete. E, per questo, m'hanno spinto qui per imbasciadore, oratore, legato, procuratore o poeta, pigliatel come v'entra meglio nella memoria. Io mi truovo il mandato ampio, in buona forma. Prestatemi la fede vostra; altrimenti gli è forza ch'io vel mostri, ché l'ho portato meco. Dico ch'io so' qui a posta per far questa pace e rappiccarvi insieme con loro, se ne sète contente; ché, a dirvi il vero, le lor faccende, senza voi, son fredde e presso che perdute e, se non ci si ripara, se ne vanno in un zero. Fatelo, eh! fatelo, donne; ché ve ne metterà bene. Voi conoscete pur la natura loro: che, se voi gli volgete una volta gli occhi un poco pietosi, e' si lasceranno maneggiare, portar per bocca (da voi, però, non da altri, ché non starebbon forti) e straziare, toccar nel vivo con le parole, coi fatti, star di sopra a ogni cosa e esser sempre le prime voi. O che volete? sète contente? faretelo o no?... Voi non rispondete? Non lo negando, questo è buon segno. Mirate s'elli hanno voglia di farlo, questo accordo! che, quasi in tre dí, hanno fatto una comedia; e oggi ve la voglion far vedere e udire, se voi vorrete. Ecco che voi sapete ora quel che vuol dire questo apparecchio, chi io sono e quello ch'io vi faccio d'intorno. Questa comedia, per quanto io ne abbia inteso, la chiamano L'ingannati: non perché fussero mai ingannati da voi, no, ché mai non l'ingannaste e vi conoscan pur troppo bene (ma ben gli avete sforzati sempre né se ne son possuti guardar tanto che basti); ma la chiamano cosí perché poche persone intervengono nella favola che, nel compimento, non si trovino ingannate. Ma e' ci son degli inganni, tra gli altri, d'una certa sorte che volesse Iddio, per il mal ch'io vi voglio, che voi fusse ingannate spesso cosí, voi, ed io fussi l'ingannatore! ché io non mi curarei di

The Deceived

they did, burning all that stuff that excited their dreams and worked up their appetites for you and all your beauty.[1]

But now I want to allay your astonishment. These Intronati are really regretting their crazy behaviour. This is the truth, and I know it to be so because I heard them say it. They're worried sick that they've hurt you with their nasty taunts and that from now on you'll stop talking to them, that you'll give them the cold shoulder whenever they show up — which they know you can. That's why I've been pushed out here. I'm to be their emissary, their spokesman, ambassador, legal consultant, sweet talker — whatever you want to call me — commissioned to make you bury this whole affair, however it fits best into the deepest cleft of your forgetfulness.

So here I am in front of you with a jutting whopper of a task, and if you don't believe me, I can haul it out and show you.[2] It is my objective to work a truce between you to draw you back together, by your kind consent, for the truth is that without you their market has gone soft and lacklustre, and without your forgiveness it may waste away completely. So forgive, dear ladies, forgive. The pleasure will be yours as well. And you know their natures. Just a glance of compassion and you have them under your spell, like puppets in your hands. These are your skills alone, for not all women have such powers. With sweetness you can torture them, take hold of their,... of their minds with your words, put yourself in control, and always come out on top. So do I carry the day? Are you happy with this and willing? Why aren't you saying anything? Well, at least you're not refusing, so there's a bit of hope. They were all so keen to make up to you that in scarcely three days' time, they built this comedy for you, hoping you'd all agree to see it and hear it today.

That's why all these stage props are out.[3] And it explains why I'm here, too, and what I'm trying to do. As I understand it, they've entitled their comedy *The Deceived*, not because you've ever deceived them. Ah, no, that you could never have managed because they know you all too well. Even so, you've teased them a lot in ways that stopped them from getting back at you. No, the play got its name because most of

rimaner sotto all'ingannato. La favola è nuova e non altronde cavata che della loro industriosa zucca onde si cavorno anco, la notte di beffana, le sorti vostre; per le quali vi parve che l'Intronati vi mordesser tanto in su quel fatto del dichiarare e diceste che gli avevan cosí mala lingua. Ma e' si par ben che voi non l'avete assaggiate; ché forse non direste cosí, ma gli difendereste e terreste la parte loro da buone compagne in tutti quei luochi che bisognasse. So ben che non ci mancherà chi dica che questa è una insalata di mescolanza. A questi tali io non voglio, io, rispondere, perché, come ella si sia, gli basta ch'ella piaccia a voi sole: alle quali essi, con ogni loro studio, si sono ingegnati sempre di piacere principalmente; e questo pensano che gli verrà fatto di leggero e maggiormente se ce n'è tra voi delle pregne a cui soglion spesso piacere, non pur di questi cotali spettacoli, ma i carboni pesti, la cocitura dell'accia, la polver dei mattoni, i calcinacci e cosí fatte cose. Agli uomini non importa ch'ella piaccia o no, perché l'Intronati hanno ordinato un modo che nissun di loro la potrà né vedere né udire, se già non son ciechi. E però, se qualche sacciuto maligno, tirato dal desiderio che gli ha d'apontarci, avesse una gran voglia di vederla o udirla, cavisi gli occhi perché altrimenti non la corrà. Io so che vi parrà strano che i ciechi la vegghino. E pur sarà vero; e intendarete come, se voi arete tanta pazienzia ch'io vel mostri.

Quanto ha di bello il mondo, senza dubbio, è oggi in Siena; e quanto ha di bel Siena si truova al presente in questa sala. Questo non si può negare; perché quelle che non ci sono non poss'io credere che sieno né belle né appresso, poi ch'elle fuggono il parragon di voi altre. Come volete voi, adunque, che costoro stieno a mirar scene o comedie o sentino o vegghino cosa che noi faciamo o diciamo, essendoli voi dinanzi? Che piú bel giuoco, che piú bello spettaculo, che cosa piú piacevole o piú vaga si può veder di voi? Certo, nissuna. Ora

the characters are deceived before it's over. But anyway, my precious ladies, despite the bad feelings I still have for you, I wouldn't mind being the prankster who makes you fall for my tricks, God permitting, and then you could win out again and end up on top for all I care. As for the plot, it's totally new. The only source for it came right out of their teeming pumpkins — the same heads that spoke your doom on Twelfth Night.[4] That's when you all decided the Intronati had let such evil things escape their lips that you'd never forgive them. But don't despise those lips, for touching yours to theirs will make you relent. Then you'd be back on their side, taking up their cause whenever occasion requires.

I'm betting there will be folk who'll see our play as a hodgepodge. I've got nothing to say to them. However events work themselves out, if you all have fun in the process, the Intronati will be satisfied, because giving delight is all they've ever desired. And tickling your ladies' fancies should be a cinch for this play — especially the pregnant among you, who can crave almost anything: coal powder, hemp tea, brick dust, chalk, you name it. As for the men out there, the Intronati don't care whether they're pleased or not, having designed matters so that only the blind will actually see or hear any of it. And if there's still some supercilious pedant driven by his zeal to find fault, if he really wants to understand what's going on, he'd have to gouge out his eyes first. You must be thinking it odd that only the blind be allowed see this entertainment, but that's as it is. Patience and you'll understand why, because I'm about to explain.

If there's beauty for viewing anywhere on earth, you'll have to look for it in Siena, and if there's any to be found in Siena, you'll have to find it in this very room. No one could possibly deny this. I'll always believe that if they aren't here now, they've got nothing to rival your looks. They've all stayed away just to avoid the comparison. So how could any man find wonder in the dramatic action and stage scenery or listen to a thing that's said with so many gorgeous women around them? Can there be a more beautiful pastime, a more splendid sight, anything at all more delightful for a man to look upon than

eccovi mostro come gli uomini non vedranno né udiranno questa comedia, se non son ciechi, che già vi pareva ch'io avesse detta cosí gran pappolata. Ma voi, donne, la vedrete e odirete benissimo perché, in vero, non vi conosciamo tanto cortesi che vi siate per perdere o uscir di voi stesse nel mirarci. Né si pensin questi che fanno tanto il bello, questi acconci, questi spelatelli che, per aver una bella barba, per calzar bene uno stivale o per fare una riverenzia di beretta accompagnata con un sospiro che si senta fin da Fonte Becci, voi abbiate a lasciar questa cosa per attendere a loro: ché ne restarebbeno ingannati e cosí torrebbeno il nome alla nostra comedia. E' potrebbe bene essere che uno spagnuolo, che voi vedrete venire, vi rompesse un poco la fantasia e che non pigliasse cosí bene la nostra materia. Ma io v'insegnarò un bel colpo. Non vi curate di lui, ché, non avendo voi la lingua sua, non vi potete intendere insieme; e attendete a questi, che son tutti taliani: e, prestandoli voi la vostra attenzione, non perderete cosa che ci si dica e sarà bello e fatto. Ma, poi ch'io veggio questi uomini cosí intenti a mirarvi che non sentan ciò ch'io mi dica, mi giova di ragionar con voi un poco in sul sodo e domesticamente. È possibil però, ingrate che voi sète, che questi Intronati s'abbin sempre a lamentar di voi e che, sempre, in ogni luoco, vi s'abbi a ritoccare il medesimo e che le tante fatiche che duran per voi e 'l tanto studio che vi mettano intorno per lodarvi non vi possa piegare a fargli, un tratto, un piacere? Oh! Ponetevi una volta giú, col nome di Dio; e chiamateli tutti ad uno ad uno; e vogliate intendere quel che dicono e quel che cercano da voi: ché so certo che quel che vogliono è una frascaria e voi ne sète tanto copiose e ricche che, senza perdern'oncia, ne potreste dare, non solo a loro, ma a tutta questa città. Ditemi per vostra fè: che credete però che voglino? E' non cercano altro da voi che la grazia vostra; e che vogliate conoscere gli ingegni loro, chi l'ha grosso e chi l'ha sottile; e diciate: - Questo mi piace - e - Questo non mi piace, - acciò che quelli

The Deceived

you ladies? No, nothing at all. So now do you understand why they can't see or hear this comedy unless they're blind? Look, I'm not as stupid as you thought! Of course, you ladies won't have any trouble at all seeing and hearing the play, because, well-mannered as you are, you won't be falling for the likes of us. All those guys who get decked out to look handsome shouldn't think for a second that you'll lose interest in our play just to admire them — you know the ones, all spiffed up, shaved, sporting fashionable sets of whiskers, and top end boots, the chaps who make deep bows with their hats in their hands or make sighs that can be heard all the way out to the Becci Fountain.[5] If that's their notion of things, they'll be the deceived ones and steal the title of our comedy. I should warn you, as well, that you'll be seeing a Spaniard whose far-fetched yammering could set your teeth on edge and cloud up the plot. But take my bit of advice: just ignore him. You don't speak his language, so there's no way you can get what he's saying. Just listen to the Italians, and it'll all come out just fine.

But wait. There are some fellows up there so absorbed in looking you over that they haven't taken in a word I've been saying. Let me just mention a few things to you ladies frankly and personally for a minute. Considering your thanklessness, can it be that the Intronati will have to go on carping about you, repeatedly harping on this same issue wherever they go? After all the suffering they've been through for you, all the efforts they've expended in your praise, and still no willingness on your part to offer them a bit of consolation? Can't you lighten up a little, for God's sake? You should offer them your company, one by one, turn a careful ear to what they're saying and what they desire from you. I'm certain its but a bagatelle, a little something you have in such abundance that it would cost you nothing to share, not only with them, but with the entire city. Let's hear from you in all frankness what you think they're really after. I can tell you, they want nothing more than to share in your graces. When you come to know their searching wit, however straight or twisted, all you have to say is, "his wit's for me," or "the other's wit isn't." That way, the

che non v'aggradaranno possin volgere il pensiero altrove e attender dietro ad altro studio. Ma gli è una gran cosa che voi gli vogliate tener sempre in questo cimbello e non vogliate risolvervi, un tratto, a questo benedetto "sí!" Sapete quel ch'io vi vo' dire? Guardatevi di non li fare, un tratto, disperar da vero; e tenete a mente ben le mie parole, ch'io so quel ch'io me dico. Voi ne li perderete, una volta, a fatto; e non gli potrete poi tanto andare a versi che ci sia ordine a porvi riparo; e ve ne dorrete, quando non sarete piú a tempo. E tenete questo per fermo: che non si sta sempre a un modo. E questo basti. Oh! Or ch'io mi ricordo: non v'aspettate altro argomento perché quello che ve lo aveva a fare non è in punto. Fatevi senza, per ora. E bastivi sapere solamente che questa città è Modana, per questo anno, e le persone che intervengono nella favola sono, i piú, modanesi. Però, se facessino qualche errore nel muover della lingua, non sarà gran fatto perché non l'hanno ancora cosí ben presa. L'altre cose, io penso che voi siate cosí capaci che la materia v'entrarà per se stessa senza troppa fatica. Due ammaestramenti sopra tutto ne cavarete: quanto possa il caso e la buona fortuna nelle cose d'amore; e quanto, in quelle, vaglia una longa pazienzia accompagnata da buon consiglio. Il che due fanciulle, con il lor saper, vi mostraranno; il quale se, seguendolo, poi vi giovarà, arete questo obligo con esso noi. Questi uomini, se non aranno piacere delle cose nostre, assai ci aranno da ringraziare, ché, per quattr'ore al manco, gli daremo commodità di poter contemplare le vostre divine bellezze. Ma, perch'io veggo duo vecchi ch'escon fuore, mi partirò, benché mal volentieri, da mirar sí belle cose, ancor ch'io penso che vi tornarò a vedere. Addio tutti.

ones you can't abide can seek to place it elsewhere. It is no laughing matter that you keep them in perpetual turmoil and do nothing to put things right simply by saying "yes." Beware of provoking their despair, and mark my words, because I know exactly what I'm saying here. In time, you could lose them forever. There'll be no way to bring them back. And once it's too late, you'll be really sorry. Rest assured, they've got alternatives. Well, I've had my say.

Oh, and as for the play, don't think there will be a summary of the action because the person chosen for the job couldn't get it ready in time. So for now, you'll have to manage on your own. All you need to know is that the setting for this year — the one you see behind me — represents Modena. That means that most of the people you're about to encounter are Modenese. If they make a mess of the local dialect, just ignore it. They just haven't had enough time to get the hang of it. As for everything else, you're all smart enough to catch on without much difficulty. You should be taking away with you two points in particular: that good luck and picking the right moment are crucial to success in love, and that keeping patient and following good advice are essential factors. You can learn and master these lessons by watching the examples provided by the two young ladies you're about to see. And if what you learn helps you out later on, you can thank the Intronati. As for the men — well, if they don't enjoy our play, they'll still owe us for the four hours, give or take, we've provided them to meditate on your heavenly beauty. Ah, here come two old men so I must be off, despite my regret in losing sight of all you gorgeous ladies. But I plan to return. Goodbye.

The Intronati of Siena

Atto Primo

Scena prima

GHERARDO *e* Virginio *vecchi.*

GHERARDO: Fa' adunque, Virginio, se desideri in questa cosa farmi piacere, come hai detto, che quanto piú presto sia possibile si faccino queste benedette nozze; e cavami una volta di cosí intrigato laberinto nel quale non so come disavedutamente son corso. E, se pur qualche cosa ti tenesse, come il non aver danari per le veste (ché ben so che 'l tutto perdesti nel miserabil sacco di Roma) e paramenti per la casa, o per aventura ti trovasse male agiato di proveder per le nozze, dimelo senza rispetto: ché a tutto provederò io; né mi parrà fatica, pur che questa cosa segua un mese prima, per cavarmi questa voglia, spendere un dieci scudi piú, ché, per grazia di Dio, so dove sono. E ben cognosci tu che ormai niun di noi è piú erba di marzo, ma sí ben di maggio e forse... E quanto piú si va in là piú si perde tempo. Né ti maravigliar, Virginio, che tanto te ne importuni, ch'io ti do la mia fede che, perch'io sono entrato in questa girandola, non dormo la metà della notte; e, che sia vero, guarda a che ora mi son levato questa mattina e sappi che, prima ch'io venissi a te per non destarti, avevo udita la prima messa a duomo. E, se forse avessi mutata fantasia e paresseti che con gli anni di tua figliuola non s'affacesseno i miei, che già sono agli "anta" e forse gli passano, dimmelo arditamente: perché a tutto provederò, voltando i pensieri altrove; e te e me libererò, in un punto, di fastidio, ché ben sai s'io son ricerco d'imparentarmi con altri.

VIRGINIO: Né questo né altro rispetto mi terrebbe, Gherardo, se fusse in arbitrio mio di poterti fare oggi sposar mia figliuola, ch'io non lo facesse; e, avenga che quasi ogni mia facultà perdesse nel sacco (ed insieme Fabrizio, quel mio benedetto figliuolo), per grazia di Dio, mi

The Deceived

ACT I

Scene 1

A street in front of Virginio's house.
GHERARDO *and* VIRGINIO, *old men.*

GHERARDO: Just do it, Virginio. If you want to make me happy in the matter, like you promised, let's get this blessed wedding over with as soon as we can. I don't know how I managed to get myself into this stupid maze, but now I just want out for good and for all. Look, I realize you got hit pretty hard by the wretched Sack of Rome,[6] so if it's money for the gowns or the furniture or the ceremony that's holding you up, just be up front with me. I can handle everything — no problem. For the love of God, if I could get this whole thing advanced by a month just to know where I stand and satisfy my cravings, ten scudi more would be nothing.[7] We're neither of us spring grass any more, as you know. We've hit the summer sear, so the longer the delay, the more time we're losing. Don't look so baffled that I'm crowding you on this, Virginio. Once this notion got hold of my brain, my nights have been cut in half, trust me. Do you realize what time I was up this morning? I was at the Duomo for the early Mass before I showed up here so as not to wake you. Then again, if you've changed your mind — maybe thinking that your daughter's a little young for a fellow at his prime or a little past — clue me in so I can use my time to find somebody who could save both of us from all this trouble. There are plenty out there who'd still like to have me for kin.

VIRGINIO: Nothing in all this is stopping me. If it were just my doing, Gherardo, you'd be married to my girl today. And you're right about what I lost in that miserable Sack, not only nearly all my possessions, but my beloved son Fabrizio. Still, by God's grace, I've got enough of

è rimaso ancor tanto di patrimonio ch'io spero poter vestire e far le nozze di mia figliuola senza gravare alcun che mi sovenga. Né pensar ch'io mi sia per mutare di quel ch'io t'ho promesso, quando la fanciulla se ne contenti; ché ben sai tu che non sta bene a mercatanti mancar di quello ch'una volta promettono.

GHERARDO: Cotesta è una cosa, Virginio, che piú si sente in parole che non si truova in fatti fra' mercatanti de' nostri tempi. Ben credo che non sia tu di quelli. Non di meno il vedermi menar d'oggi in domane e di domane nell'altro mi fa sospettar non so che; né ti cognosco io per cosí da poco che, quando vorrai, non facci far tua figliuola a tuo modo.

VIRGINIO: Ti dirò. Tu sai che m'accadde l'andare a Bologna per saldar la ragione d'un traffico che aveamo insieme messer Buonaparte Ghisilieri, il cavalier da Casio ed io. E perch'io sono in casa solo, ed abitavo in villa, non volsi lasciar mia figliuola in man di fantesche; ma la mandai nel monister di San Crescenzio, a suor Camilla sua zia: ove è ancora, ché sai ch'io tornai iersera. Ora io ho mandato il famiglio a dirgli che la torni.

GHERARDO: Sai tu certo ch'ella sia nel monistero e ch'ella non sia altrove?

VIRGINIO: Come s'io il so? dove vuo' tu ch'ella sia? che domanda è questa?

GHERARDO. Dirotti. Son stato certe volte là per mie facende ed honne domandato; e mai non l'ho potuta vedere; e alcune mi hanno detto ch'ella non v'è.

VIRGINIO: Gli è perché quelle buone madri la vorrebon far monaca per redare, dopo la morte mia, questo poco di resto. Ma non per questo gli riuscirebbe il pensiero, ch'io non son però sí vecchio ch'io non sia atto ad avere un par di figliuoli quando io tolga moglie.

GHERARDO. Vecchio? Oh! Ti prometto ch'io mi sento cosí bene in gambe ora come quando io ero di vinticinque anni; e massimamente la mattina, prima ch'io pisci. E,

my own without burdening my friends to afford a trousseau and a wedding for my daughter. So I'm not about to go back on the promise I made you, as long as my girl's in agreement. It's ill-becoming of merchants to back out of their sworn word as you know.

GHERARDO: Merchant's promises these days, Virginio, are more in the talk than in the doing. I'm not making you out to be one of them, but I'm having my thoughts. Aren't I being led on day after livelong day? I mean, it seems to me that if you really wanted to, you could make that daughter of yours do what you tell her to do.

VIRGINIO: Will you hear this? I went to Bologna to close an account with Buonaparte Ghisilieri and the Cavalier of Casio — you knew that. I'm entirely on my own in that villa of mine, so I'm not about to leave my daughter alone with the servants.[8] That's why I sent her over to the convent of San Crescenzio to be with Sister Camilla, her aunt,[9] and she's still there because I just got back last night — you knew that too. My servant's been sent to bring her back.

GHERADO: And you're convinced she's in the convent and not somewhere else?

VIRGINIO: Sure I'm sure. Where else do you think she'd be? What are you getting at, anyway?

GHERARDO: Let me tell you. Business took me that way, so I stopped and asked for her on several occasions. But I never laid eyes on her, and some of the sisters told me she wasn't even there.

VIRGINIO: That's because the nuns are trying to turn her into one of them so that after I die, they can put their hands on what little I've got left. But that'll never happen. I'm not too old to get me another wife and have a few more kids.

GHERARDO: You or me old? I've got the vim of a twenty-five year old, strong, especially in the morning before I take a leak. So what if my whiskers are white. I've still got

s'io ho questa barba bianca, nella coda son cosí verde come il poeta toscano. E non vorrei che niun di questi sbarbatelli, che van facendo il bravo per Modena col pennacchio ritto alla guelfa, con la spada alla coscia, col pugnal di dietro, con la nappa di seta, mi vincessero in cosa nissuna, eccetto che nel correre.

VIRGINIO: Tu hai buono animo. Non so come le forze riusciranno.

GHERARDO: Vorrò che tu ne domandi Lelia, come sarà, la prima notte, dormita con me.

VIRGINIO: Or, col nome di Dio, ti bisogna avergli discrezione, perché l'è pure ancor fanciulla e non è buono, in principio, d'esser cosí furioso.

GHERARDO: Che tempo ha?

VIRGINIO: Quando fu il sacco di Roma, ch'ella ed io fumo prigioni di que' cani, finiva tredici anni.

GHERARDO: Gli è appunto il mio bisogno. Io non la vorrei né piú giovane né piú vecchia. Io ho le piú belle veste e' piú bei vezzi e le piú belle collane e' piú bei finimenti da donne che uom di Modena.

VIRGINIO: Sia con Dio. Son contento d'ogni suo bene e tuo.

GHERARDO: Sollecita.

VIRGINIO: Della dote, quel ch'è detto è detto.

Gherardo. Credi ch'io mi mutassi? Addio.

VIRGINIO: Va' in buona ora. Certo, che ecco la sua balia: che mi torrà fatica di mandarla a chiamare perché accompagni in qua Lelia:

Scena seconda

CLEMENZIA *balia e* VIRGINIO *vecchio.*

CLEMEZIA: Io non so quel che si vorrà indovinare che tutte le mie galline hanno fatto, questa mattina, sí fatto il

The Deceived

a tough carrot, as the Tuscan poet says.[10] You know those greenhorns running around Modena these days, making the fashion with their Guelph feathers sticking in the air, their swords at their sides and daggers on their butts, and their silk tassels? Not a one of them can beat me at anything except scampering off.

VIRGINIO: You've got the spirit, all right, but will your strength hold out?

GHERARDO: You just ask Lelia about that after our first night together.

VIRGINIO: Well, for God's sake, be a little gentle. She's just a girl, you know, so don't start off with brute force.

GHERARDO: How old is she then?

VIRGINIO: Back in the Sack of Rome times when those dogs[11] put the two of us in prison, she was close to the end of thirteen.

GHERARDO: Just what I'm looking for. I wouldn't want her a day older or younger. The clothes and jewelry and necklaces and trappings I've got for her are the most beautiful in all of Modena.

VIRGINIO: With God's blessings, I'm really pleased by her good fortune and yours too.

GHERARDO: Just bring on the day.

VIRGINIO: What we said about the dowry still stands?

GHERARDO: I'm not the kind to change my mind. Well, so long for now.

VIRGINIO: Good luck to you. *(Gherardo leaves.)* Heh, so now I don't have to find her first to send her after Lelia.

Scene 2

CLEMEZIA, *a nursemaid, and* VIRGINIO.

CLEMEZIA: *(To herself)* It's got to mean something. This morning the hens were cackling to turn the house

cicalare che pareva che mi volesser metter la casa a romore o arricchirmi d'uova. Qualche nuova cosa m'interverrà oggi; ché non mi fanno mai questa cantèppola che quel dí, non senta o non m'avvenga qualche cosa mal pensata.

VIRGINIO: Costei debbe testé parlar con gli angeli o col beato padre guardiano di Santo Francesco.

CLEMEZIA: Ed un'altra cosa m'è avvenuta, che anco di questo non so che me ne indovinare: ben ch'el mio confessore mi dica ch'io fo male a por mente a queste cose e dar fede alli augúri.

VIRGINIO: Che fai, che tu parli cosí drento a te? Egli ha pur passata la befania.

Clemenzia. Oh! Buon dí, Virginio. Se Dio m'aiuti, ch'io mi venivo a stare un pezzo con voi. Ma voi vi sète levato molto per tempo. Voi siate il ben venuto.

VIRGINIO: Che dicevi cosí fra' denti? Pensavi forse di cavarmi di mano qualche staiuol di grano o qualche boccal d'oglio o qualche pezzo di lardo, come è tua usanza?

CLEMEZIA: Sí certo! Oh che liberalaccio da cavargli di mano! E forse che fa massarizia pei suoi figliuoli?

VIRGINIO: Che dicevi adunque?

Clemenzia. Dicevo ch'io non sapevo pensare quel che si volesse dire che una gattina bella, ch'io ho, che l'ho tenuta quindici dí perduta, questa mattina è tornata; e, poi ch'ella ebbe preso un topino nel mio camarin buio, scherzando con esso, mi rovesciò un fiasco di tribiano che me lo aveva dato il predicator di San Francesco perch'io gli fo le bocate.

VIRGINIO: Cotesto è segno di nozze. Ma tu vuoi dir ch'io te ne desse un altro, è vero?

CLEMEZIA: Cotesto è vero.

VIRGINIO: Or vedi s'io so' indivino! Ma che è di Lelia, la tua allieva?

The Deceived

upside down or lay eggs to make me rich. Today, something's up. When they make that kind of ruckus, there's bad news or a disaster coming.

VIRGINIO: *(Aside)* Will you look at her. She's been gabbing with angels or with the holy father at the convent of St. Francis.[12]

CLEMEZIA: *(To herself)* I know my confessor says it's wrong to put faith in omens and such, but there's another weird thing that happened, and I don't know what it means.

VIRGINIO: The Befana's time has come and gone,[13] so what are you muttering to yourself about?

CLEMEZIA: O, Virginio, good day to you. As God's my defense, I was on my way to stay a while with you.[14] You're up pretty early! Welcome back.

VIRGINIO: So what's all this talking to yourself about? Up to your usual tricks trying to light-talk grain, lard chunks, or bottles of oil out of me?

CLEMEZIA: Well, I was actually. *(Aside)* Just try talking a generous skinflint like him out of something. Is he hoarding everything for his children?

VIRGINIO: What's that you say?

CLEMEZIA: That my beautiful little kitten that I lost fifteen days ago has come home, and I'm wondering what it can mean. Already it's caught a mouse in the closet, and while frisking about tipped over the bottle of Trebbiano wine the priest at Saint Francis gave to me for washing his clothes.

VIRGINIO: Ah, that presages a marriage. So you want another bottle, is that it?

CLEMEZIA: I wouldn't say "no."

VIRGINIO: See, I can read signs too, but first what's become of Lelia?

CLEMEZIA: Eh! povera figliuola, quanto era meglio ch'ella non fusse mai nata!

VIRGINIO: Perché?

CLEMEZIA: Perché, dici, eh? Gherardo Foiani non va dicendo per tutto che gli è sua moglie e che gli è fatto ogni cosa?

VIRGINIO: Dice il vero. Perché? Non ti par forse ch'ella sia bene allogata, in una casa onorevole, a un ricco, ben fornito di tutti i beni, senza avere niuno in casa, che non avrà a combattere né con suocera né con nuora né con cognate che sempre stanno come cani e gatte? E trattaralla da figliuola.

CLEMEZIA: È cotesto il male: ché le giovani vogliono essere trattate da mogli e non da figliuole; e voglion chi le strazi, chi le morda e chi l'accenci ora per un verso e ora per un altro, e non chi le tratti da figliuole.

VIRGINIO: Tu credi che tutte le donne sien come te? ché sai che ci conosciamo. Ma e' non è cosí; benché Gherardo ha un buono animo di trattarla da moglie.

CLEMEZIA: E come, che ha degli anni passati cinquanta?

VIRGINIO: Ch'emporta cotesto? Io so' pur quasi al medesimo; e tu sai pur s'io son buon giostrante o no.

CLEMEZIA: Oh! De' par vostri se ne trovan pochi. Ma, s'io credesse che voi glie la desse, prima l'affogarei.

VIRGINIO: Clemenzia, io perdei ciò ch'io avevo. Ora mi bisogna fare il meglio ch'io posso. Se Fabrizio, un dí, si trovasse ed io avesse dato ogni cosa a costei, si morrebbe di fame; che non vorrei. Ora io la marito a Gherardo con condizione che, se Fabrizio non si truova infra quattro anni, abbi mille fiorini di dote; se ritornasse, ne abbi aver solamente dugento; e, del resto, la dota egli.

CLEMEZIA: Povera figliuola! So che, se la farà a mio modo...

The Deceived

CLEMEZIA: The poor child! Better she'd never been born.

VIRGINIO: Why's that?

CLEMEZIA: You ask why? Isn't Gherardo Foiani going around telling everyone that she's his wife and that it's all arranged?

VIRGINIO: It's the plain truth he's telling. Think about it. She'll have a nice house, with a rich man, honored by everyone, with no relatives, and supplied with the best of everything. She can run her own affairs without having to squabble with a mother-in-law or sisters-in-law, who are like a bunch of scratching cats. And Gherardo will treat her just like a daughter.

CLEMEZIA: That's the hard bit. Girls don't want to be daughters. They want to be wives. They want someone to tousle and nudge them, give them little bites, warm up one side and then warm up the other. They don't want to be daughters.

VIRGINIO: You assume all women reason like you? I know your way of thinking just as well as you know mine! As for Gherardo, he's a good soul. She'll get the wife treatment.

CLEMEZIA: At fifty and counting?

VIRGINIO: What's that got to do? I'm just about that age myself, and you know how good I am in the saddle.

CLEMEZIA: Sure, not many are a match for you. But if you're really planning on sending her off with him, I'll drown her first.

VIRGINIO: But Clemenzia, my fortune's nearly gone. I've got to make shift as I can. If they find Fabrizio, someday, and I give everything to her, he'd starve to death. I can't do that. Gherardo's willing to take her on condition that if Fabrizio doesn't turn up in the next four years, I'll make that dowry one thousand florins, but if he does, she only gets two hundred, and he supplies the rest.

CLEMEZIA: Poor thing. *(Aside)* If she did what I'm telling her to do....

VIRGINIO: Che n'è? Quant'ha che tu non l'hai veduta?

CLEMEZIA: Son piú di quindici giorni. Oggi volevo andarla a vedere.

VIRGINIO: Intendo che quelle monache la voglion far monaca e dubito che non gli abbin messo qualche grillo nel capo, come è lor costume. Va' fin là, tu, e digli da parte mia che ella se ne venga a casa.

CLEMEZIA: Sapete? Vorrei che mi prestasse due carlini per comprare una soma di legna, ché non n'ho stecco.

VIRGINIO: Diavolo, empiela tu! Orsú! Va', ché te le comprarò io.

CLEMEZIA: Voglio andare prima alla messa.

Scena terza

LELIA *da ragazzo chiamata per finto nome* FABIO *e* CLEMENZIA *balia*.

LELIA: Gli è pure un grande ardire il mio, quando io 'l considero, che, conoscendo i disonesti costumi di questa scorretta gioventú modanese, mi metta sola in questa ora a uscir di casa! Oh come mi starebbe bene che qualcun di questi giovani scapestrati mi pigliasse per forza e, tirandomi in qualche casa, volesse chiarirsi s'io son maschio o femina! E cosí m'insegnasseno a uscir di casa, cosí di buona ora. Ma di tutto questo è cagione l'amore ch'io porto a questo ingrato e a questo crudel di FLAMMINIO: Oh che sorte è la mia! Amo chi m'ha in odio, chi sempre mi biasma; servo chi non mi conosce; ed aiutolo, per piú dispetto, ad amare un'altra (che, quando si dirà, nissun sarà che lo creda) senza altra speranza che di poter saziare questi occhi di vederlo, un dí, a mio modo. Ed infino a qui mi è andato assai ben fatto ogni cosa. Ma, da ora innanzi, come farò? che partito ha da essere il mio? Mio padre è tornato. Flamminio è venuto ad abitar nella città. E qui non

VIRGINIO: What's she been doing, and anyway, when did you see her last?

CLEMEZIA: A couple of weeks ago, maybe more. I meant to go see her today.

VIRGINIO: I hear the nuns are trying to make another one out of her. They'll be stuffing her head full of fibs, like they always do. So go over to the convent and arrange for her to come home.

CLEMEZIA: Seriously? But first I was hoping you'd lend me a couple of carlins[15] to buy some wood for the fire. There's not a twig left.

VIRGINIO: What the devil. Just get going, scram, and I'll go buy it for you myself.

CLEMEZIA: I'm going to hear Mass first.

Scene 3

The street in front of Flamminio's house.
LELIA, *disguised as a boy and going by the name of Fabio, and* CLEMEZIA, *her nursemaid.*

LELIA: Pretty bold of me when I think about it, leaving the house alone at this time of day, what with all those beastly punks going around Modena. Nice mess I'd be in if one of those dissolutes hauled my carcass indoors somewhere just to confirm my sex! Then I'd be regretting my early up and away. But that's how love goes when it's for that mean and thankless Flamminio. Such is my destiny — to be in love with a man who scorns, even hates me. I'm in service to a fellow who doesn't even know who I am. And worse than that, I help him out with courting another girl. Who would ever believe me if I let that out? But this is the only way there is to please my eyes with seeing him whenever I want. Things have been all right so far. But what will I do from now on? What tack should I follow? My father's back and Flamminio has moved to town. I'll be

poss'io stare senza esser conosciuta: il che se avviene, io resto vituperata per sempre e divento una favola di tutta questa città. E, per questo, sono uscita fuora a questa ora; per consigliarmi con la mia balia, che da la finestra ho veduta venire in qua, ed insieme con lei pigliarci quel partito che giudicaremo il migliore. Ma prima vo' vedere s'ella in questo abito mi conosce.

CLEMEZIA: In buona fè, che Flamminio debbe essere tornato a stare in Modena, ch'io veggio l'uscio suo aperto. Oh! Se Lelia lo sapesse, gli parrebbe mill'anni di tornare a casa di suo padre. Ma chi è questo fraschetta che tante volte m'attraversa la strada, questa mattina? Ché pur mi ti metti fra' piei? ché non mi ti levi dinanzi? ché pur ti vai attorniando? che vuoi da me? Se tu sapesse come i tuoi pari mi piacciono...

LELIA: Dio vi dia il buon dí, mona Scrocca-il-fuso.

CLEMEZIA: Va'. Dallo pure a chi tu debbi aver dato la buona notte.

LELIA: Se ad altro ho data la buona notte, a voi darò il buon dí, se lo vorrete.

CLEMEZIA: Non mi rompare il capo, ché tu mi faresti, questa mattina... ti so dir io.

LELIA: Sète forse aspettata dal guardian di San Francesco? o pure andate a trovar fra' Cipollone?

CLEMEZIA: Doh! che te venga la febre ben ora! Che hai a cercar tu i fatti miei né dov'io vo né dov'io stia? che guardiano? che fra' Cipollone?

LELIA: Oh! Non v'adirate, mona Molto-mena-e-poco-fila.

CLEMENZIA: Per certo, io conosco costui; e, non so dove, mi pare averlo veduto mille volte. Dimmi, ragazzo: e dove mi conosci tu, che vuoi saper tanto delle cose mie? Levati un poco questa cappa dal volto.

LELIA: Orsú! Fai vista di non mi conoscere, eh?

found out if I stay here, and if that happens, the whole city will zero in on me with their slander and gossip for the rest of my days. That's why I'm heading out early to talk to my nursemaid who's on her way. I saw her out the window. We can decide together what's best to do. But first, let's see if she knows me in this get-up. *(Clemenzia enters.)*

CLEMEZIA: Good Lord! Flamminio must be back in Modena because his door's hanging wide open. If Lelia knew, she'd get herself back to her father's house as fast as she could. Who's this scamp who keeps cutting in front of me? — Who are you to get underfoot? Why don't you buzz off and stop circling me? Are you after something, because if you knew what I think of the likes of you....

LELIA: Well, if it isn't Mother Lightfinger. May God make your day a good one.

CLEMEZIA: Scram. Use that line on whoever you say "good night" to.

LELIA: You've given others a good night, so I'm giving you a good day. Even if I hand out "good nights" elsewhere, I'm telling you "good day" now, if you don't mind.

CLEMEZIA: You want to sass me this morning? I'm one who can sass you back.

LELIA: So is the priest of St. Francis looking for you? Or are you looking for Brother Cipollone?[16]

CLEMEZIA: Drop dead! It's none of your business what I do or where I go. What priest are you on about? What Brother Cipollone?

LELIA: O, don't go off half cocked, Mother Partyup.

CLEMEZIA: *(Aside)* I must know this rapscallion. Can't say where, but I've seen him a bunch of times. — So let's hear it, boy, how do you know me and all my affairs? Pull that hood back from your face so I can get a better look.

LELIA: So you're pretending not to know me, is that it?

CLEMEZIA: Se stai nascosto, né io né altri ti conoscerà.

LELIA: Tirati un poco piú in qua.

CLEMEZIA: Ove?

LELIA: Piú in qua. Ora cognoscimi?

CLEMEZIA: Se' tu forse Lelia? Dolente a la mia vita! Sciagurata a me! Sí, che gli è essa. Oimè! Che vuol dir questo, figliuola mia?

LELIA: Di' piano. Tu mi pari una pazza, a me. Io m'andarò con Dio, se tu gridi.

CLEMEZIA: Parti forse che si vergogni? Saresti mai diventata femina del mondo?

LELIA: Sí, che io son del mondo. Quante femine hai tu vedute fuor del mondo? Io, per me, non ci fu' mai, ch'io mi ricordi.

CLEMEZIA: Adunque, hai tu perduto il nome di vergine?

LELIA: Il nome no, ch'io sappi, e massimamente in questa terra. Del resto si vuol domandarne gli spagnuoli che mi tenner prigiona a Roma.

CLEMEZIA: Questo è l'onor che tu fai a tuo padre, a la tua casa, a te stessa ed a me che t'ho allevata? che ho voglia di scannarti con le mie mani. Entrami innanzi, veh! Ch'io non voglio che tu sia piú veduta in questo abito.

LELIA: Oh! Abbi un poca di pazienzia, se tu vuoi.

CLEMEZIA: O non ti vergogni d'esser veduta cosí?

LELIA: So' io forse la prima? "ho vedute a Roma le centinaia. E, in questa terra, quante ve ne sono che, ogni notte, vanno in questo abito ai fatti loro!

CLEMEZIA: Coteste son ribalde.

LELIA: Oh! Fra tante ribalde non ne può andare una buona?

The Deceived

CLEMEZIA: Hidden in there, neither I nor anyone else could figure it out.

LELIA: Get a bit closer.

CLEMEZIA: How close?

LELIA: Right up here. Now do you recognize me?

CLEMEZIA: Lelia, can that be you? Sorrow of my life, you'll be the death of me. It's you for sure. Heavenly day, what do you mean by this, my dear child?

LELIA: Not so loud. You look like you're going crazy. Start yelling, and I'm off and gone.

CLEMEZIA: It's your shame that will take you off. Have you become a woman of the world?

LELIA: Of the world, all right. How many women do you know out of the world? I've never been out of it as far as I know.

CLEMEZIA: I mean can you still name yourself a virgin?

LELIA: I certainly can, especially in this town. As for elsewhere, you'll have to ask the Spaniards who kept me in a Roman prison.

CLEMEZIA: So this is how you honor your father, your family name, your very self, and me who brought you up? I should use these hands to choke you. Get yourself inside. I don't want you seen in these clothes again.

LELIA: For heaven's sake, if you don't mind — a little patience.

CLEMEZIA: You don't feel ashamed to be seen like this?

LELIA: You think I'm the first one? There've been hundreds like me in Rome. And in this city, think how many there are who go about their business every night in gear like this?

CLEMEZIA: Whores, you mean.

LELIA: Can't there be at least one honest girl among all the ladies of the night?

CLEMEZIA: Io vo' saper perché tu vi vai e perché sei uscita del monistero. Oh! Se tuo padre il sapesse, non t'uccidarebbe, povara te?

LELIA: Mi cavarebbe d'affanni. Tu credi forse ch'io stimi la vita un gran che?

CLEMEZIA: Perché vai cosí? Dimmelo.

LELIA: Se m'ascolti, io tel dirò; e, a questo modo, intenderai quanta sia la disgrazia mia e la cagion per ch'io vada in questo abito fuor del monistero e quel ch'io voglio che in questa cosa tu faccia. Ma tirati piú in qua: ché, se alcun passasse, non mi conoscesse, per vedermi ragionar con teco.

CLEMEZIA: Tu mi fai consumare. Di' presto, ch'io morrò disperata. Oimè!

LELIA: Sai che, dopo il miserabil sacco di Roma, mio padre, perduta ogni cosa e, insieme con la robba, Fabrizio mio fratello, per non restar solo in casa, mi tolse dai servizi della signora marchesana con la quale prima m'aveva posta; e, costretti dalla necessità, ce ne tornamo a Modana in casa nostra per fuggir quella fortuna ed a viver di quel poco che avevamo. E sai che, per esser mio padre tenuto amico del conte Guido Rangone, non era molto ben veduto da alcuni.

CLEMEZIA: Perché mi dici tu quel ch'io so meglio di te? E so che, per questa cagion, andaste a star di fuore al vostro podere del Fontanile; ed io ti feci compagnia.

LELIA: Ben dici. Sai anco quanto, in que' tempi, fu aspra e dura la mia vita e, non pur lontana dai pensieri amorosi, ma quasi da ogni pensiero umano: pensando che, per essere io stata in mano di soldati, che ognuno m'aditasse; né credevo poter vivere sí onestamente che bastasse a far che la gente non avesse che dire. E tu 'l sai, ché tante volte me ne gridasti e mi confortasti a tener vita piú allegra.

CLEMEZIA: Se io lo so, perché mel dici? Segui.

The Deceived

CLEMEZIA: Tell me, right now, why you're traipsing around like this and why have you left the convent. Oh, if your father got wind of this, you little rogue, he'd murder you.

LELIA: That would put an end to my misery. How much do you think I rate my life anyway?

CLEMEZIA: So what's the reason? Fess up.

LELIA: If you pay attention, I'll tell you. Then you'll know just how bedeviled I am, and why I'm out of the convent, and why I'm in this gear, and what you have to do for me. Come closer will you so people going by won't figure out who's talking to you.

CLEMEZIA: You've got me worried sick. So tell me fast before I die of grief.

LELIA: You remember that after that horrible Sack of Rome, father lost his property, my brother Fabrizio, everything. He didn't want to be alone at home, so he took me out of service with the marchioness he'd placed me with. Then we came back to Modena to beat our cruel fortune and get by on what little was left — no choice. You know, too, that for being a friend of Count Guido Rangone, father drew the animosity of quite a few around here.[17]

CLEMEZIA: Why repeat stuff to me I know better than you? It's why you went out to the farm in Fontanile, and me along with you. I know.

LELIA: Right. And you know how tough it was for me at the time. There I was, hardly giving love a single thought, just trying not to think about feelings at all, knowing that everyone was pointing their fingers at me for having fallen into the hands of soldiers. What course of honor could I pursue that would stop the talking? You remember how many times you coaxed and lectured me to buck up and be happy.

CLEMEZIA: Why are you still rambling about stuff I already know? But go on.

LELIA: Perché, se questo non t'avesse ridetto, non potresti saper quel che segue. Avvenne che, in que' tempi, Flamminio Carandini, per esser de la parte che noi, prese stretta amicizia con mio padre; e, ogni giorno, ogni giorno, veniva in casa; e, alcuna volta, molto segretamente mi mirava, poi, sospirando, ancora abbassava gli occhi. E fusti cagion tu di farmene accorgere. A me cominciorono a piacere i suoi costumi, i suoi ragionamenti e i suoi modi molto piú che da principio non facevano; ma non però pensavo ad amore. Ma, durando la pratica del suo venire in casa, ed ora uno atto ed ora un segno amoroso facendomi, sospirando, sollecitando, mirandomi, m'accorsi che costui era preso di me non poco: tal che io, che non avevo mai piú provato amore, parendomi egli degno dov'io potesse porre i mie' pensieri, m'invaghii sí fieramente che altro ben non aveva che di vederlo.

CLEMEZIA: Tutto questo ancor sapevo.

LELIA: Sai ancor che, essendo partiti li soldati di Roma, volse mio padre tornar là per veder se niente del nostro fusse salvato ma, molto piú, per veder se nuova alcuna sentiva del mio fratello; e, per non lassarmi sola, mi mandò a stare alla Mirandola, fin che tornava, con la zia Giovanna. Quanto mal volentieri mi separasse dal mio Flamminio tu lo puoi dire, che tante volte me ne asciugasti le lagrime! Alla Mirandola stei uno anno. Poi, essendo tornato mio padre, sai ch'io tornai a Modena e piú che prima innamorata di colui che, essendo il mio primo amore, tanto mi era piaciuto, pensandomi che ancor egli m'amasse come prima aveva mostrato.

CLEMEZIA: Pazzarella! E quanti modanesi hai tu trovati che durin d'amare una donna sola un anno e che un mese non dien la berta a questa e un mese a quell'altra?

LELIA: Trovailo che tanto apponto si ricordava di me quanto se mai veduta non m'avesse; e, ch'è peggio, ch'ogni suo animo, ogni sua cura ha posta in acquistar l'amor d'Isabella di Gherardo Foiani come quella che, oltre

The Deceived

LELIA: You need a refresher to make complete sense of what's coming. Back in those days, Flamminio Carandini, a supporter of our party, became one of dad's closest friends.[18] Every single day he was at the house, and sometimes he'd steal a glance at me, let slip a sigh, and then look away. Remember, it was you who told me it was happening. So I took a shine to him. More and more I liked his conversation and his polite ways. It wasn't about love, not then. But as the visits went on, with a gesture here, a love sign there, his sighing, beseeching, and gazing — it dawned on me that he really liked me. Then there was me, knowing nothing about love, who started to think of him as worthy of it, and who desired nothing more with all my heart than just to look at him.

CLEMEZIA: Still nothing new.

LELIA: Nor in this either, that when the Spanish soldiers left Rome, father went back to see if there was anything of ours to be salvaged, and more importantly whether there was any news of Fabrizio. That's when he provided me with some company by sending me to my aunt Giovanna in Mirandola until he got back.[19] You know how sad I was to tear myself away from Flamminio. You dried my tears on so many occasions. There in Mirandola I stayed for a whole year before father came to take me back to Modena. By then I was more in love than ever with the first man of my heart, deeply in love, believing that he would still love me as he seemed to at first.

CLEMEZIA: Silly girl! How many men from Modena have you ever known to stick with one girl for a year without chasing after another one this month and still another the next?

LELIA: When I met up with him, I discovered that he remembered no more of me than if we'd never met. Worse yet, he was soul-deep in love with Isabella, Gherardo Foiani's daughter, who's beautiful and his

ch'è assai bella, è unica a suo padre, se quel vecchio pazzo non piglia moglie e faccia altri figliuoli.

CLEMEZIA: Egli si crede certo d'aver te; e dice che tuo padre te gli ha promesso. Ma questo che tu m'hai detto non fa a proposito del tuo andar vestita da maschio e del tuo essere uscita del monistero.

LELIA: Se mi lassi dire, vedrai che gli è a proposito. Ma, rispondendo a quel di prima, dico che me non averà egli. Tornato che fu mio padre da Roma, gli accadde il cavalcare a Bologna per certi intrighi di conti; e, non volendo io piú tornare alla Mirandola, mi messe nel monistero di San Crescenzio in compagnia di suor Amabile, nostra parente, fin che tornasse, che si pensò di tornar presto.

CLEMEZIA: Tutto questo sapevo.

LELIA: Ivi stando, né d'altro che d'amor ragionare sentendo a quelle reverende madri del monistero, m'assicurai ancor io di scoprire il mio amore a suor Amabile de' Cortesi. Ella che ebbe pietà di me, non finò mai ch'ella fece venire piú volte Flamminio a parlar seco e con altre acciò che io, in questo tempo, che nascosta dopo quelle tende mi stava, pascesse gli occhi di vederlo e l'orecchie d'udirlo; che era il maggior desiderio ch'io avesse. Venendovi un dí, fra gli altri, sentii che molto si rammaricò d'un suo allievo che morto gli era e molto diceva delle lode e ben servire suo; soggiungendo che, se un simile ne trovasse, si terrebbe piú contento del mondo e che gli porrebbe in mano quanto teneva.

CLEMEZIA: Meschina a me! Io dubito che questo ragazzo non mi facci vivere scontenta.

LELIA: Subito mi corse nell'animo di voler provare se a me potesse venir fatto d'esser questo aventuroso ragazzo (e, partito ch'ei si fu, conferii questo pensiero con suor Amabile) e, poi che Flamminio non stava per stanza a Modena, veder se seco per servidore acconciar mi potesse.

only child to boot, unless the old buzzard gets married and starts making more.

CLEMEZIA: He's talking about nailing you for the job, saying you've been contracted to him by your father. But none of this explains why you're going about in boy's clothes and why you're out of the convent.

LELIA: Just let me talk and you'll see it's all to the point. But contrary to what you just said, I want you to know that Gherardo will never have me. After father was back from Rome, he went off to Bologna on private business, and because I didn't want to go back to Mirandola, he sent me to stay with a relative in the Convent of San Crescenzio, Sister Amabile, and to wait for what he thought would be a quick return.

CLEMEZIA. Still, nothing new in that.

LELIA: So there I was, listening to those nuns talk about nothing but love, which gave me the courage to tell my plight to Sister Amabile de' Cortesi.[20] She took pity on me. She even went so far as to invite Flamminio around to chat with her and the others on numerous occasions. Hiding in the curtains, I satisfied my craving to feast on him with my eyes and ears. That was my greatest desire. The day came when, among other things, I heard him grieving the death of his page, applauding his service, and announcing that if he could find another as good, he'd be extremely happy and would put him in charge of all his things.

CLEMEZIA: *(Aside)* I can see what's coming. This lad will be my undoing.

LELIA: Then it dawned on me. Maybe I could be that lucky boy. Since Flamminio wasn't yet living in Modena, I thought I would get myself hired as his page. So as soon as he left, I talked the idea over with Sister Amabile.

CLEMEZIA: Nol diss'io che questo ragazzo... Disfatta a me!

LELIA: Ella me ne confortò; e ammaestrommi del modo ch'io avevo a tenere; e accommodommi di certi panni che nuovamente s'aveva fatti per potere ella ancora, alcuna volta, come l'altre fanno, uscir fuor di casa travestita a fare i fatti suoi. E cosí, una mattina per tempo, me ne uscii in questo abito fuor del monistero che, per esser fuor della terra come gli è, mi die' molto animo e fu molto a proposito. E andamene al palazzo ove Flamminio abitava, che sai che non è molto discosto dal monistero; ed ivi mi fermai tanto che gli uscí fuora. E, in questo, non posso se non lodarmi della fortuna perché subito Flamminio mi voltò gli occhi addosso e molto cortesemente mi domandò se alcuna cosa domandavo e d'onde io era.

CLEMEZIA: È possibil che tu non cadesse morta della vergogna?

LELIA: Anzi, aiutandomi Amore, francamente gli risposi ch'io ero romano che, per essere rimasto povero, andavo cercando mia ventura. Mirommi piú volte dal capo ai piedi tal che quasi ebbi paura che non mi cognoscesse; poi mi disse che, se mi fusse piaciuto di star seco, mi terrebbe volentieri e mi trattaria bene e da gentile uomo. Io, pur vergognandomi un poco, gli risposi di sí.

CLEMEZIA: Io non vorrei esser nata, sentendoti. E che util ne vedesti, per te, di far questa pazzia?

LELIA: Che utile? Part'egli che poco contento sia d'una innamorata veder di continuo il suo signore, parlargli, toccarlo, intendere i suoi segreti, veder le pratiche che gli ha, ragionar seco ed esser sicura, almeno, che, se tu nol godi, altri nol gode?

CLEMEZIA: Queste son cose da pazzarelle; e non è altro ch'agiugner legna al fuoco, se non sei certa che, facendolo, piaccino al tuo amante. E di che 'l servi tu?

LELIA: Alla tavola, alla camera. E conosco essergli venuta, in questi quindici dí ch'io l'ho servito, in tanta grazia che, se in tanta gli fusse nel mio vero abito, beata a me!

The Deceived

CLEMEZIA: *(Aside)* Didn't I say this boy would be the ruin of me?

LELIA: She gave me her blessings, taught me how to act, and gave me a man's suit only recently made for her so she could tend to business in the town — like all the others do. Then, early one morning, dressed in these clothes, and full of courage, I left the convent, conveniently situated outside the city, and made my way to Flamminio's villa to wait for him. It's not all that far from the convent, as you know. All I can do is thank my lucky stars that as soon as he spied me, he asked me in the politest way where I was from and if I was looking for something.

CLEMEZIA: How did you keep from dying of shame?

LELIA: Love coached me. Bald-faced I know, but I said I was a Roman, that I was poor, and had set off to seek my fortune. He looked me over several times from top to bottom. I was terrified he'd recognize me. When he asked me if I wanted a place in his household, telling me that he'd gladly take me in and treat me like a gentleman, of course I said "yes," though I felt pretty sheepish.

CLEMEZIA: Listening to you makes me regret I was born. What good can come of this insanity?

LELIA: What good? Can't you think that someone who loves like I do would find a little pleasure in seeing her master all the time, talking to him, touching him, sharing in his secrets, watching all his doings, and trying to make sure that if she can't have him, no one else will either?

CLEMEZIA: Folly, all of it. You're just adding wood to the fire. You've no idea whether your beloved would be happy about all this stuff you're doing. What kind of service does he ask for anyway?

LELIA: Service at his table — in his room. What I know is that during the last fifteen days I've been there, I've brought him a lot of pleasure. What a bounty it would be if I could bring him as much dressed in my own clothes.

CLEMEZIA: Dimmi un poco: e dove dormi tu?

LELIA: In una sua anticamara, sola.

CLEMEZIA: Se, una notte, tentato dalla maladetta tentazione, ti chiamasse ché tu dormisse con lui, come andarebbe?

LELIA: Io non voglio pensare al mal prima che venga. Quando cotesto fusse, ci pensarei e risolvereimi.

CLEMEZIA: Che dirà la gente, quando questa cosa si sappia, cattivella che tu sei?

LELIA: Chi lo dirà, se non lo dici tu? Or quello ch'io vorrei che tu facesse è questo (perch'io ho veduto che mio padre tornò iersera e dubito che non mandi per me): che tu facesse sí che, fra quattro o cinque giorni, non ci mandasse; o gli desse ad intendere ch'io sono andata con suor Amabile a Roverino e, fra questo tempo, tornarò.

CLEMEZIA: E questo perché?

LELIA: Ti dirò. Flamminio, com'io ti dissi poco fa, è innamorato d'Isabella Foiani e spesso spesso mi manda a lei con lettere e con imbasciate. Ella, credendo ch'io sia maschio, si è sí pazzamente innamorata di me che mi fa le maggior carezze del mondo; ed io fingo di non volerla amare, se non fa sí che Flamminio si levi dal suo amore; e ho già condotta la cosa a fine. Spero, fra tre o quattro giorni, che sarà fatto e che egli la lasciarà.

CLEMEZIA: Dico che tuo padre m'ha detto ch'io venga per te; e ch'io voglio che tu te ne venga a casa mia, ché mandarò pe' tuo' panni; e non voglio che sia veduta cosí, se non che dirò ogni cosa a tuo padre.

LELIA: Tu farai ch'io andarò in luogo che mai piú mi vedrete né tu né egli. Fa' a mio modo, se tu vuoi. Ma non ti posso finir di dire ogni cosa. Sento che Flamminio mi chiama. Signore! Aspettami fra un'ora in casa, ché ti verrò a trovare. E sai? abbi avertenzia che, domandandomi, mi chiami Fabio degli Alberini, ché cosí mi fo chiamare; sí che non errare. Vengo, signore! Addio.

The Deceived

CLEMEZIA: Where do you sleep?

LELIA: By myself in the next room.

CLEMEZIA: If an evil desire got the best of him to call you to his bed some night, what would you do then?

LELIA: I'm not going to think about evil desires till they pop up. When it happens, I'll consider and decide then.

CLEMEZIA: And when people find out, you little minx, what do you think they'll be saying?

LELIA: If you don't talk about it, who else is going to talk about it? Now, here's what I want you to do, since dad's back home as of last night and very likely to send for me. Find some way to stop him for four or five days. Make him believe I've gone to Roverino[21] with Sister Amabile and will be coming back after that.

CLEMEZIA: Why do that?

LELIA: Here's why. As I explained a short time ago, Flamminio is in love with Isabella Foiani and is constantly sending me there on errands or to carry letters. And now she's fiercely in love with me. She thinks I'm a guy and comes on to me really passionately, so I make out that I can't love her back till she gets Flamminio to abandon his claims. The whole situation is nearly there, and I'm hoping it'll end soon — that he'll drop her in the next three or four days.

CLEMEZIA: You're father's sent me to fetch you. So you come to my house while I send for some proper clothes. I don't want you seen looking like this. Otherwise, I'm spilling everything to your father.

LELIA: If you make me do that, I'll end up where neither you nor dad will ever see me again. Please! Can't we do it my way? Flamminio's calling me. There's no time for more words. — Yes, my lord! — I'll be at your place in an hour. Wait for me there. And if you ever ask for me, don't forget to call me Fabio degli Alberini. That's my name. Don't mess up. — Coming, Master! — I've got to run.

CLEMEZIA: In buona fé, che costei ha veduto Gherardo che viene in qua; e però s'è fuggita. Or che farò io? Di costei non è cosa da dire al padre e non è da lasciarla star qui. Tacerò fin che di nuovo gli parli.

Scena quarta

GHERARDO *vecchio,* SPELA *suo servo e* CLEMENZIA *balia.*

GHERARDO: Se Virginio fa quanto m'ha promesso, io mi vo' dare il piú bel tempo ch'uom di Modena. Che ne dici, Spela? Non farò bene?

SPELA: Credo che molto meglio fareste a far qualche bene ai vostri nepoti, che stentano, e a me, che v'ho servito tanto tempo e non mi so' pure avanzato un par di scarpe; ch'io ho paura che questa moglie non vi mandi qui o che la vi faccia... So ben io.

GHERARDO: Vorrò che tu vegga s'ella si terrà ben pagata da me.

SPELA: Credolo: ché, dove un altro la pagarebbe di grossi e di cinquine, e voi la pagarete di doppioni e di piccioli.

GHERARDO: Ecco la sua balia. Taci, ch'io voglio astutamente domandare che è di Lelia.

CLEMEZIA: Oh che bel giglio d'orto da voler moglie sí tenera! Credi che fusse ben condotta, quella povera figliuola, nelle man di questo vecchio rantacoso? Alla croce di Dio, che io la strozzerei prima che voler ch'ella fusse data a questo vieto, muffato, baboso, rancido, moccioso. Io ne voglio un poco di pastura. Lassamigli accostare. Dio vi dia il buon dí e la buona mattina, Gherardo. Voi mi parete, questa mattina, un cherubino.

GHERARDO: E a te ne dia centomila e altri tanti ducati.

SPELA: Cotesti starebbon meglio a me.

The Deceived

CLEMEZIA: In fact, it's Gherardo who's coming. That's why she took off. Now what am I going to do? It's not something I can tell her father, but I can't leave her there either. I'll keep mum till I talk to her again.

Scene 4

GHERARDO, SPELA, *his servant, and* CLEMEZIA.

GHERARDO: If Virginio keeps his word, there'll be no man in Modena who's ever had it better than me. Pretty good, eh, Spela? What do you think?

SPELA: Better if you gave something to your needy nephews, or me. I've been in your service for so long my shoe soles are down to nothing. You know what scares me? This wife of yours will send you round the bend, or plant a set of.... I'm dead certain of that.[22]

GHERARDO: Find out if she thinks I'll be rewarding her well enough.

SPELA: Sure you will. Except that other men would give her some real bullion, while you'll just be dropping teensy coins in her purse.[23]

GHERARDO: *(As Clemenzia comes along)* Here's her nursemaid. Watch me find out about Lelia on the sly.

CLEMEZIA: *(Aside)* That Gherardo takes himself for a lily of the valley now that he's hankering after a young wife. Who could possibly think it smart to hand over this poor girl to a wheezing old fogie? Cross of God, I'd cut her throat before I'd see her turned over to that run-down, mouldy, drooling, and rotten old stinker. I'll work him over and give him a run for it. — Good day to you Gherardo, and a glorious morning. You're looking just like a cherub today.

GHERARDO: God repay you with a hundred thousand ducats — even more.

SPELA: *(Aside)* You can send those my way.

GHERARDO: O Spela, quanto sarei stato contento s'io fusse costei!

SPELA: Perché avreste, forse, provati molti mariti, ove non avete provato se non una moglie? O pur il dite per altro?

CLEMEZIA: E quanti mariti ho io provati, Spela? che Dio te faci spelar da le mosche! Hai tu forse invidia di non esser stato un di quelli?

SPELA: Sí, per Dio! ché la gioia è bella, almanco.

GHERARDO: Tace, bestia, ché non lo dico per cotesto, io, no.

SPELA: Perché lo diceste adunque?

GHERARDO: Perché arei tante volte abbraciata, baciata e tenuta in collo la mia Lelia dolce, di zuccaro, d'oro, di latte, di rose, di non so che mi dire.

SPELA: Oh! ohu! Padrone, andiamo a casa. Sú! presto!

GHERARDO: Perché?

SPELA: Voi avete la febbre e vi farebbe male lo star qui a questa aria.

GHERARDO: Io ho il malan che Dio ti dia. Che febbre! Io mi sento pur bene.

SPELA: Dico che voi avete la febbre: lo conosco ben io, certo; e grande.

GHERARDO: So ch'io mi sento bene.

SPELA: Duolvi il capo?

GHERARDO: No.

SPELA: Lasciatemivi toccare un poco il polso. Duolvi lo stomaco o pur sentite qualche fumo andare al cervello?

GHERARDO: Tu mi pari una bestia. Vuo' mi far Calandrino, forse? Io dico ch'io non ho altro male che di Lelia mia, delicata, inzuccarata.

SPELA: Io so che voi avete la febbre e state molto male.

The Deceived

GHERARDO: Heh, Spela, if I were Clemenzia, I'd be really happy.

SPELA: Why's that? Because if you were her you'd have tried a whole bunch of husbands instead of being stuck with just one wife? Am I getting that right?

CLEMEZIA: And just how many husbands do you think I've tried, Mr. Spela? Jealous because you didn't get picked? Well, may God have the flies chew off your hide.

SPELA: By God, you got me there. The joy of it, at least, is a beautiful thing!

GHERARDO: Not what I meant at all, so you can close your trap.

SPELA: So what did you mean, then?

GHERARDO: I meant that if I were her, I'd have been hugging and kissing my honey-pie Lelia, all sugar and gold and milk and roses — I haven't got words for them all.

SPELA: Whoa, boss, better head indoors. Come on! Get a move on!

GHERARDO: What are you doing?

SPELA: A fever's taken you and the outside air will only make it worse.

GHERARDO: My only pain is in my ass — may God give it to you. Fever, what? I'm perfectly fine.

SPELA: Ah no, it's a fever, a really big one, trust me.

GHERARDO: No, I'm feeling fine I tell you.

SPELA: What about your head. Aching?

GHERARDO: No!

SPELA: Here, let me feel your pulse. Stomach hurting? Feel any vapours heading for your brain?

GHERARDO: You're out of your gourd. Who do you take me for, Calandrino?[24] I'm telling you, no problems. I'm only feeling sick with missing my dainty sugarplum, Lelia.

SPELA: No, you've got the fever — really sick.

GHERARDO: A che te ne accorgi tu?

SPELA: A che? Non vi accorgete che voi sète fuor di gangari, farneticate, affannate e non sapete che vi dire?

GHERARDO: Gli è Amor che vuol cosí, non è vero, Clemenzia? Omnia vincit Amor.

SPELA: Ohu! Che bel detto da napoletani. Facetis manum, brigata. Mai piú fu detto.

GHERARDO: Quella crudelina, traditorina di tua figliana...

SPELA: Questa non sarà febbre, ma scemamento di cervello. Ohu! Povero a me! come farò?

GHERARDO: O Clemenzia, mi vien voglia d'abracciarti e di baciarti mille volte.

SPELA: Qui bisognaranno le funi, dissi ben io.

CLEMEZIA: Di cotesto guardatevi molto bene, ch'io non voglio esser baciata da vecchi.

GHERARDO: Paioti cosí vecchio?

SPELA: Che credi? Al mio padrone non sono ancor caduti gli occhi fuor di bocca; volsi dire, i denti.

CLEMEZIA: In ogni modo, non avete il tempo che si crede, veggo ben io.

GHERARDO: Dillo a LELIA: E sai? Se mi metti in sua grazia, ti vo' donare un mongile.

SPELA: Ehi, liberalaccio! E a me che darete?

CLEMEZIA: Tanto fusse voi in grazia del duca di Ferrara quanto voi sète in grazia di Lelia, che buon per voi! Ma sí! Voi la dileggiate: ché, se voi gli volesse bene, non la terreste in queste trame né cercaresti di tuorgli la sua ventura.

GHERARDO: Come torgli la sua ventura? Io cerco di darglila, non di torgliela.

The Deceived

GHERARDO: What tells you that?

SPELA: Easy. Aren't you out of your mind, talking gibberish, in a frenzy, and rambling?

GHERARDO: Love makes me do it. Isn't that so, Clemenzia? *Omnia vincit amor!* [Love conquers all!][25]

SPELA: *(Aside)* Sure, just what they'd say in Naples and tell the crowds, *"facetis manum."* [Clap your hands.] There's no more to say.

GHERARDO: Ah, so sweet, so cruel, your little daughter, such a traitor....

SPELA: *(Aside)* This is no fever, it's incurable insanity. Oh boy. Not good for me, but what's to be done?

GHERARDO: Oh, Clemenzia, I could just squeeze and kiss you a thousand times.

SPELA: *(Aside)* Lunatic, we'll need a straitjacket.

CLEMEZIA: Easy there! No desire here to be kissed by an old geezer.

GHERARDO: You think I look old?

SPELA: *(Aside)* What's your opinion? He's still got his eyes. At least they haven't fallen out of his mouth, er, rather his teeth.

CLEMEZIA: Well, now with a bit of inspection, you're not as old as they claim.

GHERARDO: Tell that to Lelia. And hey, if you build me up a bit with her, I'll offer you a nice veil.

SPELA: *(Aside)* Amazing! So generous. And what'll you offer me?

CLEMEZIA: You'd be a lucky man if you had the same favor from the Duke of Ferrara as you have from Lelia. But you're just toying with her. If you really had any feelings for her, you wouldn't be messing her around and ruining her life.

GHERARDO: Ruining her life? I'm out to give her the best life possible, not ruin it.

CLEMEZIA: Perché la tenete, tutto questo anno, in su le pratiche di volerla o di non volerla?

GHERARDO: Ché! Pensasi Lelia che rimanga da me, adunque? S'io non sollecito ogni dí suo padre, se non è la maggior voglia ch'io abbi al mondo, s'io non volesse che si facesse piú presto oggi che domane, che tu mi vegga, fra pochi dí, sovr'una bara.

CLEMEZIA: E questo non mancarà, se a Dio piace. Io gli dirò ogni cosa. Ma sapete? La vi vorrebbe vedere andare altramenti; ché cosí gli parete un pecorone.

GHERARDO: Come "un pecorone"? che gli ho io fatto?

CLEMEZIA: No. Ma perché voi andate sempre avviluppato ne le pelli.

SPELA: Sarà buon, dunque, che per amor suo si faccia scorticare o che, almanco, corra ignudo per questa terra. Ha' veduto?

GHERARDO: Io ho piú be' panni ch'uom di Modena. Ho caro che me l'abbi detto. Vorrò che, di qua a un poco, mi vegga altrimenti. Ma dove la potrei vedere? quando tornerà dal monistero?

CLEMEZIA: Alla porta Bazzovara. Or ora voglio andare a trovarla.

GHERARDO: Ché non mi lassi venir con te, che andarem ragionando?

CLEMEZIA: No, no. Che direbben le genti?

GHERARDO: Io muoio. Oh amore!

SPELA: Io scoppio. Oh bastone!

GHERARDO: Oh beata a te!

SPELA: Oh pazzo che tu se'!

GHERARDO: Oh Clemenzia avventurata!

SPELA: Oh bestia mal cignata!

GHERARDO: Oh latte ben contento!

SPELA: Oh capo pien di vento!

The Deceived

CLEMEZIA: Then why is she still waiting after an entire year while you make up your mind to marry her or not?

GHERARDO: What? Can Lelia believe that was my fault? I've been asking her father every day — check it out. If this wasn't my sole longing to marry her as fast as I could, then stretch me out in my coffin right now.

CLEMEZIA: Well, if it's God's will, nothing can get in the way. I'll tell her the whole story. She wouldn't mind, though, if you changed your appearance. Right now, you look like an old goat.

GHERARDO: An old goat! What's wrong with me now?

CLEMEZIA: Oh nothing, but you're always muffled up in some kind of fur or other.

SPELA: *(Aside)* Now, she'll have him fleeced for love, or at least make him run around town half naked.

GHERARDO: My clothes are the best of any worn in Modena. But thanks for the advice. She'll see me looking different. When's she back from the convent? Where can I see her?

CLEMEZIA: At the Bazzovara Gate.[26] I'm on my way to fetch her now.

GHERARDO: Why don't I just go along with you? We can chat on the way.

CLEMEZIA: Ah no. Think what folks would be saying. *(Exit)*

GHERARDO: *(To himself)* O my love. I'm dying for you!

SPELA: *(Aside)* O my God, I'm splitting in two.

GHERARDO: Oh, what a blessed little thing you are!

SPELA: *(Aside)* Oh, you're madder than a Naar.

GHERARDO: O Clemenzia, happy she!

SPELA: *(Aside)* Oh, and what a blockhead he!

GHERARDO: Oh, the milk of tenderness!

SPELA: *(Aside)* Oh, the brain that holds much less!

GHERARDO: Oh Clemenzia felice!

SPELA: Oh! in culo avestu una radice!

GHERARDO: Orsú, Clemenzia! Addio. Viene, Spela, ch'io mi voglio ire a raffazzonare. Ho deliberato di vestirmi altrimenti per piacere alla mia moglie.

SPELA: L'andarà male.

GHERARDO: Perché?

SPELA: Perché già cominciate a fare a suo modo. Le brache saran pur le sue.

GHERARDO: Vanne alla buttiga di Marco profumiere e comprami un bossol di zibetto, ch'io voglio andare in su l'amorosa vita.

SPELA: I denari ove sono?

GHERARDO: Eccoti un bolognino. Va' presto. Io m'avvio a casa.

Scena quinta

SPELA *servo e* SCATIZZA *servo di Virginio.*

SPELA: Se ad alcuno venisse voglia di racchiuder tutte le sciocchezze in un sacco, mettivi il mio padrone, ché sarà fatto a punto quanto e' vuole. E magiormente, or che gli è entrato in questa frenesia d'amore, egli si spela, si pettina, passeggia intorno alla dama, va fuor la notte a' veglini con la squarcina, canticchia tutto 'l dí con una voce rantacosa, ribalda e con un leutaccio piú scordato di lui. E essi dato infino a far le fistole (che gli venghino!) e i sognetti e i capogirli, gli strenfiotti, i materiali e mill'altre comedie: cosa da far creppar di ridere gli asini, non che i cani. Or vuol portare il zibetto. Al corpo di Dio, che c'impazzerebben le palle. Ma ecco Scatizza che debbe tornar da le monache.

The Deceived

GHERARDO: O Clemenzia, blithe and merry!

SPELA: *(Aside)* Oh, your arse holds more than it can carry.

GHERARDO: Goodbye Clemenzia, goodbye! — So, Spela, follow me. I'm in for a total makeover. I've got to fit myself out in fashion to please my lovey.

SPELA: Nothing good can come of this.

GHERARDO: Why say that?

SPELA: Because you're already doing everything her way. Pretty soon she'll be wearing the pants.

GHERARDO: Head over to Marco the cosmetician's shop and buy me a pot of musk. It's the lover's life I'm after.

SPELA: What about the money?

GHERARDO: Here's a bolognino for you. No dawdling. I'm going back to the house.

Scene 5

SPELA *and* SCATIZZA.

SPELA: *(Alone)* If you want to wrap up all the stupidity of the whole wide world in a parcel, just wrap up the boss, and your work is done. And now that he's been caught in the frenzies of love, it's even worse. There he is, shaving, combing his hair, sauntering back and forth in front of her house, going to parties at night carrying his dagger and singing love songs all day, with that croaking voice of his, to a jangling, ill-tuned lute. And now he's taken to writing pistols — he should be shot with one — and sornets, rinds, strampedes, and madrigals, and hundreds of other things that should be put in farces.[27] It could make a dog guffaw, if not kill all the asses on the globe with laughing. And now he's adding musk. For God's sake, it could make your balls dance in their sack. And here comes Scatizza on his way back from the convent.

SCATIZZA: Ti so dir che questi padri che fan le lor figliuole monache debbono esser di que' buoni uomini del tempo antico di Bartolommeo Coglioni. E forse che non si credono ch'elle stien sempre dinanzi al Crocefisso a pregare Iddio che facci del bene a chi ve l'ha messe? È ben vero che pregano Dio e 'l diavolo; ma che gli faccia rompare il collo a chi è cagion ch'elle ci sieno.

SPELA: Voglio intender questa novella.

SCATIZZA: Com'io bussai alla ruota, subito tutta la stanza s'empí di suore; e tutte giovane e tutte belle come angeli. Comincio a domandar di Lelia, chi ride di qua, chi sghignazza di là; tutte si facevan beffe del fatto mio, come se io fusse stato un zugo melato.

SPELA: Addio, Scatizza. E donde si viene? Oh! Tu hai delli zuccarini. Dammene.

SCATIZZA: Il cancar che ti venga, a te e quel pazzo di tuo padrone!

SPELA: Lasciame andare e tira a te. Donde vieni?

SCATIZZA: Dalle monache di Santo Crescenzio.

SPELA: Or be', che è di Lelia? È tornata a casa?

SCATIZZA: La forca tornarà per te! Po' fare Iddio che quel mentecatto di tuo padrone se la crede avere?

SPELA: Perché? Non lo vuole?

SCATIZZA: Credo di no, io. Parti ch'ella sia carne da' suo' denti?

SPELA: Ella ha ragione, in fine; ma che dice?

SCATIZZA: Niente non dice. Che vuoi ch'ella dica, quando io non l'ho potuta vedere? ché, come io gionsi là e domanda' la, quelle sgherracce di quelle monache volevan la pastura di me.

The Deceived

SCATIZZA: *(Talking to himself)* Our fathers who turn their daughters into nuns are about as bright as the great ones back in Bartolomeo Coglioni's time.[28] Do they really think their girls bruise their knees for hours a day in front of a crucifix asking God to bless and reward the folks who put them there? They pray to God all right, and the devil too, asking them to break the necks of those who got them locked away.

SPELA: *(Aside)* Here's a story I have to hear.

SCATIZZA: As soon as I rattled the door-wheel of their cloistered convent — which they pretend to keep locked up — the nuns drifted in from all sides, youthful and pretty as angels. And when I asked for Lelia, laughter broke out on one side and sniggering on the other, and then they started to horseplay with me, like I was a stick of hard sugar candy.

SPELA: Hey, Scatizza, God bless. Where you in from? Nice sweets you've got there. How about a few for me?

SCATIZZA: You can drop dead, and that idiot master of yours.

SPELA: Stop pulling on me! Go pull on yourself! Where're you coming from?

SCATIZZA: Over talking to the sisters of San Crescenzio.

SPELA: Fine, but what's up with Lelia? Is she back home now?

SCATIZZA: May your head meet up with a noose. As for that idiot boss of yours, how does God let him think he's going to marry her?

SPELA: Why not? Isn't she perfectly willing?

SCATIZZA: I doubt that. You think she's the kind of morsel to put in his mouth?

SPELA: Can't blame her for not wanting him. So what'd she say?

SCATIZZA: Nothing at all. How could she if I wasn't allowed to see her? After I arrived and asked about her, those starving sisters wanted me for their pasture.

SPELA: Altro volevan che la pastura! Piú presto il pastorale. Tu non le conosci bene.

SCATIZZA: Le conosco meglio di te, cosí gli venisse il cancaro! Vo' che tu vegga. Chi mi domandava s'io ne sto male; chi s'i' la torrei per moglie; chi diceva ch'ell'era in molle in dormentorio, che s'asciugava; chi ch'ell'era in soppresso nel chiostro. Un'altra mi disse: "Tuo padre ebbe figliuoli maschi?" Oh! Io fui per dire: "Ebbe un ca...cameto". Tanto che pur m'accorsi che m'uccellavano, ché non volevano ch'io le parlasse.

SPELA: Tu fosti un da poco. Dovevi entrar dentro e dir che la volevi cercar tu.

SCATIZZA: Cancaro! Entra dentro solo! Va' là, va' là: tu mi conciaresti! Oh! Non c'è stallone in Maremma che ci regesse col fatto loro, solo. Monache? Cancaro! Ma io non posso star piú con te; ché ho da rispondere al mio padrone.

SPELA: Ed io ho a comprare il zibetto a quel pazzo del mio.

ATTO SECONDO

Scena prima

LELIA *da ragazzo sotto nome di Fabio e* FLAMMINIO *giovene innamorato.*

FLAMMINIO: Gli è pure una gran cosa, Fabio, che, in fino a qui, non abbi potuto cavare una buona risposta da questa crudele, da questa ingrata d'Isabella. E pur mi fa creder il vederti dare sempre grata audienzia e l'accoglierti sí volentieri ch'ella non m'abbi in odio; però ch'io non gli feci mai cosa, ch'io sappi, che le dispiacesse. Tu ti potresti accorgere, ne' suoi ragionamenti, di ch'ella si

The Deceived

SPELA: You're not getting into a sheep may safely graze situation, my friend; their comfort is your rod and staff. You don't know how they are.

SCATIZZA: I know their antics better than you do — may they all get the scabies. You should have seen them. One of them wanted to know if I was lovesick for her, another if I'd marry her. Another one told me that Lelia was towelling down after soaking herself in the bath, and another that she was drying her clothes with a twin-roller mangle.[29] "Hey there, did your daddy have any boy children?" came another, and I was just on the verge of saying that he had a pretty big co... er, clothes beater, but hey, they were just joshing around to keep me from finding out about Lelia.

SPELA: Not good enough on your part, I'd say. Best just to barge right in and announce to them you're going to case the place on your own.

SCATIZZA: You're nuts! Barge in there alone? Get serious, man. Are you trying to have me done in? Whoa, there's not a stallion in the Maremma[30] who could deal with that lot. The sisterhood? A clap on them all. But I can't loaf around here any longer. I've got to go find my master.

SPELA: Me too, I have to buy musk for my loopy boss.

ACT 2

Scene 1

The street in front of Flamminio's house.
LELIA, *dressed as Fabio, and* FLAMMINIO.

FLAMMINIO: Very strange, Fabio, that as of now you've not gotten a single polite answer for me out of that cruel and thankless Isabella. But she's always glad to see you and invite you in, so I can't imagine she hates me. I've never done a thing to annoy her. Maybe from what she says you can figure out what I've done wrong. So

dolga di me? Ridimmi, di grazia, Fabio: che ti disse ella iersera, quando v'andasti con quella lettera?

LELIA: Io ve l'ho già replicato vinti volte.

FLAMMINIO: Oh! Ridimelo un'altra volta. Questo che importa a te?

LELIA: Oh! Che m'importa? Importami: ch'io veggo che voi ne pigliate dispiacere; il che cosí duole a me come a voi. Essendovi, com'io vi sono, servidore, non doverei cercare altro che di piacervi; ché, forse, di queste risposte ne volete poi male a me.

FLAMMINIO: Non dubitar di questo, il mio Fabio, ch'io t'amo come fratello. Conosco che tu mi vuoi bene e però sia certo ch'io non so' per mancarti mai; e vedra'lo col tempo. Prega Iddio e basti. Ma che diss'ella?

LELIA: Non ve l'ho detto? che il maggior piacere che voi le possiate fare al mondo è di lasciarla stare e non pensar piú a lei, perché l'ha volto l'animo altrui; e che, insomma, la non ha occhi con che la vi possi pur guardare; e che voi perdete il tempo e quanto fate in seguirla, perché, alla fine, vi trovarete con le mani piene di vento.

FLAMMINIO: E pare a te, Fabio, che queste cose le dica di cuore o pur ch'ella abbia qualche sdegno con esso me? Ché pur soleva, qualche volta, farmi favore, da un tempo in là; né posso creder ch'ella mi voglia male, accettando le mie lettere e le mie imbasciate. Io so' disposto di seguirla fino alla morte. Ben vo' vedere quel che n'ha da essere. Che ne dici, Fabio? non ti pare?

LELIA: A me no, signore.

FLAMMINIO: Perché?

LELIA: Perché, s'io fusse in voi, vorrei ch'ella l'avesse di grazia ch'io la mirasse. Forse ch'a un par vostro, nobile, virtuoso, gentile, delle bellezze che sète, mancaranno dame? Fate a mio modo, padrone. Lasciatela e attaccatevi a qualcun'altra che v'ami; che ben ne trovarete, sí, e forse di cosí belle come ella. Ditemi: non

Fabio, please tell me again what she said to you last night when I sent you with the letter.

LELIA: I've told you twenty times already.

FLAMMINIO: But just one more time, all right? What does it matter to you?

LELIA: It matters to me. It matters that you're unhappy because that makes me as sad as you are. I'm your servant. It's my job to make you as happy as I can. And I worry that her replies will only make you mad at me.

FLAMMINIO: Never think that, Fabio. You know I love you like a brother, and I'm sure you care for me too, so God willing, I'll never let you down. Just say your prayers and don't worry about it. All right, what did she say?

LELIA: What I've told you already: that the greatest pleasure you could give her is just to leave her alone. Best not to think about her anymore. In her heart she's somewhere else. She's got no eyes for you, so you're wasting your time chasing after her. By the time the end rolls 'round, you'll find yourself alone.

FLAMMINIO: What do you think, Fabio? Is this from her heart, or is she just upset with me? She was warm enough with me only a short while ago. Surely she can't hate me now, the way she accepts my letters and messages. I'm pursuing her to the bitter end. I need to see what's going to happen. Why shouldn't I, eh Fabio? What do you say?

LELIA: That you shouldn't.

FLAMMINIO: Your reason?

LELIA: In your place, I'd want some respect from her for my attentions. Surely there must be plenty of women around for a man as noble and worthy and gentle and good-looking as you are. Take my advice, Master, and drop her. Hook up with somebody new who loves you. There are plenty of them out there for you, no doubt

avete voi nissuna che avesse caro che voi l'amasse, in questa terra?

FLAMMINIO: Come s'io n'ho? Ve n'è una, fra l'altre, chiamata Lelia, che mille volte ho voluto dire che ha tutta l'effigie tua, tenuta la piú bella, la piú accorta e la piú cortese giovane di questa terra (che te la voglio, un dí, mostrare), che si terrebbe per beata pur ch'io le facesse una volta un poco di favore; ricca e stata in corte; ed è stata mia innamorata presso a uno anno, che mi fece mille favori, di poi s'andò con Dio alla Mirandola. E la mia sorte mi fece innamorar di costei: che tanto m'è stata cruda quanto quella mi fu cortese.

LELIA: Padrone, e' vi sta bene ogni male perché, se avete chi v'ama e non l'apprezzate, è ragionevol cosa che altri non apprezzi voi.

FLAMMINIO: Che vuo' tu dire?

LELIA: Se quella povera giovane fu prima vostra innamorata, e anco piú che mai v'ama, perché l'avete abbandonata per seguire altri? Il qual peccato non so se Iddio ve lo possa mai perdonare. Ahi, signor Flamminio! Voi fate, per certo, un gran male.

FLAMMINIO: Tu sei ancora un putto, Fabio, e non puoi conoscere la forza d'amore. Dico ch'io son forzato ad amar quest'altra ed adorarla; e non posso né so né voglio pensare ad altri che a lei. E però tornagli a parlare e vede se gli puoi cavare di bocca destramente quel ch'ella ha con me, ch'ella non mi vòl vedere.

LELIA: Voi perdete il tempo.

FLAMMINIO: E perder questo tempo mi piace.

LELIA: Voi non farete nulla.

FLAMMINIO: Pazienzia!

LELIA: Lasciatela andar, vi dico.

FLAMMINIO: Io non posso. Va' là, ch'io te ne prego.

about it, and maybe just as pretty as she is. Can't you think of someone else in this city who loves you? Think.

FLAMMINIO: Well, yes, among others there's this girl called Lelia, who looks quite a bit like you I've been meaning to say. The resemblance has struck me a thousand times. Folks call her the most beautiful, gifted, and elegant young lady in the entire region. Someday, I'll have to point her out to you. She'd be in the clouds if I showed her even the slightest interest. She's rich, she's been at court, and she's been in love with me for almost a year. She did a thousand things to please me, but then she got shipped off to Mirandola,[31] and now fate has made me fall in love with a girl who's as mean to me as she was kind.

LELIA: Well, then, you deserve to suffer, Master, if you can't fancy a girl who loves you. It's only fair that this new one hates you.

FLAMMINIO: What do you mean by that?

LELIA: If that unfortunate girl was in love with you before, and she goes on loving you more than ever, why ditch her in pursuit of another? God may never forgive you for such bad behavior. Ah, it's plain wrong what you've done, Signor Flamminio.

FLAMMINIO: You're just a boy, Fabio. Love's power? What can you know about that? It drives me to cherish and dote on this one. There's only her. I can't think about anyone else. So go back to her, talk to her, use all your wits to get from her lips what she has against me. Find out why she won't see me anymore.

LELIA: You're wasting your time.

FLAMMINIO: I like to waste my time this way.

LELIA: It'll gain you nothing.

FLAMMINIO: I'm patient.

LELIA: Set her free.

FLAMMINIO: I can't do that. So do as I say and go back.

LELIA: Io andarò; ma...

FLAMMINIO: Torna con la risposta, subito. Io andarò fino in duomo.

LELIA: Com'io veggo el tempo, non mancarò.

FLAMMINIO: Fabio, se tu fai questa cosa, buon per te!

LELIA: A tempo si parte, ché ecco Pasquella che mi viene a trovare.

Scena seconda

PASQUELLA *fante di Gherardo e* LELIA *da ragazzo detto Fabio.*

PASQUELLA: Io non credo che nel mondo si truovi il maggior affanno né il maggior fastidio che servire, una mia pari, una giovane innamorata; e massimamente a quella che non ha d'aver timore di madre, di sorelle o d'altre persone, quale è questa padrona mia: che, da certi dí in qua, è intrata in tanta frega e in tanta smania d'amore che né dí né notte ha posa. Sempre si gratta il petinicchio, sempre si stropiccia le cosce, or corre in su la loggia, or corre a le finestre, or di sotto, or di sopra; né si ferma altrimenti che s'ella avesse l'ariento vivo in su piedi. Gesú! Gesú! Gesú! Oh! I' so' pure stata giovana ed innamorata la mia parte, ed ho fatto qualche cosetta; e pur mi posavo, talvolta. Almanco si fusse messa a voler bene a qualche uomo di conto, maturo, che sapesse fare i suo' fatti e gli cavasse la pruzza! Ma la s'è imbarbugliata d'un fraschetta che a pena credo che, quando gli è sdilacciato, si sappia allacciare, s'altri non gli aita. E, tutto 'l dí, mi manda a cercar questo drudo come s'io non avesse che fare in casa. E forse che 'l suo padrone non si crede che facci l'ambasciate per lui? Ma gli è, per certo, questo che viene in qua. Ventura! Fabio, Dio ti dia il buon dí. Vezzo mio, ti venivo a trovare.

LELIA: Ed a te mille scudi, la mia Pasquella. Che fa la tua bella padrona? e che voleva da me?

The Deceived

LELIA: I'll go, but if....

FLAMMINIO: And come straight back with her answer. I'm going on to the cathedral.

LELIA: When the moment is right, I'll do what I can.

FLAMMINIO: If you do, Fabio, it will be to your benefit too. *(Flamminio departs.)*

LELIA: He's off in the nick of time. Here comes Pasquella looking for me.

Scene 2

PASQUELLA, *housekeeper of Gherardo, and* LELIA *as Fabio.*

PASQUELLA: I can't think of anything more troublesome and irksome in the whole world than serving a young girl in love. And to make it worse, she's not afraid of anyone, not even her mother. Over the last five days she's gotten herself into such a frenzy of passion that she can't get a minute of rest day or night. She's rubbing her crotch or scratching at her legs and thighs or running out on the balcony or over to the window, then going downstairs and back up again, never ceasing, like her feet were made of mercury. God Almighty! I know what it's like to be young and in love. I did a few bad things in my time. But at least I found time to rest now and again. And why, for a start, couldn't she have found someone worth her time, some grown-up guy who can look after his affairs and scratch her where she itches? But no, my ward's fallen for a pipsqueak who needs help just to lace up his clothes. Not a day passes that she doesn't send me looking for this flame of hers, as if I don't have things to do at home. And the lad's master thinks he's carrying messages for him. But hey, I'm in luck. Here he is now. — Good day, Fabio, and perfect timing my charmer. I was just on my way to find you.

LELIA: Ah, Pasquella, a thousand scudi to you.[32] What's your beautiful little mistress up to now, and what does she need from me?

PASQUELLA: E che ti credi che la facci? Piagne, si consuma, si strugge, che stamattina non sei ancor passato da casa sua.

LELIA: Oh! Che vuol ch'io ci passi innanzi giorno?

PASQUELLA: Credo ch'ella vorrebbe che tu stesse con lei tutta la notte ancora, io.

LELIA: Oh! Io ho da fare altro. A me bisogna servire il padrone; intendi, Pasquella?

PASQUELLA: Oh! Io so ben che a tuo padron non faresti dispiacere a venirci, non. Dormi forse con lui?

LELIA: Dio il volesse ch'io fusse tanto in grazia sua! Ch'io non sarei ne' dispiaceri ch'io sono.

PASQUELLA: Oh! Non dormiresti piú volentieri con Isabella?

LELIA: Non io.

PASQUELLA: Eh! Tu non dici da vero.

LELIA: Cosí non fusse!

PASQUELLA: Or lasciamo andare. Dice la mia padrona che ti prega che tu venga tosto fin a lei, che suo padre non è in casa e ha bisogno di parlarti d'una cosa che importa.

LELIA: Digli che, se non si leva dinanzi Flamminio, che perde il tempo: che la sa ben ch'io mi rovinarei.

PASQUELLA: Viene a dirgliel tu.

LELIA: Io dico che ho altro da fare. Non odi?

PASQUELLA: E che hai da fare? Dacci una corsa; e tornarai subito.

LELIA: Oh! Tu mi rompi il capo, ora. Vatti con Dio.

PASQUELLA: Non vuoi venire?

LELIA: Non, dico: non m'intendi?

The Deceived

PASQUELLA: She's doing just what you think. She's crying and wasting away because you didn't pass by her house this morning.

LELIA: Really? She expecting me there even before daybreak?

PASQUELLA: It's more like she'd have you there all night if she could.

LELIA: Sorry, other matters to attend to. Serving my master is all I've got time for. I'm sure you catch my meaning, don't you Pasquella?

PASQUELLA: Your master wouldn't care all that much if you spent time over here. Or maybe you're sharing his bed?

LELIA: Would to God I had such favor with him. Then I wouldn't be so miserable.

PASQUELLA: But wouldn't you prefer sleeping with Isabella?

LELIA: Nope.

PASQUELLA: What? You can't be honest.

LELIA: I'm afraid so.

PASQUELLA: Well, nevermind. Shall we go? My mistress wants me to ask you over — as soon as you can make it. She has to talk to you. It's important. And her father's not home right now.

LELIA: Tell her that without dropping Flamminio first, she's wasting her time. She knows I'd be massacred.

PASQUELLA: You go tell her yourself.

LELIA: You're not listening. I'm preoccupied elsewhere, like I said.

PASQUELLA: So what's on for you now? Just run over there, and you'll be back in no time at all.

LELIA: For the love of God, get going. You're giving me a headache.

PASQUELLA: So you're not coming?

LELIA: No, I'm telling you. That's clear now?

PASQUELLA: In buona fede, in buona verità, Fabio, Fabio, che tu sei troppo superbo. E sai che ti ricordo? che tu sei giovinetto e non conosci il ben tuo. Questo favore non ti durerà sempre, no. Ne verrà la barba; non arai sempre sí colorite le gotuzze né cosí rossette le labbra; non sarai cosí sempre richiesto da tutti, non. Allora conoscerai quanto sia stata la tua pazzia; e te ne pentirai, quando non sarai piú a tempo. Dimmi un poco: quanti ne sono, in questa città, che arebben di grazia ch'Isabella gli mirasse? E tu par che ti facci beffe del pane onto.

LELIA: Perché non gli mira, donque? E lasci star me che non me ne curo.

PASQUELLA: Oh Dio! Gli è ben vero che i giovani non han tutto quel senno che gli bisognarebbe.

LELIA: Orsú, Pasquella! Non mi predicar piú, ché tu fai peggio.

PASQUELLA: Superbuzzo, superbuzzo, ti mancarà questo fumo! Orsú, il mio Fabio caro, anima mia! Vien, di grazia, presto; se non, mi rimanderebbe un'altra volta a cercarte né crederebbe ch'io t'avesse fatto l'ambasciata.

LELIA: Orsú! Va', Pasquella, ch'io verrò. Burlavo teco.

PASQUELLA: Quando, gioia mia?

LELIA: Presto.

PASQUELLA: Quanto presto?

LELIA: Tosto. Va'.

PASQUELLA: T'aspettarò all'uscio di casa, veh!

LELIA: Sí, sí.

PASQUELLA: Uh! Sai? Se tu non vieni, m'adirarò.

The Deceived

PASQUELLA: You're a cocky kid, Fabio. But let me remind you of something. You're too young to know what's in your best interests. Your come-on won't last forever. Pretty soon you'll have a beard. Those pink cheeks and red lips will disappear. Not everyone will be running around after you. Then you'll see how silly you were. You'll be sorry after it's too late. Do you realize how many guys there are in this town who'd relish just one of her smiles? Such a tasty morsel of bread and butter, and you take it all for a joke.

LELIA: So why don't you go look at her and leave me alone? I couldn't care less.

PASQUELLA: Oh for God's sake, it's true what they say. Adolescents are short on brains.

LELIA: That's the end of your sermon, Pasquella. You're no good at it, so please just head off.

PASQUELLA: An arrogant brat is what you are, but you'll learn soon enough. Come on, darling and treasured Fabio, you have to come over right away. If not, she'll think I'm not delivering her messages. She'll only send me after you again.

LELIA: Go on ahead, Pasquella. I was just kidding. I'll be over.

PASQUELLA: Joy of my life, when?

LELIA: Pretty soon.

PASQUELLA: How soon?

LELIA: Soon enough, so go on!

PASQUELLA: Is it all right if I wait for you outside the house?

LELIA: Sure, sure.

PASQUELLA: You understand that if you don't show up I'll be hopping mad.

The Intronati of Siena

Scena terza

GIGLIO *spagnuolo e* PASQUELLA *fante.*

GIGLIO: Por mia vida, que esta es la vieia biene avventurada que tiene la mas hermosa moza d'esta tierra per sua ama. Oh se le puodiesse io ablar dos parablas sin testigos! Voto a la virginidad de todos los prelatos de Roma que le hara io dar gritos como la gatta de heniero. Mas quiero veer se puedo, con alguna lisonia, pararme tal con esta vieia vellacca alcahueta que me aga alcanzar algo con ella. Buenos dies, madonna Pasquella galana, gentil. Donde venís vos tan temprana?

PASQUELLA: Oh! Buon dí, Giglio. Io vengo dalla messa. E tu dove vai?

GIGLIO: Buscando mi ventura, se puedo toppar alguna muger che me haga alguna carizia.

PASQUELLA: Oh sí! In buona fé, che vi mancano a voi spagnuoli! che non ce n'è niun di voi che non n'abbi sempre una decina a sua posta.

GIGLIO: Io verdade es che ne tiengo dos; mas non puedo andar à ellas senza periglo.

PASQUELLA: Ché! Son gentildonne, forse, di casa porcina, eh?

GIGLIO: Sí, à fé. Mas io queria trovar una madre que me blancasses alguna vez las camisas e me rattopasses calzas y el giuppon y que me tenesse por fiolo; e io la serviria di buona gana.

PASQUELLA: Cerca, cerca, ché non te ne mancarà, no; ché chi ha le gentildonne, come tu, non gli mancan le fantesche.

GIGLIO: Ya trobada sta, se voi volite.

PASQUELLA: Chi è?

GIGLIO: Voi misma.

The Deceived

Scene 3

GIGLIO, *a Spaniard, and* PASQUELLA.

GIGLIO: *(Aside)* Well, bless my soul if this isn't the lucky old biddy who looks after the sweetest señorita in town. I'd give anything to get in a couple of palabras with her, just enough to get her yowling like a cat in heat — I swear I would by all the celibate padres in Rome. But for now I can just butter up this old crone here the better to get through to her mistress. — Buenas días to you, my dear, dear Madonna Pasquella. What brings you out this morning?

PASQUELLA: Ah, Giglio, good day to you. I'm on my way back from Mass. And where are you headed?

GIGLIO: In search of my fortune. I hope to find a lady who will pamper me.

PASQUELLA: That's right. Just what you Spaniards are always looking for. You've got a dozen of them lingering about — you all do.

GIGLIO: I've got a couple, I have to say, but it's too risky to go see them these days.

PASQUELLA: Must be elites. Surely not the fine ladies of the Porcini household?[33]

GIGLIO: By God, how did you guess? But now I'm looking for a dream of a homebody who'll wash a few shirts and mend a few socks, a jacket or two, and look after me like her own boy. I'll be loyal to her in service, trust me.

PASQUELLA: Keep up the good search. There are plenty of them out there. A fellow like you with ladies in his entourage can get servants, no problems.

GIGLIO: Yes, but I've already found the one I want, if you'll allow.

PASQUELLA: Who then?

GIGLIO: You're own good self.

PASQUELLA: Eh! Io son troppo vecchia per te.

GIGLIO: Vieia? Voto alla Virge Maria di Monsurat que me parecceis una moza di chinze o veinte annos. Vees, non le digais mas, per vostra vida, que non le puedo soffrir. Vedite piú presto se volite farmi qualche piazer, que vederite se vos trattaré da giovane o da vieia.

PASQUELLA: No, no. Galli, via. Non mi voglio impacciar con spagnuoli. Sète tafani di sorte che o mordete o infastidite altrui; e fate come il carbone: o cuoce o tegne. V'aviam tanto pratichi oramai che guai a noi! E vi conosciamo bene, Dio grazia; e non c'è guadagno coi fatti vostri.

GIGLIO: Guadagno? Giuro a Dios que piú guadagnarite con à mi que con el primo gentil ombre de esta tierra; y, aunque vos paresque cosí male aventurade, io son de los buenos y bien nascidos ydalgos de toda Spagna.

PASQUELLA: Un miracolo non ha detto signore o cavaliere! poi che tutti gli spagnuoli che vengon qua si fan signori. E poi mirate che gente!

GIGLIO: Pasquella, tomma mia amistade, que buon por à ti!

Pasquella. Che mi farai? signora, eh?

GIGLIO: Non quiero se non que seays mia matre. E io quiero ser vostro figliolo y, allas vezes, aun marido, se vos verrà bien.

PASQUELLA: Eh lasciami stare!

GIGLIO: Reiose: eccha es la fiesta.

PASQUELLA: Che dici?

GIGLIO: Que vi voglio donare un rosario para dezir quando es la fiesta.

PASQUELLA: E dove è?

GIGLIO: Veiolo aqui.

PASQUELLA: Oh! Questa è una corona. Ché non me la dài?

PASQUELLA: Honestly? But I'm much too old for you.

GIGLIO: Too old? Mary, Mother of Monserrat,[34] you look no more than sweet fifteen or twenty. Never say "old" again, which offends my ears. Give me your favor and you'll see in no time whether I take you for young or old.

PASQUELLA: Ah, no, my fine Spanish cock, not a chance. Spaniards aren't my type. You make me think of horse flies, either biting or buzzing, or of coal, either burning or charring and smoking. Too bad for us, all the dealings we've had with your type already. Praise God, we know you now. There's nothing in it for us to get involved in anymore.

GIGLIO: In it for you? There's lots, I swear. More than from any gent in the town. Maybe I look to you now like I'm out of pocket, but I can assure you my family is among the noblest in Spain.

PASQUELLA: I'm surprised you haven't claimed to be Don This or Cavalier That already. All of your countrymen do. And then just look how they act.

GIGLIO: Let's be friends, Pasquella. You won't regret it.

PASQUELLA: You'd make me a lady, I suppose. Is that what you'd do?

GIGLIO: No, I'm only asking you to be my mother. I just want to be your son — and also your husband from time to time, if you're up for that.

PASQUELLA: *(With a guffaw)* You'd better back off.

GIGLIO: *(Aside)* Now she's laughing, so it's in the bag.

PASQUELLA: What are you going on about?

GIGLIO: That I'll give you a rosary to use on holy days.

PASQUELLA: Where are you keeping it?

GIGLIO: Right here.

PASQUELLA: A rosary, yes, that's what it is. Aren't you giving it to me?

GIGLIO: Se volite ser mia madre, io vos la daré.

PASQUELLA: Sarò ciò che tu vuoi, pur che tu me la dia.

GIGLIO: Quando podremos ablar giuntos una hora?

PASQUELLA: Quando tu vuoi.

GIGLIO: Dove?

PASQUELLA: Oh! Io non so dove.

GIGLIO: Non tení in casa algun logar donde me possa poner io à questa sera?

PASQUELLA: Sí, è; ma se 'l padron lo sapesse?

GIGLIO: E que! Non saprà nada, no.

PASQUELLA: Sai? Vedrò stasera se ci sarà ordine. Tu passa dinanzi a casa e io ti dirò se potrai venire o no. Or dammi la corona. Oh! Gli è bella!

GIGLIO: Orsú! Io starò avertido allas vintiquattr'oras.

PASQUELLA: Or sí, eh! ma dammi i paternostri.

GIGLIO: Io los portarò con me quando verrò aglià, que les quiero primiero far un poghetto profumar.

PASQUELLA: Non mi curo di tante cose. Dammegli pur cosí; io non gli voglio piú profumati.

GIGLIO: Vedi à qui: esto stocco sta gasto. Io ci harò metter un poco de oro; e questa sera ve los darò. Vòi tu altro se non que sarà la tuya?

PASQUELLA: Mia sarà quand'io l'arò. È da far gran fondamento nelle parole degli spagnuoli, alla fede! Non diss'io che voi sète formiche di sorbo, che non uscite per bussare?

GIGLIO: Que dezis, matre?

PASQUELLA: Io voglio andare in casa, ché la padrona me aspetta.

GIGLIO: E spera un pochitto! Vos teneis una gran priessa. Que teneis de azer con vostra padrona?

GIGLIO: Only if you'll be my mother. Then you can have it.

PASQUELLA: If you give it to me, I'll be whatever you want.

GIGLIO: So when can we have an hour together for a chat?

PASQUELLA: Any time.

GIGLIO: Where, then?

PASQUELLA: Uh, no idea where.

GIGLIO: Haven't you got a place in the house where I can stay tonight?

PASQUELLA: There is, I suppose. But what if my master finds out?

GIGLIO: Don't worry about that. He'll never find out.

PASQUELLA: For tonight? I'll look into it. Just drop by the house and I'll tell you "yes" or "no." So how about the rosary now? It's really pretty.

GIGLIO: Fine. Come sundown, I'll arrive.

PASQUELLA: It's a deal. So let me have the rosary.

GIGLIO: I'll have it with me when I come back. I'll get it scented for you in the meantime.

PASQUELLA: No, you needn't bother. No perfume. Just give it to me as it is.

GIGLIO: Look, this tassel's a bit frayed. Let me get a bit of gold put in and then you can have it tonight. There's no hurry. You're going to have it.

PASQUELLA: *(Aside)* Going to have it when it's in my hands. The promise of Spaniards? Not too reliable. Like the ants in the mountain ash. They don't come out even when you shake it like crazy.

GIGLIO: Mother, dear, what are you mumbling?

PASQUELLA: I've got to run now. My mistress is waiting for me.

GIGLIO: What's the hurry? Can't you hold on for a bit longer? What does your mistress want from you, anyway?

PASQUELLA: Oh! che ti credi? Che '' diavol mi porti, se le fanciulle d'oggi non son prima innamorate che gli abbino asciutti gli occhi e se prima non volesseno il punteruolo che l'aco.

GIGLIO: Que quereis dezir?

PASQUELLA: Chiachiare? E' non son miga chiachiare! La vorrebbe far da vero.

GIGLIO: Pos dimmi, de grazia. De quien es innamorada? que non es possibile, que es aun troppa gioven.

PASQUELLA: Cosí non fusse o almen si fusse messa con un par suo!

GIGLIO: Dimme, por tu vida: quien es?

PASQUELLA: E' non si vuol dire. Vedi: fa' che tu non ne parli. Non cognosci quel ragazzo di Flamminio de' Carandini?

GIGLIO: Quien? aquel mucciaccio qu'es todo vestido de blanco?

PASQUELLA: Sí, cotesto.

GIGLIO: Valeme Dios! Es possibile? Que quiere azer d'aquel, ch'es megior per ser sanado que per sanar?

PASQUELLA: E tu odi.

GIGLIO: Y el mucciaccio quiere ben à la gioven?

PASQUELLA: Eh! Cosí, cosí.

GIGLIO: Mas el patre d'ella non s'accorge d'esta trama?

PASQUELLA: Non pare, a me. Anzi, l'ha trovato due volte in casa; ed hagli fatto mille carezze, presolo per la mano, toccato sotto 'l mento, come se fusse suo figliuolo. E dice che gli par che s'assomigli a una figliuola di Virginio Bellenzini.

GIGLIO: Ah reniego del putto, vieio puerco, vellacco! Ya, ya. Sé io lo que quiere.

PASQUELLA: Uh! Tu m'hai tenuta troppo; me ne voglio ire.

The Deceived

PASQUELLA: You're not going to believe this. Devil take me if the girls of today aren't in love before they can add or subtract. Nowadays, they're out to put pestle into the mortar before they put thread into a needle.

GIGLIO: What's this? Your talk is hazy.

PASQUELLA: My talk is crazy? Not at all, when I see how ready they are to do it.

GIGLIO: Isn't she a bit young for that? So who's this fellow she's after?

PASQUELLA: No one if I had my way. At the least, she might have chosen someone of her own class.

GIGLIO: Come on, fess up, who is it?

PASQUELLA: I shouldn't say. But if you keep it a secret, you know the kid serving Flamminio de'Carandini?

GIGLIO: What? That little guy? The one all dressed in white?

PASQUELLA: That's him.

GIGLIO: Jumpin' Jesus. Really? Why's she after his services? He's better suited for in-put than out-put.

PASQUELLA: So, see what I mean?

GIGLIO: As for the boy, does he care anything about her?

PASQUELLA. Sort of.

GIGLIO: What about her father? Hasn't he noticed anything?

PASQUELLA: Nothing that I know of. He's found the boy in the house a couple of times and gives him little hugs, and holds his hand and tickles him under the chin as he would a son. And he says the boy looks like one of Virginio Bellenzini's daughters.

GIGLIO: Well, the lecherous old bugger! It's pretty clear what he's after.

PASQUELLA: Pew! I've got to get going. I've been out here long enough.

GIGLIO: Mira que verrò, à esta nocce. Non te scordar della promessa.

PASQUELLA: Né tu di portar la corona.

Scena quarta

FLAMMINIO, CRIVELLO *suo servo e* SCATIZZA *servo di Virginio.*

FLAMMINIO: Tu non sei ito a veder se tu vedi Fabio; ed egli non viene. Non so che mi dire di questa sua tardanza.

CRIVELLO: Io andavo; e voi mi richiamaste indietro. Che colpa è la mia?

FLAMMINIO: Va' adesso: e, caso che ancor fusse in casa d'Isabella, aspettalo fin che gli esca e fallo poi venir subito.

CRIVELLO: Oh! Che saprò io se v'è o se non v'è? volete forse ch'io ne domandi alla casa di lei?

FLAMMINIO: Mira che asino! Parti che cotesto stesse bene? Credelo a me ch'io non ho servidore in casa che vaglia un pane altro che Fabio. Iddio mi dia grazia ch'io gli possa far del bene. Che borbotti? che dici, poltrone? non è vero?

CRIVELLO: Che volete ch'io dica? Dico di sí, io. Fabio è buono, Fabio è bello, Fabio serve bene. Fabio con voi, Fabio con madonna... Ogni cosa è Fabio; ogni cosa fa Fabio. Ma...

FLAMMINIO: Che vuol dir "ma..."?

CRIVELLO: ...non sarà sempre buona robba.

FLAMMINIO: Che dici tu di robba?

CRIVELLO: Che non è da fidargli cosí sempre la robba. Sí, ché gli è forestiero e potrebbe, un dí, caricarvela.

GIGLIO: Don't forget about tonight, or your promise, because I'll be here.

PASQUELLA: What about you? Don't forget the rosary.

Scene 4

The street in front of Flamminio's house.
FLAMMINIO, CRIVELLO, *his servant, and* SCATIZZA.

FLAMMINIO: You haven't gone to find out what's become of Fabio. He doesn't show up, and I don't know what to think. What's keeping him?

CRIVELLO: I was on my way but you called me back. How's that my fault?

FLAMMINIO: Well, go then, and if you find him at Isabella's place, wait for him to come out and then bring him right back here.

CRIVELLO: How will I know if he's coming out or not? Shouldn't I just go to her house and ask?

FLAMMINIO: You're an idiot! Does that make any sense to you? Fabio's the only servant in the household worth his salt. Pray God I can treat him as he deserves. So what are you grumbling about? What's on your mind, blockhead? Don't you agree?

CRIVELLO: What should I say? Sure, sure, Fabio's great, Fabio's good-looking, Fabio does your every bidding, Fabio with you, Fabio with the lady, Fabio the be-all, Fabio the end-all. But....

FLAMMINIO: "But," you add? But what?

CRIVELLO: He may not always be the right kind of thing for you.

FLAMMINIO: What "thing" is that?

CRIVELLO: That he might not be all that trustworthy. You don't really know him, and one day he could make a mockery of you.

FLAMMINIO: Cosí fidati fusse voi altri! Domanda un poco lo Scatizza, che è là, se l'avesse veduto. E io sarò al banco de' Porrini.

CRIVELLO: Scatizza, addio. Ha' tu veduto Fabio?

SCATIZZA: Chi? quella vostra buona robba? Oh cagnaccio! Tu ti dài il bel tempo.

CRIVELLO: Ove andavi?

SCATIZZA: A trovare il mio grimo.

CRIVELLO: Gli è passato di qui or ora.

SCATIZZA: Dove è andato?

CRIVELLO: In qua sú. Viene, ché 'l trovaremo. Eh viene! ché t'ho da contare una facezia, che m'è intervenuta con la mia Caterina, la piú bella del mondo.

Scena quinta

SPELA *servo di Gherardo, solo.*

Può esser peggio al mondo che servire a un padron pazzo? Gherardo mi manda a comprare il zibetto. Quando lo domandai al profumiere e dissi ch'io non avevo piú d'un bolognino, cominciò a dire ch'io non avevo tenuto a mente e che Gherardo doveva aver detto un bossol d'onguento da rogna: ché n'aveva bisogno; ché sapeva che non usava zibetto. Cominciagli a dire, acciò che egli mel credesse, di questo suo amorazzo: e fu per crepar di ridere con certi giovani che eran lí; e voleva pur ch'io gli portasse un bossol d'assafetida; tal che, cosí dileggiato, me ne partii. Or, se 'l padrone il vuole, diemi piú quattrini.

The Deceived

FLAMMINIO: If only the rest of you were as trustworthy as he is. Here comes Scatizza. Ask if he's seen him. I've got business at the Porrini Bank. *(Exit Flamminio)*

CRIVELLO: Hey, Scatizza. You seen Fabio around?

SCATIZZA: The boss's prissy pet? His little spaniel! You're having your fun!

CRIVELLO: So where are you off to?

SCATIZZA: I'm trying to find my old man.

CRIVELLO: He was here a minute ago.

SCATIZZA: Which way was he headed?

CRIVELLO: He went that way. Follow me, we'll catch up to him. Make it snappy. I've got a great story to tell you about me and Caterina — she's the beauty of the world.

Scene 5

SPELA, *alone.*

SPELA: You tell me what's worse in the whole world than working for a daft master. Gherardo sends me to get some civet musk. So I tell the pharmacist that I've only got one bolognino. Then he tells me I mistook what Gherardo asked for, and adds that he probably wants a jar of mange ointment, because that's what he needs. Then he tells me my boss wouldn't know which end to apply the musk to if he had it. So to make him believe me, I start to tell him about Gherardo's crazy infatuation. But then he and a bunch of other guys in the shop end up killing themselves with laughter. After that he tries to foist a jar of asafetida on me,[35] so I got out of there fast with all that laughing still in my ears. If the boss wants musk, he's got to give me more money.

Scena sesta

CRIVELLO, SCATIZZA, LELIA *da ragazzo e* ISABELLA.

CRIVELLO: Or hai inteso; e, se tu vuoi venire, mi basta l'animo di trovarne una per te ancora.

SCATIZZA: Fa' un poco di pratica, ch'io ti prometto che, se tu trovi qualche fantesca che mi piaccia, che noi ci daremo il piú bel tempo del mondo. Io ho la chiave del granaio, della cantina, della dispensa, delle legna; e, s'io avesse dove poter scaricar le some a piano, mi basterebbe l'animo che noi faremmo una vita da signori. In ogni modo, da questi padroni non se ne cava altro.

CRIVELLO: Io t'ho detto: io 'l vo' dire a Bita, che ti provegga di qualche cittona acciò che tutti a quattro insieme possiam darci buon tempo in questo carnovale.

SCATIZZA: Oh! Noi siamo all'ultimo.

CRIVELLO: Daremcelo questa quaresima, mentre ch'i padroni saranno alla predica a vagheggiare. Ma sta', ché l'uscio di Gherardo s'apre. Tirate un poco piú qua.

SCATIZZA: Perché?

CRIVELLO: Oh! Per buon rispetto.

LELIA: Orsú, Isabella! Non vi dimenticate di quanto m'avete promesso.

ISABELLA: E voi non vi dimenticate di venirmi a vedere. Ascoltate una parola.

CRIVELLO: S'io fusse in questa fregàgnuola, so che 'l padrone mi perdonarebbe!

SCATIZZA: Mangiaresti i polli per te, eh?

CRIVELLO: Che ne credi?

LELIA: Or volete altro?

ISABELLA: Udite un poco.

LELIA: Eccomi.

The Deceived

Scene 6

A street in front of Gherardo's house.
CRIVELLO, SCATIZZA, LELIA *in boy's clothes, and* ISABELLA.

CRIVELLO: Now you're catching on. If you want in on it, I'll find another girl for you.

SCATIZZA: Put some effort into it, will you. Find me a serving wench to my liking and I guarantee us the best time in the world. I've got the keys — granary, cellar, pantry, woodshed, the lot. If there were somewhere quiet where I could unload the goods, we could live like princes. With masters like ours, this is about as much as we can hope for.

CRIVELLO: Like I said, I'll ask Bita to find you a great big girl. Then the four of us will have a blast for Carnival.

SCATIZZA: Well, today's the last day for it.[36]

CRIVELLO: All right then, we wait for Lent to do it when the bosses are in church to pray and ogle the girls. But check out Gherardo's door. Somebody's coming out, so step back over here.

SCATIZZA: How come?

CRIVELLO: As a precaution. *(Lelia and Isabella enter. Crivello and Scatizza hide to spy on them.)*

LELIA: Come on Isabella, don't you forget your promise.

ISABELLA: Don't you forget to visit me. And one more thing.

CRIVELLO: *(Aside to Scatizza)* If I were in the same place as that little bugger, I know what the boss would do to me.

SCATIZZA: You'd claim the chick, right?

CRIVELLO: What would you do?

LELIA: Anything else?

ISABELLA: Just listen for a second.

LELIA: All ears.

ISABELLA: Ecci nissun costí fuora?

LELIA: Non si vede anima nata.

CRIVELLO: Che diavol vòl colei?

SCATIZZA: Questa dimestichezza è troppa.

CRIVELLO: Sta' a vedere.

ISABELLA: Udite una parola.

CRIVELLO: Costor s'accostan molto.

SCATIZZA: Che sí! che sí!

ISABELLA: Sapete! Vorrei...

LELIA: Che vorreste?

ISABELLA: Vorrei... Accostatevi.

SCATIZZA: Accostati, salvaticaccio!

ISABELLA: Mirate se v'è niuno.

LELIA: Non ve l'ho detto? Non si vede persona.

ISABELLA: Oh! Io vorrei che voi tornasse dopo disinare quando mio padre sarà fuora.

LELIA: Lo farò; ma, come passa il mio padron di qui, di grazia, fuggite e serrategli la finestra in fronte.

ISABELLA: S'io non lo fo, non mi vogliate piú bene.

SCATIZZA: Dove diavol gli tien la man, colei?

CRIVELLO: Oh povero padrone! Che sí, che sí, ch'io sarò indivino!

LELIA: Addio.

ISABELLA: Udite: vi volete partire?

SCATIZZA: Basciala, che ti venga il cancaro!

CRIVELLO: L'ha paura di non esser veduta.

LELIA: Orsú! Tornatevi in casa.

ISABELLA: Voglio una grazia da voi.

ISABELLA: Is anyone around?

LELIA: Not a soul alive.

CRIVELLO: *(Aside to Scatizza)* What the deuce is she after?

SCATIZZA: Pretty cozy. This beats everything.

CRIVELLO: Gotta see this.

ISABELLA: There's something I want to say.

CRIVELLO: They're huddled up close.

SCATIZZA: You said it.

ISABELLA: Know what? I really want....

LELIA: Really want what?

ISABELLA: I really want.... But get closer.

SCATIZZA: *(Aside)* Wild! "Get closer."

ISABELLA: Make sure no one's around.

LELIA: Like I said, nobody.

ISABELLA: I really want you to slip back after supper when father's away.

LELIA: I'll be there. But if my master goes past, don't fail to slam the window on him and run away.

ISABELLA: I will, or you're free to love another.

SCATIZZA: *(Aside to Crivello)* Devil, look where she's putting his hand.

CRIVELLO: You said it. Too bad for the boss! I suspected as much.

LELIA: Time to go.

ISABELLA: You want to leave me?

SCATIZZA: *(Aside)* Just plant the damned kiss, and the plague take you.

CRIVELLO: She's scared of being seen.

LELIA: Best go back in.

ISABELLA: I need a favor from you.

LELIA: Quale?

ISABELLA: Entrate un poco dentro a l'uscio.

SCATIZZA: La cosa è fatta.

ISABELLA: Oh! Voi sète salvatico!

LELIA: Noi sarem veduti.

CRIVELLO: Oimè! oimè! O seccareccio, altrettanto a me.

SCATIZZA: Non ti diss'io che la baciarebbe?

CRIVELLO: Or ben ti dico ch'io non vorrei aver guadagnato cento scudi e non aver veduto questo bacio.

SCATIZZA: Il veggio. Cosí fusse tócco a me!

CRIVELLO: Oh! Che farà il padrone, come egli 'l sappia?

SCATIZZA: Oh diavol! Non si vòl dirglielo.

ISABELLA: Perdonatemi. La vostra troppa bellezza e 'l troppo amar ch'io vi porto è cagion ch'io fo quello che forse voi giudicarete esser di poca onesta fanciulla. Ma Dio lo sa ch'io non me ne son potuta tenere.

LELIA: Non fate queste scuse con me, signora; ché so ancor io come io sto e quel che, per troppo amore, mi son messo a fare.

ISABELLA: E che cosa?

LELIA: Oh! Che? A ingannare il mio signore, che non sta però bene.

ISABELLA: Il malan che dio gli dia!

CRIVELLO: Vatti po' fida di bagasce! Ben gli sta. Non è maraveglia che 'l fegatello confortava il padrone a lasciar questo amore.

SCATIZZA: Ogni gallina ruspa a sé. In fine, tutte le donne son fatte a un modo.

LELIA: L'ora è già tarda ed io ho da trovare il padrone. Rimanete in pace.

ISABELLA: Udite.

The Deceived

LELIA: What now?

ISABELLA: Come here into the doorway.

SCATIZZA: *(Aside)* It's nearly done.

ISABELLA: Oh, you're just plain mean.

LELIA: Someone will see us.

CRIVELLO: *(Aside)* Holy crap, I want one too.

SCATIZZA: Didn't I tell you he'd plant one?

CRIVELLO: Yeah, and better to have seen this kiss than get a hundred scudi.

SCATIZZA: My eyes took it in, but not my lips, damn it!

CRIVELLO: Oh boy, what if the master finds out?

SCATIZZA: Heck, don't ever tell him.

ISABELLA: I'm sorry, I'm sorry. You're so beautiful, and my love for you — I couldn't help myself, immoral or not. God only knows.

LELIA: No need for apologies, my lady. From an excess of love, I too know what I've become and what I'm determined to do.

ISABELLA: What's that?

LELIA: That I'll do? It's wrong, but I'll deceive my master.

ISABELLA: God plague him is all I can say.

CRIVELLO: *(Aside)* Why, the cheating vixen. No wonder the kid's been telling the master to dump her.

SCATIZZA: *(Aside)* Goes to show people always look after themselves first. Said and done, all women are alike.

LELIA: It's gotten late. I'd better go find my master. So I'll leave you here in peace.

ISABELLA: No wait. *(She kisses him again.)*

CRIVELLO: Ohi! e due! Che ti si secchi, che ti faccia il mal pro!

SCATIZZA: Al corpo di Dio, che m'è infiata una gamba che par che la voglia recere.

LELIA: Serrate. Addio.

ISABELLA: Mi vi dono.

LELIA: Son vostro. Io ho, da un canto, la piú bella pastura del mondo di costei che si crede pur ch'io sia maschio; dall'altro, vorrei uscir di questa briga e non so come mi fare. Veggio che costei è già venuta al bacio; e verrà, la prima volta, piú avanti; e trovarommi aver perduta ogni cosa: tal che forza è ch'e' si scuopra la ragia. Voglio andare a trovar Clemenzia di quanto gli par ch'io faccia. Ma ecco FLAMMINIO:

CRIVELLO: Scatizza, il padrone mi disse aspettarmi al banco de' Porrini. Vo' dargli questa buona nuova. Caso non mi creda, fa' che non mi facci parer bugiardo.

SCATIZZA: Io non ti posso mancare. Ma, facendo a mio modo, te ne starai queto e arai sempre questo calcio in gola a Fabio per poterlo far fare a tuo modo.

CRIVELLO: Dico ch'io gli vo' male, ché m'ha rovinato.

SCATIZZA: Governatene come ti piace.

Scena settima

FLAMMINIO *e* LELIA *da ragazzo.*

FLAMMINIO: È possibil, però, ch'io sia tanto fuor di me e mi stimi sí poco ch'io voglia amare a suo dispetto costei e servir chi mi strazia, chi non fa conto di me. Che non mi vuol pur compiacer sol d'uno sguardo? Sarò io sí da poco e sí vile ch'io non mi sappi levar questa vergogna e questo strazio da dosso? Ma ecco Fabio. Or ben, che hai fatto?

CRIVELLO: *(Aside)* Smokes! There's two of them. May you get parched and blow away.

SCATIZZA. Body of God, she's made one of my legs swell up till it spits.[37]

LELIA: Bolt the door and good bye.

ISABELLA: I love you.

LELIA: And I love you too. *(Isabella goes in.)* In one sense, this is the best lark there is, her thinking I'm a boy. In another, though, I'd like to have this mess over with, but I don't have a clue how to do it. Now she's at the kissing stage, and she'll want more the first chance she gets. But if she discovers my secret, it's all up with me. I need Clemenzia's advice, but here comes Flamminio.

CRIVELLO: *(Aside to Scatizza)* Well, Scatizza, the boss will be waiting for me at the Porrini Bank. I've got to take him the good news. And if he doesn't believe me, you back me up that it's the truth.

SCATIZZA: Trust me. But if you'd listen to me you wouldn't let this out. You're spilling because you want to get even with Fabio. You want him by the throat so you can boss him around.

CRIVELLO: Hate his guts. I'm wiped out because of him.

SCATIZZA: Then make it work to your advantage.

Scene 7

Outside Flamminio's house.
FLAMMINIO *and* LELIA *in boy's clothes.*

FLAMMINIO: Am I out of my mind or what? Do I despise myself so much as to go on loving someone against her will — serving someone who torments me without a care and won't even glance my way? Am I so shrunken and depraved that I can't shake off this shame and affliction? Here comes Fabio. — So, what have you achieved?

LELIA: Nulla.

FLAMMINIO: Perché sei stato tanto a tornare? Tu vorrai diventar un forca, sí?

LELIA: Io ho indugiato perch'io volevo pur parlare a Isabella.

FLAMMINIO: E perché non gli hai parlato?

LELIA: Non mi ha voluto ascoltare. E, se voi facesse a mio modo, pigliaresti altro partito e vi risolvaresti de' casi vostri: ché, per quel ch'io n'ho potuto comprendere insino a qui, voi vi perdete il tempo; ché la si mostra ostinatissima a non voler far mai cosa che vi piaccia.

FLAMMINIO: E, se 'l dicesse Iddio, l'ha pure il torto. Non sai che, or ora, passando di là, si levò subito, come la mi vidde, dalla finestra con tanto sdegno e con tanta furia come s'ell'avesse visto qualche cosa orribile o spaventosa?

LELIA: Lasciatela andar, vi dico. È possibil che, in tutta questa città, non sia un'altra che meriti l'amor vostro quanto lei? Non vi è piaciuta mai altra donna che lei?

FLAMMINIO: Cosí non fusse! Ch'io ho paura che questo non sia la cagion di tutto 'l mio male: perché io amai già molto caldamente quella Lelia di Virginio Bellenzini di ch'i' ti parlai; e ho paura ch'Isabella non dubiti che questo amor duri ancora e, per questo, non mi voglia vedere. Ma io gli farò intendere ch'io non l'amo piú; anzi, l'ho in odio e non la posso sentir ricordare. E gli farò ogni fede ch'ella vorrà di non arrivar mai dove lei sia. E voglio che glie lo dica tu, a ogni modo.

LELIA: Oimè!

FLAMMINIO: Che hai? Par che tu venga meno. Che ti senti?

LELIA: Oimè!

FLAMMINIO: Che ti duole?

LELIA: Oimè! Il cuore.

FLAMMINIO: Da quanto in qua? Appoggiati un poco. Duolti forse il corpo?

LELIA: Not much.

FLAMMINIO: Why have you been gone so long? You're not pulling a fast one on me?

LELIA: I stayed around to talk to Isabella.

FLAMMINIO: So did you?

LELIA: She wouldn't listen to me. If I were you, I'd call this affair off and look somewhere else. Just a waste of time from everything I've seen. It's looking like you won't get a single favor out of her.

FLAMMINIO: If I heard this from God I'd call Him a liar. But you might as well know that as I passed her place just now, as soon as she saw me she backed away from the window with a look of anger and scorn as if she'd seen a monster.

LELIA: I'm telling you to drop her. Isn't there someone else in this whole city that's more deserving of your devotion? Haven't you loved another one as much as this one?

FLAMMINIO: I wish I hadn't. I think that's behind my whole calamity. I was once passionate over Lelia, the daughter of Virginio Bellenzini, the one I mentioned to you. But now I'm afraid Isabella refuses to see me because she thinks it isn't over. She'll have to be made to understand that I don't love Lelia, that I hate her, that I can't even stand the sound of her name. I'll promise her any way she wants to hear it that I'll never see Lelia again. It's your job to tell her this.

LELIA: Aye yai!

FLAMMINIO: Now what's the matter? You look like you're about to faint.

LELIA: Aye yai!

FLAMMINIO: Where is it hurting?

LELIA: In my heart, aye yai!

FLAMMINIO: How long have you had this? Here, lean on me. Is your body hurting?

LELIA: Signor no.

FLAMMINIO: E forse lo stomaco ch'è indebilito?

LELIA: Dico ch'è il cuore che mi duole.

FLAMMINIO: Ed a me, forse, molto piú. Tu hai perduto il colore. Vattene a casa: e fatti scaldare qualche panno al petto e far qualche frega dietro alle spalle; ché non sarà altro. Io sarò or ora là e, bisognando, farò venire il medico che ti tocchi il polso e vegga che male è il tuo. Da' qua, un poco, il braccio. Tu sei gelato. Orsú! Vattene pian piano. A che strani casi è sottoposto l'uomo! Non vorrei che costui mi mancasse per quanto vale tutto 'l mio: ch'io non so se fusse mai al mondo servidor piú accorto, meglio accostumato di questo giovanetto; e, oltre a questo, mostra d'amarmi tanto che, se fusse donna, pensarei che la stesse mal di me. Fabio, va' a casa, dico; e scaldati un poco i piei. Io sarò or ora là. Di' che apparecchino.

LELIA: Or hai pur, misera te, con le tue proprie orecchie, dall'istessa bocca di questo ingrato di Flamminio, inteso quanto egli t'ami. Misera, scontenta Lelia! Perché piú perdi tempo in servir questo crudele? Non ti è giovata la pazienzia, non i preghi, non i favori che gli hai fatti; or non ti giovan gl'inganni. Sventurata me! Rifiutata, scacciata, fuggita, odiata! Perché serv'io a chi mi rifiuta? Perché domando chi mi scaccia? perché seguo chi mi fugge? perché amo chi m'ha in odio? Ah Flamminio! Non ti piace se non Isabella. Egli non vuole altro che Isabella. Abbisela, tenghisela; ch'io lo lasciarò o morrò. Delibero di non piú servirli in questo abito né piú capitargli innanzi, poi che tanto m'ha in odio. Andarò a trovar Clemenzia che so che m'aspetta in casa; e con essa disporrò quel che abbi da essere della vita mia.

The Deceived

LELIA: No, no sir.

FLAMMINIO: Probably just an upset stomach.

LELIA: The pain's in my heart, I'm telling you.

FLAMMINIO: Not as big as mine. You're looking pale. Better go home, get a warm plaster for your chest, and have your back rubbed. That'll do it. I'll be there soon to call the doctor if you need your pulse taken. He'll know what's wrong. Here give me your arm. You're awfully cold. Let's get going, but easy, easy. *(Aside)* What strange things can happen to a person. I don't want to lose this boy, not for all I own. He's been the best, most polite, and well-behaved page in the world. More than that, he's really devoted. If he were a girl, I'd say he's lovesick over me. — Fabio, time to go home and get your feet warm. I'll be right there. Tell the others to get the supper ready.

LELIA: *(Aside)* Wretched me. Your ears have heard it straight from his mouth how little this hard-heart loves you. It's too shocking. No more time wasted in the service of so much cruelty. Your patience, your prayers, your attention — none of it to any avail. Nor your deceptions either. I'm plain miserable. I feel slighted, scorned, discarded, hated. Why go on with one who rejects me? Why yearn for someone who disdains me? Why chase after a man who's in full flight? Why love where I'm loathed? Ah, Flamminio! You only love Isabella, you want her alone. So have her, take her. I'd rather be dead than stay with him now. I'll not be needing these clothes anymore to serve him. Being so much hated, I'll not put myself between them. With Clemenzia's help, I'll map a new life for myself. She's waiting for me at the house.

Scena ottava

CRIVELLO e FLAMMINIO.

CRIVELLO: E, se non è cosí, fatemi impicar per la gola; non tanto tagliar la lingua. Vi dico che gli è cosí.

FLAMMINIO: Da quanto in qua?

CRIVELLO: Quando voi mi mandasti a cercar di lui.

FLAMMINIO: Come andò? Dimmelo un'altra volta, perché egli mi niega d'averle oggi potuto parlare.

CRIVELLO: Sarà buon che vel confessi! Dico che, aspettando io di vedere s'egli dava di volta intorno a quella casa, lo vidi uscir fuore. E, volendosi già partire, Isabella lo richiamò dentro: e, guardando se fuore era alcuno che gli vedesse, non vi vedendo persona, si baciorno insieme.

FLAMMINIO: Come non vider te?

CRIVELLO: Perch'io m'era ritratto in quel portico rincontro, e non me potevan vedere.

FLAMMINIO: Come gli vedesti tu?

CRIVELLO: Con gli occhi. Credete forse ch'io gli abbi veduti con le gombita?

FLAMMINIO: E basciolla?

CRIVELLO: Io non so s'ella baciò lui o egli lei; ma io credo che l'un basciassi l'altro.

FLAMMINIO: Accostorono il viso l'uno a l'altro tanto che si potessen baciare?

CRIVELLO: Il viso no, ma le labbra sí.

FLAMMINIO: Oh! Possonsi accostar le labbra senza il viso?

CRIVELLO: Se l'uomo avesse la bocca nelle orecchie o nella cicottola, forse; ma, stando dove le stanno, credo che no.

FLAMMINIO: Guarda che tu vedesse bene, che tu non dica poi: "E' mi parve"; ché questa è una gran cosa che tu mi dici.

The Deceived

Scene 8

CRIVELLO *and* FLAMMINIO.

CRIVELLO: If you don't find it true, hang me by the neck or lop out my tongue. I'm telling you it's true.

FLAMMINIO: When did it happen?

CRIVELLO: Just after you sent me off to find him.

FLAMMINIO: So what exactly did you see? Repeat it to me, because he wasn't able to speak to her today.

CRIVELLO: He'd better tell you the truth! I was checking to make certain he was still in the house, and then he came out. He was leaving, but Isabella called him back, and when they thought no one was watching, they kissed each other.

FLAMMINIO: So why didn't they see you?

CRIVELLO: I stepped out of sight into the doorway across the street.

FLAMMINIO: Then how could you see them?

CRIVELLO: With my eyeballs. You think I see with my elbows, maybe?

FLAMMINIO: So he kissed her?

CRIVELLO: Maybe he did, or maybe she kissed him, but what I know is one of them kissed the other.

FLAMMINIO: And their faces were close enough for kissing?

CRIVELLO: Not faces, just lips.

FLAMMINIO: Oh, so lips can touch without faces closing in?

CRIVELLO: Maybe, if a man's mouth were on his ears or the top of his head. But with lips where they are, probably not.

FLAMMINIO: You'd better be sure of what you saw. Don't be saying to me later, "I was under the impression." This is a big deal you're telling me.

CRIVELLO: Maggiore è il Mangia che sta in cima alla torre di Siena.

FLAMMINIO: Come vedesti?

CRIVELLO: Vegliando, con gli occhi aperti, stando a vedere né avendo a far altra cosa che mirare.

FLAMMINIO: Se questo è vero, tu m'hai morto.

CRIVELLO: Questo è vero. Lo chiamò, se gli accostò, l'abbracciò, lo basciò. Or, se tu vuoi morir, muore.

FLAMMINIO: Non è maraviglia che 'l traditor negava di non esservi stato! Or so perché il ribaldo mi confortava a lasciarla: per goderla lui. Se io non fo tal vendetta che, fin che questa terra dura, sarà essempio ai servidori che non sieno traditori a' padroni, non voglio esser tenuto uomo. Ma, in fine, se altra certezza non n'ho, io non tel vo' credere. So che tu sei un tristo e gli debbi voler male; e fai perch'io me lo levi dinanzi. Ma, per quel Dio che s'adora, ch'io ti farò dire il vero o t'ammazzarò. Di' su! Hailo veduto?

CRIVELLO: Signor sí.

FLAMMINIO: Baciolla?

CRIVELLO: Baciârsi.

FLAMMINIO: Quante volte?

CRIVELLO: Due volte.

FLAMMINIO: Ove?

CRIVELLO: Nel suo ridotto.

FLAMMINIO: Tu menti per la gola. Poco fa, dicesti in su l'uscio.

CRIVELLO: Volsi dir vicino all'uscio.

FLAMMINIO: Di' il vero!

CRIVELLO: Ohi! ohi! M'increscie d'avervel detto.

FLAMMINIO: Fu vero?

CRIVELLO: Signor sí. Ma io mi so' scordato ch'io avevo un testimonio.

CRIVELLO: Yeah, as big a deal as Mangia the giant ringing the hours in Siena.[38]

FLAMMINIO: You're sure you could see them?

CRIVELLO: My eyes were wide open. I was there for looking, and there was nothing to distract me.

FLAMMINIO: If it's true, you're the death of me.

CRIVELLO: Well, what I said's the truth. She called out to him, then got close to him, then hugged and kissed him. So if you're going to die, get on with it.

FLAMMINIO: The traitor! An incredible lie saying he was never there. It explains why the rogue kept urging me to leave her. He wanted her for himself. Well, if there's any manhood left in me, when my vengeance is finished, servants down to the day of doom will know the cost of betraying their masters. But why should I believe it? I need more proof. You're just a grumbler, anyway. You wish him ill because you want me to give him the boot. Well, you're going to tell me the truth, by God, or prepare to die. Is this what you really saw?

CRIVELLO: Really.

FLAMMINIO: That he kissed her?

CRIVELLO: That they were kissing.

FLAMMINIO: For how many times?

CRIVELLO: Two.

FLAMMINIO: Where?

CRIVELLO: In the archway.

FLAMMINIO: That's a lie. Before, you said in the doorway.

CRIVELLO: That's what I meant.

FLAMMINIO: Speak the truth. *(Beats him)*

CRIVELLO: Aye, aye. I'm sorry I ever said it.

FLAMMINIO: So was it true?

CRIVELLO: You bet, and did I mention I've got a witness?

FLAMMINIO: Chi era?

CRIVELLO: Lo Scatizza di Virginio.

FLAMMINIO: Vidde egli ancora?

CRIVELLO: Come me.

FLAMMINIO: E se egli nol confessa?

CRIVELLO: Ammazzatemi.

FLAMMINIO: Farollo.

CRIVELLO: E s'egli il confessa?

FLAMMINIO: Amazzarò tutt'e due.

CRIVELLO: Oimè! Perché?

FLAMMINIO: Non dico te; ma Isabella e Fabio.

CRIVELLO: E che voi abbruciate quella casa, con Pasquella e con chi v'è dentro.

FLAMMINIO: Andiamo a trovar lo Scatizza. S'io non nel pago, s'io non fo dir di me, se tutta questa terra non lo vede... Ne farò tal vendetta!... Oh traditore! Vatti poi fida.

Atto Terzo

Scena prima

PEDANTE, FABRIZIO *giovine figliuol di Virginio e* STRAGUALCIA *servo.*

PEDANTE: Questa terra mi par tutta mutata poi ch'io non vi fui. Vero è ch'io non vi fui se non per transito con li oratori d'Ancona; e alloggiammo al "Guicciardino". Pur vi stemmo da sei giorni. Tu ricognoscine cosa alcuna?

FABRIZIO: Come mai piú non l'avessi veduta.

PEDANTE: Credotelo, perché te ne partisti sí piccolo che non è maraviglia. Or pur conosco la strada dove siamo. Quello è il palazzo de' Rangoni; qui sotto passa il canal

The Deceived

FLAMMINIO: Who?

CRIVELLO: Scatizza, Virginio's man.

FLAMMINIO: He saw it too?

CRIVELLO: Same as me.

FLAMMINIO: And what if he doesn't back you up?

CRIVELLO: Kill me.

FLAMMINIO: Count on it.

CRIVELLO: And if he backs me up?

FLAMMINIO: I'll kill two people.

CRIVELLO: How come? Not fair.

FLAMMINIO: No, not you. Isabella and Fabio.

CRIVELLO: And burn down their house with Pasquella and the others inside.

FLAMMINIO: Where's Scatizza? If those two don't get what's coming to them.... If I don't set the city talking.... If the whole world doesn't witness.... There'll be revenge, the traitor. So much for trust. Let's go.

ACT 3

Scene 1

PIERO, FABRIZIO, *young son of Virginio,* and STRAGUALCIA, *servant.*

PIERO: I barely recognize this place, it has changed so much. I was once here for a short time with a group of orators from Ancona. We were at the Guicciardino for six days as I recall. Anything familiar to you?

FABRIZIO: No, it's like seeing it for the first time.

PIERO: Not surprising. You left here when you were a tot, so that's logical. Oh, wait, this street I know. That's the Rangoni Palace, and the Grand Canal's just beyond,

grande; quel che vedi là in capo è il duomo. Hai tu sentito dire "Sarestú mai la potta da Modana?" o vero "Gli pare esser la potta da Modana"?

FABRIZIO: Mille volte. Mostratemela, di grazia.

PEDANTE: Vedila sopra il duomo.

FABRIZIO: È quella?

PEDANTE: Quella.

FABRIZIO: Oh! Questa è una baia!

PEDANTE: Tu vedi.

FABRIZIO: Ho sentito ancor dire "Tu hai tolto a menar l'orso a Modana". Che vuol dire? Dov'è questo orso?

PEDANTE: E' son dettati antiqui de quibus nescitur origo.

FABRIZIO: Certo, maestro, che questa terra par che mi venga di buono.

STRAGUALCIA: Ed a me vien di migliore, ch'io sento qua presso uno odor d'arosto che mi fa morir di fame.

PEDANTE: Oh! Non sai quel che dice Cantalicio? "Dulcis amor patriae". E Catone: "Pugna pro patria". Hoc. Insumma, e' non c'è la piú dolce cosa che la patria.

STRAGUALCIA: Io credo che sia molto piú dolce il tribiano, maestro. Cosí n'avess'io un boccale! Ch'io sono spallato, a portar questa valigia.

PEDANTE: Queste strade paion fatte di nuovo. Quand'io ci fui, eran tutte sordide e fangose.

STRAGUALCIA: Aviamo a contare i mattoni? Ci sarà facenda! Vorrei che noi andassemo piú presto in qualche luogo che facessemo colazione, io.

PEDANTE: Iandudum animus est in patinis.

The Deceived

and the cathedral's there at the top of the street.[39] You know the old saying, "Does she think she's the pussy of Modena?"[40]

FABRIZIO: Heard it a thousand times. Let's go have a look at it.

PIERO: See over the door of the cathedral? See that statue there?

FABRIZIO: That one?

PIERO: That's the very one.

FABRIZIO: Fantastic. What a hoot.

PIERO: So you've got the connection?

FABRIZIO: There's another one about trying to lead the bear to Modena.[41] What's that all about? Is there a bear somewhere?

PIERO: It's an old proverb of the *antiqui de quibus nescitur origo* [the ancients of unknown origin].

FABRIZIO: Teacher, I've got a good feeling that things are going to go well for me here.

STRAGUALCIA: And even better for me. I'm getting a whiff of sweet odors rising from a roast, and my hunger's killing me.

PIERO: Well, you know what Cantalicius says: "Dulcis amor patriae" [the love of one's country is sweet].[42] Then there's Cato: "Pugna pro patria" [fight for the fatherland]. Well, this is it. *In summa* [So, in brief] your fatherland is the sweetest thing there is.

STRAGUALCIA: Trebbiano wine is sweeter than that, Mr. Teacher, and I could really use a cup of that about now. All this luggage has broken my back.

PIERO: The streets look freshly paved. Last time I was here they were grit and muck.

STRAGUALCIA: So are we just going to stand here and count the paving stones? What a job that would be. Let's find ourselves a place to eat — that's all I want.

PIERO: *Iandundum animus est in patinis* [His soul already resides among pots and pans].[43]

FABRIZIO: Che arma è quella di quei succhielli?

PEDANTE: Quella è l'arma di questa communità e chiamasi la Trivella. E, come a Fiorenza si grida: "Marzocco! Marzocco!" e a Vinegia: "San Marco! San Marco!" e a Siena: "Lupa! Lupa!", cosí qui esclamano: "Trivella! Trivella!".

STRAGUALCIA: Io vorrei piú tosto che noi gridassemo: "Padella! Padella!".

FABRIZIO: Quella la conosco. È l'arme del duca.

STRAGUALCIA: Maestro, vorrei che voi portasse un poco questa valigia, voi. Io ho sí secche le labbra ch'io non posso parlare.

PEDANTE: Orsú, che ti cavarai la sete poi!

STRAGUALCIA: Quand'io son morto, fatemi un brodetto agli archi.

FABRIZIO: Basta che, ne la prima gionta, questa terra mi piace assai. E a te, Stragualcia?

STRAGUALCIA: A me pare un paradiso, ché non vi si mangia e non vi si beve. Orsú! Non perdiam piú tempo a veder la terra, ché la vedremo a bello agio.

PEDANTE: Tu vedrai qui il piú solenne campanile che sia in tutta la machina mondiale.

STRAGUALCIA: È quello al qual i modanesi volevon far la guaina? e che dicono che la sua ombra fa impazzar gli uomini?

PEDANTE: Sí, cotesto.

STRAGUALCIA: Io so ch'io non uscirò di cucina, per me. Chi ci vuole andar ci vada. Or sollecitiam d'alloggiare.

PEDANTE: Tu hai una gran fretta.

STRAGUALCIA: Cancaro! Io mi muoio di fame e non ho mangiato altro, stamattina, ch'una mezza gallina che v'avanzò in barca.

The Deceived

FABRIZIO: What is that insignia over there with the augur on it?

PIERO: Ah the "Trivella" it's called, the coat of arms of the town.[44] In Florence the cry is "Marzocco, Marzocco," in Venice "San Marco, San Marco," in Siena "Lupa, Lupa," so here it's "Trivella, Trivella."

STRAGUALCIA: How about "Kettle, Kettle?" That's my recommendation.

FABRIZIO: That one there I know. It's the duke's arms.

PIERO: Correct!

STRAGUALCIA: Hey teacher, are you going to carry the bags for a while? My lips are so dry from thirst I can hardly talk.

PIERO: Courage man. You can deal with your thirst later.

STRAGUALCIA: Once I'm dead, make me a soup based on yawning, because when you start doing that, you know you're hungry.

FABRIZIO: Enough of that! Even at a first glance I like this city so much it makes me happy. What about you, Stragualcia?

STRAGUALCIA: Looks like heaven, all right. Nobody eats or drinks around here either. Let's stop wasting our time sightseeing and move on. We've got time for that after we eat.

PIERO: Right here you'll see the most magnificent campanile in the whole order of the universe.

STRAGUALCIA: Is that the one these Modenese want to hide in a sheath because its shadow drives men bonkers?[45]

PIERO: That's the one.

STRAGUALCIA: Well, for all of me, the kitchen's where I'll be staying. Let the gawkers gawk. Let's find a place to stay.

PIERO: What's your great hurry?

STRAGUALCIA: The clap take me! I'm famished to death, with nothing to eat today except that half a hen you left in the boat.

FABRIZIO: Chi trovarem noi che ci meni a casa di mio padre?

PEDANTE: Non. A me pare che noi ci andiamo a metter prima in una ostaria, e quivi assettarci un poco e con commodità poi investigarne.

FABRIZIO: Mi piace. Queste debbono esser l'ostarie.

Scena seconda

L'AGIATO *oste,* FRULLA *oste,* PEDANTE, FABRIZIO, STRAGUALCIA.

AGIATO: Oh gentili uomini! Questa è l'ostaria, se volete alloggiare. Allo "Specchio"! allo "Specchio"!

FRULLA: Oh! Voi siate i ben venuti. Io v'ho pure alloggiati altre volte. Non vi ricorda del vostro Frulla? Entrate qua dentro, ove alloggiano tutti e' par vostri.

AGIATO: Venite a star con me. Voi arete buone camere, buon fuoco, buonissime letta, lenzuola di bocata; e non vi mancarà cosa che voi aviate.

STRAGUALCIA: Di cotesto mel sapevo.

AGIATO: Volsi dir che voi vogliate.

FRULLA: Io vi darò il miglior vin di Lombardia, starne tanto larghe, salciccioni di questa fatta, piccioni, polastri e ciò che voi saprete domandare; e goderete.

STRAGUALCIA: Questo voglio sopra tutto.

PEDANTE: Tu che dici?

AGIATO: Io vi darò animelle di vitella, mortatelle, vin di montagna; e, sopra tutto, starete dilicati.

FRULLA: Io vi darò piú robba e manco dilicatura. Se venite con me, trattarovvi da signori e 'l pagamento sarà a vostro modo; ove, allo «Specchio», vi metterà a conto fino le candele. Fate voi.

The Deceived

FABRIZIO: Who around here can show us where my father lives?

PIERO: Well first, we really should find ourselves an inn and rest up a little. Then we can take our time looking for him.

FABRIZIO: That seems good. Hey, these look like inns.[46]

Scene 2

AGIATO, *innkeeper*, FRULLA, *innkeeper*, PIERO, FABRIZIO, *and* STRAGUALCIA.

AGIATO: Ah, gentlemen. If it's lodging you're in need of, this is the inn for you. It's called the Mirror. Come to the Mirror.

FRULLA: Welcome, most welcome. I've hosted you before. Remember me, your Frulla? Come on in. It's where all the right people stay.

AGIATO: Come lodge with me. You're rooms will be of the best, with a good fire, comfortable beds, fresh clean sheets, and all that's yours, you'll not be without.

STRAGUALCIA: I would hope not.

AGIATO: What I mean is that whatever you desire will be supplied.

FRULLA: I've got the best wine in Lombardy for you, and plump birds, sausages this long, and pigeons, and big chickens — whatever you'll ask for. You'll love everything here.

STRAGUALCIA: That sounds mighty good to me.

PIERO: And you, what can you add to that?

AGIATO: I've got sweetbreads, mortadella, wine from the mountains — all sorts of tasty things — and above all, you'll be treated like gentlemen.

FRULLA: Forget the dainty stuff, I'll give you heaping quantities. You'll feel like lords at my establishment, and you can pay me as you see fit. At the Mirror, you pay for everything — the candles included. Your choice.

STRAGUALCIA: Padrone, stiam qui, ché gli è meglio.

AGIATO: E fate a mio modo, se volete star bene. Volete che si dica che voi siate alloggiati al "Matto"?

FRULLA: È cento mila volte meglio il mio «Matto» che non è il tuo "Specchio".

PEDANTE: Speculum prudentia significat iusta illud nostri Catonis "Nosce teipsum". Intendi, Fabrizio?

FABRIZIO: Intendo.

FRULLA: Veggasi chi ha piú osti: o tu o io.

AGIATO: Veggasi dove van piú uomini da bene.

FRULLA: Veggasi ove son meglio trattati.

AGIATO: Veggasi chi tien piú dilicato.

STRAGUALCIA: Che tanto "dilicato, dilicato, dilicato"? Io vorrei, una volta, empire il corpo meglio e star manco dilicato, per me, io; ché tanta delicatezza è cosa da fiorentini.

AGIATO: Tutti cotesti alloggian con me.

FRULLA: Alloggiavano; ma, da tre anni in qua, tutti vengono a questa insegna.

AGIATO: Garzon, pon giú quella valigia; ché m'avveggo che la ti spalla.

STRAGUALCIA: Non ti curar di questo, tu; ch'io non voglio alleggerir la spalla, s'io non veggo di caricar prima il ventre.

FRULLA: Bastarannoti un paio di capponi? Porta qua. Questi son per te solo.

STRAGUALCIA: Non, eh! Ma gli è per uno antipasto.

AGIATO: Guardate che prosciutto, se non pare un cremisi!

PEDANTE: Questo non è cattivo.

The Deceived

STRAGUALCIA: This is the place, master. It's perfectly clear.

AGIATO: If you want comfort, I'd advise you to lodge with me. You don't want people saying that you're at the Jester, do you?

FRULLA: My Jester beats your Mirror a hundred times over.

PIERO: *Speculum prudentia significat iusta illud nostri Catonis, "Nosce teipsum."* [The mirror signifies prudence according to Cato's dictum: "Know thyself."][47] You got that one, didn't you Fabrizio?

FABRIZIO: Got it.

FRULLA: Well, just check out who has more patrons, him or me.

AGIATO: Rather, take notice of where the distinguished folk stay.

FRULLA: Just look where they get better treatment.

AGIATO: Just look where the best things are.

STRAGUALCIA: Whoa, better, best, better, best. Only one thing matters. Where can I top up my entire body? Forget the finery, for all of me. All that elegant stuff you can keep for the Florentines.

AGIATO: They always stay with me.

FRULLA: Used to, you mean, but my sign's been drawing them all here for the last three years.[48]

AGIATO: Young fellow, depose your baggage here. I can see how fatigued you are.

STRAGUALCIA: Not to worry. I'm not unloading my back till I'm certain to load up my belly.

FRULLA: How about a couple of nice fat capons? Would that do it? Bring the bags over here. These are just for you.

STRAGUALCIA: Eh, no! But they're good starters.

AGIATO: How about this prosciutto? It's as fine as vermillion silk.

PIERO: Not too shabby.

FRULLA: Chi s'intende di vino?

STRAGUALCIA: Io, io, meglio che i franzesi.

FRULLA: Assaggia se ti piace: se non, te ne darò di dieci sorti.

STRAGUALCIA: Frulla, al mio parer tu sei piú prattico di questo altro che prima ci mostra il modo da far bere che sappia se 'l vin ci piace. O padrone, gli è buono. Tolle, tolle questa valigia.

PEDANTE: Aspetta un poco. Tu che dici?

AGIATO: Dico che i gentili uomini non si curan d'empire il corpo di tanta robba; ma di poca, buona e dilicata.

STRAGUALCIA: Costui debbe essere spedaliere o oste d'ammalati.

PEDANTE: Non parli male. Che ci darai?

AGIATO: Domandate.

FRULLA: Ed io mi maraveglio di voi, gentiluomini. Quando c'è de la robba assai, l'uom può mangiar quel poco o quel molto che gli piace; il che del poco non accade. Poi, come l'uomo comincia, l'appetito cresce e bisogna empirsi il corpo di pane.

STRAGUALCIA: Tu sei piú savio delli statuti. Io non viddi mai uomo che intendesse meglio il mio bisogno di te. Va', ch'io ti vo' bene.

FRULLA: Va' un poco in cucina, fratello, e vede.

PEDANTE: Omnis repletio mala, panis autem pessima.

STRAGUALCIA: Pedante poltrone! Ti rompo, un dí, la bocca, s'io vivo.

AGIATO: Venite, gentiluomini, ché lo star fuore al freddo non è cosa da savi.

The Deceived

FRULLA: Who's your wine expert?

STRAGUALCIA: That's me! I'm more in the know than the French.

FRULLA: Tell me if you like this one. If not, I've got over ten more.

STRAGUALCIA: For my money, you're the better host, Frulla. He's all backward, talking up stuff that makes you thirsty before he lets you check out the wine. *(Drinks)* Ah, this is a good one boss. Here, you can take my bags.

PIERO: Hold on there. What would you answer to that?

AGIATO: Gentlemen don't go around stuffing their bellies with all they can eat. They choose modest servings that are light and refined.

STRAGUALCIA: What's he running, an infirmary, a hospice for sick people?

PIERO: *(To Agiato)* I quite agree with you. So what do you have on offer?

AGIATO: Select according to your desires.

FRULLA: You gentlemen astound me. Where the food is abundant, it's up to you to choose as much or as little as you like. When there's little, you have no choice. Plus, once you start eating, you feel like eating more, and then there's nothing but bread to fill up on.

STRAGUALCIA: Now there's wisdom beyond anything heard in a court of law. Never have I met a man who knows me better. You've got my love, I'm going in.

FRULLA: Just head for the kitchen, my friend, and have a look around.

PIERO: *Omnis repletio mala, panis autem pessima.* [All excess is bad, but repletion by bread is the worst.]

STRAGUALCIA: One overeducated idiot! Someday I'm going to fix your teeth, if I live long enough.

AGIATO: Then you gentlemen should come with me, because standing too long in the cold is not wise.

FABRIZIO: Eh! Noi non siam cosí gelosi, no.

FRULLA: Sapiate, signori, che questa ostaria dello "Specchio" soleva esser la megliore ostaria di Lombardia. Ma, come io apersi questa del "Matto", non alloggia, in tutto uno anno, dieci persone; e ha piú nome questa mia insegna, per tutto il mondo, che ostaria che sia. Qui vengon francesi a schiera, todeschi quanti ne passano.

AGIATO: Non dici il vero, ché i todeschi vanno al "Porco".

FRULLA: Qui vengono i milanesi, i parmigiani, i piagentini.

AGIATO: Alla mia vengono i veneziani, i genovesi e i fiorentini.

PEDANTE: Ove alloggiano i napoletani?

FRULLA: Con me.

AGIATO: Lasciatevi dire. Alloggian, la piú parte, all' "Amore".

FRULLA: E quanti ne alloggian con me?

FABRIZIO: Il duca di Malfi dove alloggia?

AGIATO: Quando alla mia, quando alla sua, quando alla "Spada", quando all' "Amore", secondo che ben gli mette.

PEDANTE: Dove alloggiano i romani? perché noi siam da Roma.

AGIATO: Con me.

FRULLA: Non è vero: non trovarete un che v'alloggi in tutto l'anno. Vero è che certi cardenali antichi, per usanza, vi sono alloggiati; ma tutti questi novi dan del capo nel "Matto".

STRAGUALCIA: Io non mi partirei di qui, s'io ne fusse strascinato. Vadin costoro dove vogliono. Padrone, son tante pignatte intorno al fuoco, tanti pottaggi, tanti savoretti, tanti intengoli, spedonate di starne, di tordi, di piccioni, capretti, capponi lessi, arrosto e miramessi, guazzini, pasticci, torte che, s'egli aspettasse il carnovale o la corte di Roma tutta, gli bastarebbe.

The Deceived

FABRIZIO: You know, maybe we're not all that prone to cold.

FRULLA: Hear me, fine squires. The Mirror, over there, was once the best place in all of Lombardy. But now that I've opened the Jester, if he attracts ten a year, he's lucky. My inn is now the most famous in the world. Frenchmen galore check in, not to mention all the Germans who pass through the city.

AGIATO: That's a lie. The Germans stay at the Swine.

FRULLA: Folks from Milan, Parma, Piacenza? They all stay here.

AGIATO: Yes, but the Venetians, Genoese, and Florentines all come here.

PIERO: What about the Neapolitans?

FRULLA: Here, too.

AGIATO: Now you jest. Nearly all of them stay at the Amore.

FRULLA: Yes, but how many stay here?

FABRIZIO: What about the Duke of Amalfi?[49]

AGIATO: Occasionally with me, occasionally with him, but other times at the Sword or the Amore. It all depends on what he's looking for.

PIERO: We're coming from Rome, so where do the Romans lodge?

AGIATO: At my place.

FRULLA: Now you're fibbing. Not one's been there all year. Well, maybe out of habit, a few dilapidated old cardinals, but the new ones come to the Jester.

STRAGUALCIA: There's no getting me away from here unless you haul me out. You others can go wherever you want. Master, you should see the cauldrons around the fire: soups, spiced dishes, sauces everywhere, and giant spits with roasting pigeons, partridges, thrushes, not to mention goats, boiled meats, capons steaming, stewed delicacies, marinades, cakes. He's got enough for the whole Roman court at Carnival, and still have stuff left over.

FRULLA: Hai tu bevuto?

STRAGUALCIA: E che vini!

PEDANTE: Variorum ciborum commistio pessima generat digestionem.

STRAGUALCIA: Bus asinorum, buorum, castronorum, tatte, batatte pecoronibus! Che diavolo andate intrigando l'accia? Che vi venga il cancaro a voi e quanti pedanti si truova! Mi parete un manigoldo, a me. Padrone, entriam drento.

FABRIZIO: Dove alloggian gli spagnuoli?

FRULLA: Io non m'impaccio con loro. Cotesti vanno al "Rampino". Ma che bisogna piú cose? Non c'è persona che vada a torno che non alloggi a questa insegna. Dai sanesi in fuora, che, per esser quasi una cosa medesima coi modanesi, non giongan prima in questa terra che truovan cento amici che se gli menano a casa loro, signori e gran maestri, poveri e ricchi, soldati e buon compagni, tutti corrono al "Matto".

AGIATO: Io dico che i dottori, i giudici, i frati virtuosi, tutti vengono alla mia insegna.

FRULLA: Ed io vi dico che passan pochi giorni che qualcun di quelli che sono alloggiati allo "Specchio" non eschino fuore e non venghino a star con me.

FABRIZIO: Maestro, che faremo?

PEDANTE: Etiam atque etiam cogitandum.

STRAGUALCIA: O corpo mio, fatti capanna; ch'io so che, per una volta, alzarò il fianco.

PEDANTE: Io penso, Fabrizio, che noi aviam pochi denari.

STRAGUALCIA: Maestro, io ci ho veduto un figliuol dell'oste bello come uno angiolo.

PEDANTE: Orsú! Stiam qui. In ogni modo, tuo padre, se lo troviamo, pagarà l'oste.

The Deceived

FRULLA: Did you taste the wine?

STRAGUALCIA: Did I ever.

PIERO: *Variorum ciborum commistio pessima generat digestionem.* [Mixing so many foods will generate bad digestion.]

STRAGUALCIA: *Bus asinorum, buorum castronorum, tatte, battate, pecoronibus!* [nonsense] What's got into you to always complicate things? Get shingles and scratch, you and the body of the world's pedants. You're just a rogue. We're staying here, Master.

FABRIZIO: Where do the Spanish stay?

FRULLA: I avoid all contact with them. They put up over at the Crook.[50] What else could you ask for? Everybody coming through stays here, except for the Sienese, who are so much like the Modenese that when they show up they make a hundred friends who take them back to their houses.[51] But men of rank, famous professors, the rich and the poor, soldiers and men of quality all head straight for the Jester.

AGIATO: But at my inn, you'll find all the doctors, judges, friars, and men of learning.

FRULLA: Well, I can tell you that hardly a day goes by when lodgers at the Mirror don't end up over at my place.

FABRIZIO: Teacher, what shall we do?

PIERO: *Etiam atque etiam cogitandum.* [This matter requires careful thinking.]

STRAGUALCIA: Dear body, it's time to fill you up. Our turn to eat till we're totally stuffed.

PIERO: My worry now, Fabrizio, is that we don't have all that much money left.

STRAGUALCIA: Teacher, when I was inside, there was the innkeeper's young son as pretty as an angel.[52]

PIERO: That's it then. We'll stay at the Jester. And anyway, when we find your father, if we do, he'll settle up with the host.

STRAGUALCIA: Parti che 'l cimbel fusse a tempo per far calare il tordo? Io ho già bevuto tre volte e ho detto una. Io non mi partirò di cucina, ch'io assaggiarò ciò che v'è; e poi dormirò intorno a quel buon fuoco. E cancar venga a chi vuol far robba!

AGIATO: Ricordati, Frulla, che tu me n'hai fatte troppo e un dí, ci spezzarem la testa; e bene.

FRULLA: A tua posta. Non posso piú presto che ora.

Scena terza

VIRGINIO *vecchio e* CLEMENZIA *balia.*

VIRGINIO: Questi sono i costumi che tu gli hai insegnati? Questo è l'onore ch'ella mi fa? Oh sfortunato a me! Per questo ho io campato tante fortune? per veder la mia robba senza erede? per veder la mia casa disfatta, la mia figliuola una puttana? per diventare una fabula del vulgo? per non piú potere alzar la fronte fra gli uomini? per esser mostrato a dito da' fanciulli, deleggiato dai vecchi, messo in comedia dagli Intronati, posto per essempio nelle novelle e portato per bocca dalle donne di questa terra? E forse che non son novelliere! forse che non gli piace di dir male! Già credo che si sappia per tutto; anzi, ne son certo, ché basta ch'una sola il sappia che, fra tre ore, va per tutta la terra. Disgraziato padre! misero e doloroso vecchio troppo vissuto! Virginio, che farò io? che pensiero ha da essere il mio?

CLEMEZIA: Farai bene di farne manco romore che puoi e veder di proveder, meglio che si potrà, che la torni a casa senza che tutta questa città se ne accorga. Ma tanto avesse ella fiato, suor Novellante Ciancini, quanto io credo che sia vero che Lelia vada vestita da uomo! Guarda che elle non dichin cosí perché la vorrebbeno far monaca e che tu gli lassi tutta la robba tua.

The Deceived

STRAGUALCIA: *(Aside)* I knew that bit about the boy would be the bait to snare the old geezer. I'm three glasses of wine to the wind, but we'll say only one. I'm not out of that kitchen 'til I've sampled everything. Then a nice snooze by the fire, and a curse on anyone who gets in my way.

AGIATO: Hey, Frulla, you'd better watch your step. You've cheated me too many times. The day will come when we settle it for good.

FRULLA: Any time, I'm here and ready for you.

Scene 3

Outside Virginio's house.
VIRGINIO *and* CLEMEZIA.

VIRGINIO: Is this how you taught her to behave? Is this the respect I should have coming? Bad luck for me. Is it for this that I've gathered so much wealth? No heir to my estate? My household destroyed? My daughter a whore and the gossip of the whole town? My head bowed in public disgrace? Pointed at by children in the streets and taunted by elders as an embarrassment, featured in a comedy by the Intronati, moralized in stories, my name the chatter of every woman in town? Don't think there aren't plenty of them around to tattle and slander. But hell, it doesn't matter. It's probably already known everywhere — in fact I'm certain of it — because one female tongue can cover the city in three hours' time. I'm a tortured father and a sad old man already past my time. What's to be done, Virginio? What's there to think?

CLEMEZIA: You'd be better off making less commotion and doing more to get her home before it becomes public knowledge. I certainly don't wish for more wind in the body of that Sister Novellante Ciarcini[53] after she spread the story about Lelia disguised as a boy. You've got to watch out for their yarns, because they just want to make a nun out of her so they can lay hands on all your money.

VIRGINIO: Come non dice il vero? Ella m'ha per infin detto ch'ella sta per ragazzo con un gentiluomo di questa terra e che egli non s'è ancora accorto ch'ella sia donna.

CLEMEZIA: Potrebbe essere ogni cosa; ma, per me, non lo posso credere.

VIRGINIO: Né io non lo posso credere che non la conosca per donna.

CLEMEZIA: Non dico cotesto, io.

VIRGINIO: Il dico io, ché mi tocca: bench'io stesso mi feci il male, dandola a nutrire a te che sapevo chi tu eri.

CLEMEZIA: Virginio, non piú parole. S'io son stata una trista, m'hai fatta tu. Sai bene che, prima che tu, non mi ebbe altri che il mio marito. Io dico che le fanciulle si voglion trattare altrimenti. Non ti vergognavi di volerla maritare a un vecchio rantacoso che le potrebbe esser nonno?

VIRGINIO: E che hanno i vecchi, manigolda? Son mille volte meglio che i giovani.

CLEMEZIA: Tu sei uscito del sentimento: e però fa bene ognuno a scorgerti e darti ad intender le ciaramelle.

VIRGINIO: S'io la truovo, la strascinarò a casa pe' capegli.

CLEMEZIA: Farai pur come colui che si toglie le corna di seno e se le mette in capo.

VIRGINIO: Non me ne curo. Tanto se ne saria. Basti ch'io me le tagliarò.

CLEMEZIA: Govèrnate a tuo modo, ché non ti dorrà la testa.

VIRGINIO: Io ho avuti i segnali come la va vestita. Tanto la cercarò ch'io la trovarò. Poi bastisi.

CLEMEZIA: Fa' come tu vuoi, ch'io mi vo' partire; ch'io perderei il tempo a lavar carboni. Ma...

The Deceived

VIRGINIO: Why wouldn't she be telling me the truth? According to her, Lelia's now the servant to a gentleman in town, and that he doesn't have any idea yet she's a girl.

CLEMEZIA: It's all possible, but I still don't believe it.

VIRGINIO: Well, I think he knows perfectly well she's a girl.

CLEMEZIA: That's not what I'm saying.

VIRGINIO: But I am, and it gives me a pain. It's all my fault, anyway, letting you raise her, being what you are.

CLEMEZIA: Enough on that subject, Virginio. You think I'm a harlot, then it's you who made me one, because before you showed up, the only man I'd ever known was my husband. As for young girls, they must be handled differently. Don't you feel ashamed trying to marry Lelia off to a wheezy dodderer old enough to be her grandfather?

VIRGINIO: What do you have against senior men, your old trot? They're a thousand times better than the young ones.

CLEMEZIA: You're completely out of your mind. Everyone is right in making fun of you and pulling the wool over your eyes to make you believe things that aren't true.

VIRGINIO: When I find her, I'll haul her home by the hair of her head.

CLEMEZIA: Sure, and act like the chap who pulled the horns from his breast and stuck them on his head.

VIRGINIO: Doesn't matter to me. If people find out, they find out. Lop them off is all I can do.

CLEMEZIA: Do as you damned well please, and lop off your head while you're at it.

VIRGINIO: I know what her get-up looks like, so I can track her down. Then we'll know what's what.

CLEMEZIA: Just do whatever you want, because I'm leaving. Washing coal is a waste of my time. But....

The Intronati of Siena

Scena quarta

FABRIZIO *giovinetto e* FRULLA *oste.*

FABRIZIO: Mentre che questi due miei servidori si riposano, io andarò a vedere la terra. Come si levan, digli che venghino verso piazza.

FRULLA: Per certo, padron mio, che, se io non vi avesse veduto vestir questi panni, io giurarei che voi fusse un giovinetto, servidor d'un gentiluomo di questa terra, che veste come voi di bianco e tanto vi s'assomiglia che quasi parete lui.

FABRIZIO: Saria forse qualche mio fratello?

FRULLA: Potrebbe essere.

FABRIZIO: Direte poi al maestro che cerchi di colui che sa.

FRULLA: Lasciate l'impaccio.

Scena quinta

PASQUELLA *fante e* FABRIZIO *giovinetto.*

PASQUELLA: In buona fé, che eccolo. Avevo paura di non aver a cercar tutta questa terra prima ch'io 'l trovassi. Fabio, che tu sia il ben trovato. Ti venivo a cercare; tu m'hai tolto fatica. Amor mio, dice la padrona che, per una cosa ch'importa a te e a lei, che tu venga or ora a trovarla. Non so già quel che si sia.

FABRIZIO: Chi è la tu' padrona?

PASQUELLA: Tu lo sai ben, tu, chi ella è. In buona fé, che l'uno e l'altro s'è attaccato bene!

FABRIZIO: Io non son però attaccato; ma, s'ella vuole, ci attaccaremo, e presto.

PASQUELLA: Perché sète due da pochi. Vorrei esser giovine per potere ancor io tôrmene una corpacciata; e so che, s'io

The Deceived

Scene 4

Outside the Jester Inn, near Gherardo's house.
FABRIZIO *and* FRULLA.

FABRIZIO: I'll have a further look about town while my two servants are napping. When they wake up, tell them they'll find me in the piazza.

FRULLA: Yes, sir. If you weren't wearing your own clothes, I could swear you're the page to a gentleman in the city. He's dressed in white, just like you, and resembles you so much he could almost be you.

FABRIZIO: Do you think I've got a brother?

FRULLA: Maybe.

FABRIZIO: Tell my tutor to keep a lookout for the person we're hunting — he knows who I mean.

FRULLA: Count on it. *(Frulla leaves.)*

Scene 5

PASQUELLA *and* FABRIZIO.

PASQUELLA: My word, there he is. I was afraid I'd have to scour the whole town to find him. — Perfect timing, Fabio. I was looking for you, and now you've spared me the task. Dear boy, my mistress wants to see you right away about something really important to you both. I've no idea what it's about.

FABRIZIO: Who is this mistress of yours?

PASQUELLA: Come on, you know perfectly well, now that you're glued to each other.

FABRIZIO: Me, glued? But if that's what she wants, we can glue together right now.

PASQUELLA: You're both of you just troublemakers! Ah, to be young again and be able to stuff myself. I can tell you

fusse in voi, avrei già posti i sospetti e i rispetti da canto. Ma bene il farete, sí.

FABRIZIO: Eh madonna! Voi non mi conoscete. Andate, ché voi m'avete colto in iscambio.

PASQUELLA: Oh! Non l'aver per male, Fabio mio, ch'io 'l dico per farti bene.

FABRIZIO: Io non ho per male niente; ma io non ho questo nome e non so' chi voi credete.

PASQUELLA: Or fate pur fra voi due a vostro modo. Ma sai, figliuolo? Delle sue pari, cosí ricche e cosí belle, in questa terra ne son poche. E vorrei che voi cavasse le mani di quel che s'ha da fare; ché andar dinanzi e di dietro, ogni giorno, e tôr parole e dar parole dà che dire alle genti, senza util tuo e con poco onor di lei.

FABRIZIO: Che cosa nova è questa? Io non l'intendo. O che costei è pazza o che m'ha còlto in iscambio. Vo' pur veder dove la mi vuol menare. Andiamo.

PASQUELLA: Oh! Mi par sentir gente in casa. Fermati un poco qui intorno, ché vederò se Isabella è sola. Accennaroti che tu entri, se non vi sarà alcuno.

FABRIZIO: Voglio stare a vedere che fine ha d'avere questa favola. Forse costei è serva di qualche cortigiana e credemi fare stare a qualche scudo; ma gli è male informata, ch'io son quasi allievo di spagnuoli e, alla fine, vorrò piú presto uno scudo del suo che dargli un carlin del mio. Qualcun di noi ci sarà incòlto. Lasciami scostare un poco da questa casa e por mente che gente v'entra ed esce per saper che razza di donna sia.

that if I were in your place, all this pussyfooting and hesitating would have been out the window by now. But you'll be at it soon enough.

FABRIZIO: Madam. Shouldn't you be on your way? You've got the wrong party. You don't have a clue who I am.

PASQUELLA: Oh, my dear Fabio, don't take it the wrong way. I'm just trying to be helpful.

FABRIZIO: I'm not taking anything the wrong way. But that's not my name, and I don't know who you take me for.

PASQUELLA: Well, you two can work out the details between you. But listen here, my boy. This city doesn't offer many girls as rich and gorgeous as she is, so I think you should wrap the whole thing up. All this toing and froing with messages day after day and folks will start talking — which is no help to you or my lady's honor.

FABRIZIO: *(Aside)* What's going on here? I don't get it. She's either cracked or takes me for someone else. But let's see where this might take me. — All right, then, let's go.

PASQUELLA: Huh? Sounds like there are people in the house. Wait here in the doorway till I find out if Isabella's by herself. If no one's there, I'll motion for you to come in.

FABRIZIO: I've got to see how this story ends up. Maybe she works for a courtesan and hopes to get money off me. She's in for a disappointment there. I'm with the Spaniards on that one, taking a dollar from her before she gets a dime out of me. One of us will end up a loser. I'll put a little distance between me and the house. That way I can get an idea of the lady by seeing who goes in and out.

Scena sesta

GHERARDO, VIRGINIO e PASQUELLA.

GHERARDO: Tu mi perdonarai. Se gli è cotesto, te la renuncio. E lasciamo stare ch'io penso che, se la tua figliuola ha fatto ciò, l'abbi fatto perché la non voglia me. Ma penso anco ch'ella abbi tolto altri.

VIRGINIO: Nol creder, Gherardo. Credi ch'io tel dicesse? Ti prego che non vogli guastar quel che è fatto.

GHERARDO: Io ti priego che non me ne parli.

VIRGINIO: Oh! Vòi mancar della tua parola?

GHERARDO: A chi m'ha mancato di fatti, sí: oltra che tu non sai se la potrai riavere o no. Tu mi vòi vendere l'uccello in su la frasca. Ho ben sentito, quando tu ragionavi con Clemenzia, il tutto.

VIRGINIO: Quando io non la riabbia, io non te la vo' dare; ma, s'io la riaverò, non sei contento che le nozze si faccin subito?

GHERARDO: Virginio, io ho avuta la piú onorata moglie che fusse in questa città e ho una figliuola che è una colombina. Come vòi ch'io mi metta in casa una che s'è fuggita dal padre e va per questa casa e per quella vestita da maschio, come le disoneste donnacce? Non vedi ch'io non trovarei da maritar mia figliuola?

VIRGINIO: Passato qualche dí, non se ne ragionarà piú. Che credi che sia? E' non vi è altri che tu e io che lo sappi.

GHERARDO: E poi ne sarà piena tutta questa terra.

VIRGINIO: E' non è vero.

GHERARDO: Quant'è ch'ella è fuggita?

VIRGINIO: O ieri o questa mattina.

The Deceived

Scene 6

GHERARDO, VIRGINIO, *and* PASQUELLA.

GHERARDO: Excuse me, but if this is the case, then I don't want her anymore. If I thought that your daughter was up to this, it's clear she doesn't want me. And anyway, I think she already has other men.

VIRGINIO: Don't you believe it, Gherardo. If that were the situation, do you think I'd have let on? Come on, don't wreck all the arrangements now.

GHERARDO: And I'm asking you not to talk to me about it anymore.

VIRGINIO: Ah, so you're backing out of your promise?

GHERARDO: With someone who's gone back on his? You bet. Anyway, you've no idea whether you can get her back. You're selling me a bird still in the bush. I overheard every word you said to Clemenzia.

VIRGINIO: All right, for as long as I don't have her, I won't try to give her away. But if I do get her, wouldn't you marry her then and there?

GHERARDO: Listen Virginio, my marriage was to the most honorable woman in town, and my daughter is as innocent as a dove. So how can you ask me to take a girl who escapes her father, dresses like a boy, runs from house to house, and acts like a little whore. Can't you understand that I'd never get an honorable match for my daughter if I did that?

VIRGINIO: A few days and the gossip stops. What are you thinking? Who knows about any of this, anyway? Just you and me.

GHERARDO: In time, the whole city will know.

VIRGINIO: Not true.

GHERARDO: When did she run off?

VIRGINIO: Yesterday, or early this morning.

GHERARDO: Dio 'l voglia. Ma che sai ch'ella sia in Modena?

VIRGINIO: Sollo.

GHERARDO: Or truovala e poi ci riparleremo.

VIRGINIO: Promettimi di pigliarla?

GHERARDO: Vedrò.

VIRGINIO: Or dimmi di sí.

GHERARDO: Nol dico, ma...

VIRGINIO: Or dillo liberamente.

GHERARDO: Adagio! Che fai costí, Pasquella? Che fa Isabella?

PASQUELLA: E che! Sta in ginocchioni dinanzi al suo altaruccio.

GHERARDO: Benedetta sia ella! Io ho una figliuola che sempre sta in orazione. È la maggior cosa del mondo.

PASQUELLA: Oh quanto ben dite! La digiuna tal vigilia che Dio vel dica; dice l'officio, come una santarella.

GHERARDO: Somiglia quella benedetta anima di sua madre.

PASQUELLA: Dice il vero. Oh quanto ben faceva quella meschina! Eran piú le discipline ch'ella si dava e i cilici ch'ella portava che non è quanto bene l'altre fanno oggi: limosiniera per la vita; e, se non fusse stato per amor di voi, non capitava né frate né prete né povarello a quello uscio che non ricettasse e non gli desse ciò ch'ella aveva.

VIRGINIO: Coteste eran buone parti.

PASQUELLA: Vi dico piú oltre che la si levò dugento volte, una e due ore innanzi dí, per andar alla prima messa de' frati di San Francesco, ché non voleva esser veduta né tenuta una pòrchita come fanno certe graffiasanti ch'io conosco.

GHERARDO: Come "pòrchita"? Che vuo' tu dire?

The Deceived

GHERARDO: May that prove to be true. Who knows if she's even still in Modena?

VIRGINIO: She is.

GHERARDO: Find her first and then we'll talk.

VIRGINIO: Do you swear to have her?

GHERARDO. We'll see.

VIRGINIO: Promise me to take her.

GHERARDO: No promises, but....

VIRGINIO: Spit it out.

GHERARDO: Just a minute. *(Enter Pasquella)* — What are you up to Pasquella, and what's Isabella doing?

PASQUELLA: Uh, well, she's down on her knees in front of the altar.

GHERARDO: Blessed thing! Just like my daughter, always praying. Best you could ask for.

PASQUELLA: You can say that again. Daily fasting, as God requires, and saintly in her prayers.

GHERARDO: She's so much like her divine mother, departed from us, God rest her soul.

PASQUELLA: So true. What acts of charity that poor woman performed. There are none today to equal her in self-mortifying flagellation and the wearing of penitential clothes. Not a soul even gets close to her. She was generous all her life in giving alms. Only her love for you stopped her from giving her all to any friar, priest, or beggar who called at her door.

VIRGINIO: Remarkable virtues.

PASQUELLA: Many were the times she arose well before daybreak to attend early Mass with the Friars of St. Francis. And it wasn't for parading her piety, or making a hypocrut of herself like some sinners I know.

GHERARDO: What do you mean, hypocrut?

PASQUELLA: Pòrchita, sí; come si dice?

VIRGINIO: Cotesta è una mala parola.

PASQUELLA: So ch'io sentivo dir cosí a lei.

GHERARDO: Tu vuoi dire ipocrita, tu.

PASQUELLA: Forse. Ma vi dico che sua figliuola sarà ancor piú di lei.

GHERARDO: Dio il voglia.

VIRGINIO: Oh Gherardo, Gherardo! Questa è colei di che aviam ragionato. Oh scontento padre! Forse che si nasconde o che si fugge per avermi veduto? Accostiamoglici.

GHERARDO: Vedi di non far errore, ché forse non è essa.

VIRGINIO: Chi non la conosceria? Non vegg'io tutti i segnali che m'ha dati suor Novellante?

PASQUELLA: La cosa va male. Che sí ch'io n'arò le mie!

Scena settima

VIRGINIO, GHERARDO e FABRIZIO *giovinetto.*

VIRGINIO: Addio, buona fanciulla. Parti che questo sia abito conveniente a una tua pari? Questo è l'onor che tu fai alla casa tua? Questo è il contento che tu dài a questo povero vecchio? Almen fuss'io morto quando io t'ingenerai! ché non sei nata se non per disonorarmi, per sotterarmi vivo. Oh Gherardo! Che ti par della tua sposa? parti ch'ella ci facci onore?

GHERARDO: Cotesto non dich'io. Sposa, eh?

VIRGINIO: Ribalda, scelerata! Come ti starebbe bene che costui non ti volesse piú per moglie e non trovasse piú partito! Ma ei non guardarà alle tue pazzie; e ti vuol pigliare.

GHERARDO: Adagio!

VIRGINIO: Entra costí in casa, sciaurata! che fu ben maladetto il latte che tua madre ti porse il dí ch'io t'ingenerai.

The Deceived

PASQUELLA: Hypocrut. What would you say?

VIRGINIO: Not a nice word.

PASQUELLA: That's what I heard her say.

GHERARDO: You mean hypocrite?

PASQUELLA: Could be, but what I'm saying is that your daughter will surpass her mother.

GHERARDO: By God's grace.

VIRGINIO: Heh, Gherardo! There she is, just the one we're looking for. Sad for a father that in seeing me she tries to run or hide! Go catch her if you can.

GHERARDO: Let's not be mistaken here. It might not be her.

VIRGINIO: Anybody could recognize her. She fits Sister Novellante's description to the last detail.

PASQUELLA: This is not going to go well. I could be in deep trouble.

Scene 7

VIRGINIO, GHERARDO, *and* FABRIZIO.

VIRGINIO: So now, my dainty daughter. Do you think this get-up befits a young lady? Is this the respect you pay to your family? Is this the joy you bring to your old father? I should have died the moment you were begotten. You came into the world to disgrace me and bury me alive. So Gherardo, here's your bride. Is this the way you should honor your father?

GHERARDO: I wouldn't say so, and now she's my bride?

VIRGINIO: You're a strumpet and a tart is what you are. What a mess you'd be in if this man wouldn't marry you anymore, and nobody else would have you. But he'll overlook your nonsense and take you anyway.

GHERARDO: Not so fast.

VIRGINIO: Get back in that house, trollop. Your mother's milk was bewitched on the day you were born.

FABRIZIO: O buon vecchio, avete voi figliuoli, parenti o amici in questa terra a' quali appartenga aver cura di voi?

VIRGINIO: Guarda che risposta! Perché dici cotesto?

FABRIZIO: Perché mi maraviglio che, avendo voi tanto bisogno di medico, vi lascino uscir di casa; ché, in ogni altro luogo che voi fusse, vi terreben legato.

VIRGINIO: Legata dovevo io tener te, che mi vien voglia di scannarti! Portami un coltello.

FABRIZIO: Vecchio, voi non mi conoscete bene; e ditemi villania, forse pensando ch'io sia forestiero. Ed io son cosí ben da Modana come voi e figliuol di sí buon padre e di sí buona casa come voi.

GHERARDO: Gli è bella, in fine. Se non c'è altro errore che quanto si vede, io la vo' pigliare.

VIRGINIO: E perché ti sei partita da tuo padre e dal luogo dove io t'avevo raccomandata?

FABRIZIO: Me non raccommandaste voi mai, ch'io sappia; ma il partir mi fu forza.

VIRGINIO: Forza, eh? e chi ti sforzò?

FABRIZIO: Gli spagnuoli.

VIRGINIO: E adesso donde vieni?

FABRIZIO: Di campo.

VIRGINIO: Di campo?

FABRIZIO: Di campo, sí.

GHERARDO: Non ne sia fatto nulla.

VIRGINIO: Oh sventurata a te!

FABRIZIO: Questo sia sopra di voi.

VIRGINIO: Gherardo, di grazia, mettiamola in casa tua, ch'ella non sia veduta cosí.

GHERARDO: Non farò. Menala pure alla tua.

The Deceived

FABRIZIO: Now, now, old timer. Maybe you've got sons, or relatives, or friends in town who can look after you?

VIRGINIO: What kind of answer is that? Why do you talk like that?

FABRIZIO: You're in such urgent need of clinical care I'm surprised they let you wander free. In other places you'd be tied in a straitjacket.

VIRGINIO: That's what you should be in. Somebody fetch me a knife so I can just cut your throat.

FABRIZIO: Listen old man, you don't know who I am. Maybe you take me for a foreigner and think you can insult me. But I'm as good a citizen of this city as you are, and born into a family as respectable as yours.

GHERARDO: *(Aside)* Still, she's really beautiful. If this is the only thing she's done wrong, I'll have her all the same.

VIRGINIO: Why did you flee the paternal household and now the residence I put you in?

FABRIZIO: I'm not aware of being put anywhere, and I ran away because I was forced to.

VIRGINIO: Who forced you?

FABRIZIO: The Spaniards.

VIRGINIO: Where are you coming from now?

FABRIZIO: From the garrison.

VIRGINIO: What garrison?

FABRIZIO: The army garrison.

GHERARDO: *(Aside)* Well, then, there's nothing that can be done.[54]

VIRGINIO: You poor girl!

FABRIZIO: What happened is all your fault.

VIRGINIO: Please, Gherardo, take her to your place so she can't be seen like this.

GHERARDO: Not me. Take her to your own house.

The Intronati of Siena

VIRGINIO: Per mio amore, fa' un poco aprire l'uscio.

GHERARDO: Non, dico.

VIRGINIO: Ascolta un poco. E voi aviate cura che costei non vada altrove.

FABRIZIO: Io ho conosciuti molti modanesi pazzi li quali non contarei per nome; ma pazzi come questo vecchio, che non stesse o legato o rinchiuso, non viddi alcuno mai. Guarda che bello umore! È impazzato in questo, per quanto mi sono accorto: che i gioveni gli paion donne. Oh! Questa è molto piú bella pazzia che quella che il Molza disse della donna sanese che gli pareva essere una vettina: essendo piú propio delle donne aver poco cervello che de' vecchi che, per mille ragioni, deveno essere savissimi. E non vorrei per cento scudi non poter contar questa pazzia alle veglie, al tempo dei carnovali. Or vengono in qua. Vediamo quel che dicono.

GHERARDO: Io ti dirò il vero. Da un canto, mi pare; dall'altro, no. Pure, se gli può domandare un poco meglio.

VIRGINIO: Vien qua.

FABRIZIO: Che volete, buon vecchio?

VIRGINIO: Tu sei ben trista, tu.

FABRIZIO: Non mi dite villania, ch'io non comportarò.

VIRGINIO: Sfacciata!

FABRIZIO: Oh! oh! oh! oh! oh! oh! oh!

GHERARDO: Lascial dire: non vedi che gli è scorrucciato? Fa' a suo modo.

FABRIZIO: Che vuol da me? che ho da far né con voi né con lui?

VIRGINIO: Ancor hai ardir di parlare? Di chi sei figliuola, tu?

FABRIZIO: Di Virginio Bellenzini.

VIRGINIO: Volesse Dio che tu non fusse! ché tu mi farai morir innanzi tempo.

The Deceived

VIRGINIO: If you have the least concern for me, open your doors.

GHERARDO: My answer's still "no."

VIRGINIO: *(They leave Fabrizio and speak together.)* Listen, you have to take care she doesn't run off again.

FABRIZIO: *(Aside)* I've seen a lot of crazy people in Modena — too many to keep track of. But this old guy beats them all and is still running around the streets. What a dandy of a condition he's got! He seems to mistake young men for young women. This is crazier than the one Molza tells about the Sienese lady who thought she was an earthenware pot.[55] Better for women to be short on brains than old men. They should be the wise ones, for all kinds of reasons. Still I wouldn't have missed this occasion for 100 scudi. What a great story for Carnival or for telling at wakes. Here they come again. Now what'll they say?

GHERARDO: I'll be open with you. In one sense, maybe, in another sense, no. Ask her some more questions.

VIRGINIO: Come over here.

FABRIZIO: What now, my dear old man?

VIRGINIO: You're nothing but a little hussy.

FABRIZIO: That's enough of the insults. I won't take any more.

VIRGINIO: Impertinence!

FABRIZIO: Ouch, ouch, what are you talking about?

GHERARDO: Let her speak. She's getting into a rage. Just humor her.

FABRIZIO: What does he want from me? I've got nothing to do with him, or with you.

VIRGINIO: You want to go on talking? Then tell me, whose child are you?

FABRIZIO: Virginio Bellenzini's.

VIRGINIO: I wish to God you weren't! You'll lead me to an early grave.

FABRIZIO: Innanzi tempo muore un vecchio di sessant'anni? Tanto vivesse ognuno! Morite a vostra posta, ché sète vissuto troppo.

VIRGINIO: Tua colpa, ribalda!

GHERARDO: Eh! Lasciate queste parole. Figliuola mia e sorella mia, non si risponde cosí al padre.

FABRIZIO: Lascia andare i colombi, e' s'appaiano. Tutt'a due questi peccano d'un medesimo umore. E che bel caso! Ah! ah! ah! ah! ah!

VIRGINIO: Ancor ridi?

GHERARDO: Questo è un mal segno, a farsi beffe del padre.

FABRIZIO: Che padre? che madre? Io non ebbi mai altro padre che Virginio né altra madre che Giovanna. Voi mi parete una bestia. Che vi credete, forse, ch'io non abbi alcun per me?

GHERARDO: Virginio, sai che dubito? che, per maninconia, non abbi a questa povera giovane dato volta il cervello.

VIRGINIO: Trist'a me! Ch'io me n'accorsi fino al principio, quando vidi che con sí poca pazienzia mi venne innanzi.

GHERARDO: No: questo poteva proceder da altro.

VIRGINIO: E da che?

GHERARDO: Com'una donna ha perduto l'onore, tutto 'l mondo è suo.

VIRGINIO: Io dico che l'ha qualche pazzia nel capo.

GHERARDO: Pur, si ricorda del padre e della madre; mentre par che non ti conosca.

VIRGINIO: Faciamola entrare in casa tua, poi che gli è qui vicina, ché alla mia non la potrei far condurre senza farmi scorgere a tutta la terra.

FABRIZIO: Che se consegliano quei rimbambiti, fratelli di Melchisedec?

VIRGINIO: Facciamo in prima con le buone tanto che noi la conduciamo dentro; poi, per forza, la serraremo in camara con tua figliuola.

The Deceived

FABRIZIO: How can a man of sixty go before his time? Many would like to live as long. It's your time to go. You've been around long enough.

VIRGINIO: Little tart, you'll be to blame for it.

GHERARDO: Enough of such talk. Good daughter and sister, don't talk to your father like that.

FABRIZIO: Two peas in a pod. Both afflicted with the same disease. What a story this is. Ha, ha ha, ha ha!

VIRGINIO: You think this is funny?

GHERARDO: It's a really bad thing to mock your father.

FABRIZIO: Father? Mother? Virginio's my only father, and Giovanna's my mother. You're just an old fool. Do you suppose that I don't have anyone?

GHERARDO: *(Conferring in an aside)* Do you know what I think, Virginio? I think this poor girl's brain has gone melancholy.

VIRGINIO: Sad to think. I spotted that right off, the way she greeted me in a frenzy.

GHERARDO: Or maybe there's another cause.

VIRGINIO: Such as?

GHERARDO: When a girl loses her chastity she thinks she owns the world.

VIRGINIO: Some kind of madness in her brain, that's for sure.

GHERARDO: But she still knows the names of her parents. She just doesn't know you.

VIRGINIO: Your house is close by. Let's take her there. We can't get her back to my place without the whole city seeing us.

FABRIZIO: *(Aside)* What are the old geezers talking about now like the brothers of Melchizedek?[56]

VIRGINIO: Let's lure her inside as gently as possible. Then we'll use force if necessary to lock her in the room with your daughter.

GHERARDO: Che si faccia.

VIRGINIO: Orsú, figliuola mia! Io non voglio star teco piú in còlora. Ti perdono ogni cosa, pur che attendi a viver bene.

FABRIZIO: Vi ringrazio.

GHERARDO: Cosí fanno le buone figliuole.

FABRIZIO: Ecco l'altro rosto fresco.

GHERARDO: Orsú! Non v'è onore esser visti ragionar fuore in questo abito. Entratevene in casa. Pasquella, apre l'uscio.

VIRGINIO: Entra, figliuola mia.

FABRIZIO: Cotesto non farò io.

GHERARDO: Perché?

FABRIZIO: Perché non voglio entrar per le case d'altri.

GHERARDO: Costei sarà una Penelope, beato a me!

VIRGINIO: Non diss'io che la mia figliuola era bella e buona?

GHERARDO: L'abito 'l mostra.

VIRGINIO: Ti vo' dir solamente una parola.

FABRIZIO: Ditela di fuore.

GHERARDO: Eh che non sta bene! Questa casa è la tua; tu hai da esser la mia moglie.

FABRIZIO: Che moglie? Vecchio bugia... bugiardo!

GHERARDO: Tuo padre mi t'ha pur promessa.

FABRIZIO: Che pensate ch'io sia forse qualche bagascia che si faccia, eh?...

VIRGINIO: Orsú! Non la far corrucciar. Odi, figliuola mia. Io non vo' far se non quel tanto che tu vorrai.

FABRIZIO: Eh, vecchio! Mi conoscete male.

VIRGINIO: Ode una parola qui dentro.

FABRIZIO: Dieci, non tanto una: ho forse paura di voi?

GHERARDO: All right.

VIRGINIO: Come, daughter of mine. I won't be mad at you any longer. All's forgiven, just so you behave.

FABRIZIO: Thank you.

GHERARDO: There's a good girl.

FABRIZIO: *(Aside)* Here's another roast on the fire. He's cock-eyed too!

GHERARDO: It's not right for us to argue out here, with you dressed like this. Come on inside. — Pasquella, open the door.

VIRGINIO: Daughter, go in.

FABRIZIO: I couldn't possibly do that.

GHERARDO: Why ever not?

FABRIZIO: Into the house of a stranger?

GHERARDO: A very Penelope, thank God.[57]

VIRGINIO: I told you my daughter was good and beautiful.

GHERARDO: Her clothes make that plain enough!

VIRGINIO: Just one word more.

FABRIZIO: Say it out here.

GHERARDO: What can be wrong? This is your house. You're to become my wife.

FABRIZIO: A wife in arrears, you old liar.

GHERARDO: Your father has pledged you to me.

FABRIZIO: You take me for a whore on the make?

VIRGINIO: *(To Gherardo)* Now now, don't get her mad again. *(To Fabrizio)* Listen to me, girl. I won't accept anything you won't accept.

FABRIZIO: But you don't know who I am, old man.

VIRGINIO: Just go inside and hear one more thing.

FABRIZIO: One more, ten more. I'm not afraid of you. *(Goes into the house)*

VIRGINIO: Gherardo, ora che voi l'avete qui dentro, ordiniamo di serrarla in camara con tua figliuola fino a tanto che si rimanda pei suoi panni.

GHERARDO: Ciò che tu vuoi, Virginio. Pasquella, porta la chiave della camera da basso e chiama Isabella che venga giú.

Atto Quarto

Scena prima

PEDANTE e STRAGUALCIA.

PEDANTE: Egli ti starebbe molto bene ch'egli ti desse cinquanta bastonate per insegnarti, quando e' va fuore, a fargli compagnia e non t'imbriacassi e poi dormire, come hai fatto, e lasciarlo andar solo.

STRAGUALCIA: E voi doveria far caricar di scope, di solfo, di pece, di polvere e darvi fuoco per insegnarvi a non esser quel che voi sète.

PEDANTE: Imbriaco! imbriaco!

STRAGUALCIA: Pedante! Pedante!

PEDANTE: Lassa ch'io trovi il padrone...

STRAGUALCIA: Lasciate ch'io truovi suo padre!...

PEDANTE: Oh! A suo padre che puoi dir di me?

STRAGUALCIA: E voi che potete dir di me?

PEDANTE: Che tu sei un gaglioffo, un manigoldo, un infingardo, un poltrone, un pazzo, uno imbriaco, posso dire.

STRAGUALCIA: E io che voi sète un ladro, un giocatore, una mala lingua, un barro, un mariuolo, un frappatore, un vantatore, un capo grosso, uno sfacciato, uno ignorante, un traditore, un sodomito, un tristo, posso dire.

PEDANTE: Noi siamo conosciuti.

The Deceived

VIRGINIO: Now that she's inside, Gherardo, let's lock her into the room with your daughter until we can arrange to get her clothes.

GHERARDO: Have it your way, Virginio. Bring the key to the bedroom downstairs, Pasquella, and call Isabella here.

ACT 4

Scene 1

PIERO *and* STRAGUALCIA.

PIERO: You'd get what you deserve if he caned you with fifty blows to teach you that when he goes out, you go with him instead of getting tanked and sleeping it off as you've just done, while he's out there alone.

STRAGUALCIA: He should just load you down with brushwood, sulfur, pitch, and gunpowder and set you on fire to teach you not to be what you are.[58]

PIERO: Guzzler! Boozer!

STRAGUALCIA: Pedant, Pedant!

PIERO: Wait till I get our master.

STRAGUALCIA: Wait till I get his father.

PIERO: So, what are you going to tell him about me?

STRAGUALCIA: You, what are you going to say about me?

PIERO: That you're an idiot, a petty crook, a cheat, a bruiser, a berzerker, and a drunk.

STRAGUALCIA: Then I'll say that you're a robber, a card-sharper, a gossip, a swindler, a double-dealer, an imposter, boaster, numbskull, shamefaced imbecile, blackguard, bugger, and a general piece of crap.

PIERO: I guess we know each other.

The Intronati of Siena

STRAGUALCIA: Voi dite 'l vero.

PEDANTE: Basta: non piú parole. Non mi vo' metter con un par tuo, ché non m'è onore.

STRAGUALCIA: Sí, per Dio! Tutta la nobilità della Maremma è in voi! Sareste mai altro che figliuol d'un mulattiere? Non son io nato meglio di voi? Pare onesto a questo furfante, poi che sa dir "cuius masculini", di tener ognun sotto i piei.

PEDANTE: "Povera e nuda vai, filosofia". In bocca di chi son venute le povere lettere? D'uno asino.

STRAGUALCIA: L'asino sarete voi, se non parlate altrimenti; ché vi caricarò di legname.

PEDANTE: Sai che ti ricordo? Furor fit laesa saepius sapientia. Tu mi farai, un tratto, uscir del manico, Stragualcia. Lasciami stare, famegliaccio di stalla, poltrone, arcipoltrone!

STRAGUALCIA: Doh Pedante, arcipedante, pedante, pedantissimo! Puossi dir peggio che Pedante? trovasi la peggior genia? ecci la maggior canaglia? trovasi esercizio peggiore? Forse che non vanno gonfiati perché altri gli chiama "messer tale" e "maestro quale"? e che non rispondono con riputazione a una sbirettata discosto un miglio? Comanda, messer caca, messer stronzo, maestro squaquara, messer merda?

PEDANTE: Tractant fabrilia fabri. Tu parli proprio da quel che sei.

STRAGUALCIA: Parlo di quel che vi piace.

PEDANTE: Vòimiti levar dinanzi?

STRAGUALCIA: Io non vi ci fui mai dinanzi: benché non è restato da voi.

PEDANTE: Al corpo di...

STRAGUALCIA: Telling me.

PIERO: Enough of that. I just can't get involved with the likes of you — question of honor.

STRAGUALCIA: Sure to God! You've got all the nobility of the Maremma in you.[59] You'll never amount to more than the son of a muleteer. Isn't my lineage better than yours? Should the likes of you strut above the world just because you do bum service in Latin like a *cuius masculini*?[60]

PIERO: Oi yoi, "how philosophy creeps through the world all wretched and bare."[61] Latin's in the dregs when it comes from the mouth of an ass.

STRAGUALCIA: You're the ass, and I'll do the beating if you don't alter course.

PIERO: *Furor sit laesa saepius sapientia,* I always say. Wisdom pissed off can go berzerk, Stragualcia, so shut it down, you big shit-shoveler, you clotpole, you arch-clotpole.

STRAGUALCIA: Whoa, pedant, you arch-pedant, you *magna cum* pedant, you *summa cum* pedant! Know a worse insult than being called a pedant? Anyone more awful? Anyone more crooked? A cruddier profession? A guy could take it if they didn't go around all bloated because they're called "master" or "professor" and such, or if they at least said "hello" to someone who tips his hat before they're a mile in the dust. "Salutations to you, Mister Farten, and to you, Doctor Turdmore, and you, Professor Runnyload, and Sir Shitface Emeritus.

PIERO: *Tratant fabrilia fabri.*[62] You know the field, you talk the talk, and it describes you to a T.

STRAGUALCIA: I'm just describing your tastes.

PIERO: Your butt's in my way.

STRAGUALCIA: Mine in your way? Never, though I'm sure that's where you'd like it to be.

PIERO: Damnation to you!

STRAGUALCIA: Al corpo ci... Guarda chi mi vuol dir villania! Sa che non fece mai tristizia ch'io non sappia e che, s'io volesse, il potrei fare ardere, e pur mi sta a rompere il culo.

PEDANTE: Ti menti per la gola, ch'io non son uomo da ciò.

STRAGUALCIA: Sarebbe forse il primo.

PEDANTE: Ho deliberato, Stragualcia, o che tu non starai in casa o ch'io non ci starò io.

STRAGUALCIA: È forse la prima volta che l'avete detto? Voi non ve ne partiresti, se altri ve ne cacciasse con le granate. Ditemi un poco: chi trovareste voi che vi tenesse a tavola seco, nello studio seco, a dormire seco, se non questo giovinetto che è meglio del pane?

PEDANTE: Per Dio, sí, mi mancarebbeno i partiti, quando io gli volesse! Ho tal che mi prega.

STRAGUALCIA: Oh la buona robba! Passate, passate.

PEDANTE: Vogliam far poche parole; e farai bene. Tórnatene a l'ostaria ed abbi cura alle robbe del padrone. Poi faremo conto insieme.

STRAGUALCIA: All'ostaria tornarò io volentieri e conto farò io a vostra posta; ma pensate d'avere a pagar voi. S'io non facesse qualche volta il viso dell'arme a questo sciagurato, non potrei viver con lui. Egli è piú vil ch'un coniglio. Com'io lo bravo, non fa parola; ma, s'io me gli mettesse sotto, mi squartarebbe, sí gross'ha la discrezione! Buon per me che lo conosco!

PEDANTE: Il Frulla m'ha detto che Fabrizio sarà in verso piazza. E però sarà buono ch'io pigli di qua.

The Deceived

STRAGUALCIA: Well, damnation to you. You'd better watch your language if it's meant for me! *(Aside but audible)* He should know I'm in on all his nasty affairs. If I had a mind to it, I could have him burned. Then he'd leave my ass out of it.

PIERO: Liar! That's not my nature at all.

STRAGUALCIA: *(Aside)* He'd be about the only pedant who wasn't.

PIERO: I've made up my mind, Stragualcia. This place isn't big enough for the both of us.

STRAGUALCIA: Now there's a novel turn. Not the first time you've said it. You'll never leave unless you get chased out of here with a broom. Tell me. Who'll you find to eat with you, hit the books with you, even sleep with you, if not our young master. You'll never find a better.

PIERO: You think I couldn't get another somewhere else, for Chrissake? Somebody's already made me a splendid offer.

STRAGUALCIA: Lucky you, but isn't it time to get going?

PIERO: Give it up, and learn to keep your own mouth shut. Get back to the inn and look after our master's stuff. We can deal with this later.

STRAGUALCIA: Sure, I'll go back to the inn and do things my own way. But in the end, you're going to pay for this. *(Aside, on the way out)* If I didn't strike some fear into this wretch now and again, I couldn't stand the sight of him. He's viler than a rabbit. A little bejeez and he doesn't utter a word, but if I let him get on top of me, he'd tear me apart, given the size of his indiscretion. Good thing I know the kind he is. *(Exit)*

PIERO: Frulla said I'd find Fabrizio somewhere in the grand piazza. I'd better go have a look.

The Intronati of Siena

Scena seconda

GHERARDO, VIRGINIO e PEDANTE.

GHERARDO: De la dote quel che è detto è detto. La dotarò come tu vorrai; e tu aggiugni mille fiorini, quando tuo figliuol non si truovi.

VIRGINIO: Cosí sia.

PEDANTE: S'io non m'inganno, io ho veduto questo gentiluomo altre volte; né mi ricordo dove.

VIRGINIO: Che mirate, uomo da bene?

PEDANTE: Certo, questo è il padrone.

GHERARDO: Lascia mirar quel che gli piace. Debb'esser poco pratico in questa terra: ché, negli altri luoghi, non si pon mente a chi mira come qui; ma si lascia mirar ognuno.

PEDANTE: S'io miro, io non miro sine causa. Ditemi: conoscete voi in questa terra messer Virginio Bellenzini?

VIRGINIO: Sí, conosco; e non potrebb'esser piú mio amico di quel che gli è. Ma che volete voi da lui? Se pensate d'alloggiar seco, vi dico che gli ha altre facende e che non vi po' attendere: sí che cercate pur altro oste.

PEDANTE: Voi sète per certo esso. Salvete, patronorum optime.

VIRGINIO: Sareste mai messer Pietro de' Pagliaricci maestro di mio figliuolo?

PEDANTE: Sí, sono.

VIRGINIO: Oh figliuol mio! Trist'a me! Che nuove mi portate di lui? ove il lasciaste? ove morí? perché sète stato tanto ad avvisarmi? ammazzoronlo quei traditori, quei iudei, quei cani? Figliuol mio! Era quanto bene io avevo al mondo! O caro maestro mio, presto! Ditemelo: ve ne prego.

The Deceived

Scene 2

GHERARDO, VIRGINIO, *and* PIERO.

GHERARDO: Regarding the dowry, what we agreed to is what we agreed to. I'll come up with the dowry you want, and if you don't find your son, you'll put in a thousand florins.

VIRGINIO: Good enough.

PIERO: *(Aside, as he walks up to them)* I could be mistaken, but haven't I see this man before? I just can't remember where it was.

VIRGINIO: Hey, my good man, what are you staring at?

PIERO: *(Aside)* No mistake, it's my old master.

GHERARDO: He can stare at whatever he fancies. Must be a stranger, though, from a place where people don't care about staring as much as they do here.

PIERO: My staring is not *sine causa* [without a reason]. Can you tell me if you know Mr. Virginio Bellenzini? He's from here.

VIRGINIO: Sure, I know him. My closest friend in fact. What do you want with him? I can tell you already that if you're looking for lodging, he's tied up and can't take you in. Best to look elsewhere for that.

PIERO: Then you must be the man. *Salvete, patronorum optime.* [Greetings, best of masters.]

VIRGINIO: So does that, by chance, make you Pietro de' Pagliaricci, my son's tutor?

PIERO: Yes, that's who I am.

VIRGINIO: *(Starts to cry)* Oh, my poor son. Do you have news of him? Where did you see him last? Where did he die? What took you so long to reach me? Was he killed by those traitors, those infidels, those dogs? My pitiful son — my only good in the world. No holding back, I beg you.

PEDANTE: Non piangete, messer, di grazia.

VIRGINIO: Oh Gherardo, genero mio! Ecco chi m'allevò quel povero figliuolo mentre che visse. Oh maestro! O figliuol mio, dove se' tu sotterato? Sapetene nulla? ché non mel dite? ch'io muoio di voglia di saperlo e di paura di non intender quello ch'io intenderò.

PEDANTE: O padron mio, non piangete. Perché piangete?

VIRGINIO: Non piangerò io un cosí dolce figliuolo? cosí savio? cosí dotto? cosí bene allevato? che quei traditori me l'ammazzorono.

PEDANTE: Iddio ve ne guardi, voi e lui. Vostro figliuolo è vivo e sano.

GHERARDO: Mal per me, se questo è. Perdut'ho io mille fiorini.

VIRGINIO: Vivo e sano? Che? Se cosí fusse, saria ora con voi.

GHERARDO: Virginio, conosci ben costui, che non sia qualche barro?

PEDANTE: Parcius ista viris, tamen obiicienda memento.

VIRGINIO: Ditemi qualche cosa, maestro.

PEDANTE: Vostro figliuolo, nel sacco di Roma, fu prigione d'un capitano Orteca.

GHERARDO: State a udire, ché ora comincia la favola.

PEDANTE: E perché gli era a compagnia con due altri, pensando d'ingannarsi secretamente ci mandò a Siena. Di lí a pochi giorni venn'egli dubitando che quei gentiluomini sanesi, che sono molto amici del diritto e del ragionevole e molto affezionati a questa nazione e soprattutto uomini da bene, non glie lo tollesseno e liberasseno. Lo cavò di Siena e mandò a un castel del signor di Piombino; e per usque millies ci fece scrivere per mille ducati di taglia che gli avea posto.

The Deceived

PIERO: Good sir, please don't cry.

VIRGINIO: O Gherardo, my son-in-law, when poor Fabrizio was still alive, this was his teacher. — O Maestro! O my son! Where was he buried? Don't you know? You're not telling me, and I'm dying to find out, though I'm dying of fear that I'll learn what I dread to hear.

PIERO: Why're you crying, Master? No need to weep.

VIRGINIO: Should I not mourn so sweet a son? Such a wise, intelligent, and well-mannered boy. Those traitors, they've murdered him.

PIERO: May God bless you all, both you and him. Your son's alive. He's well.

GHERARDO: *(Aside)* If this is true, bad news for me by a thousand florins.

VIRGINIO: Alive? Well? If it's so, why is he not with you?

GHERARDO: Virginio, how well do you know this chap? Maybe it's some sort of trick.

PIERO: *Parcius ista viris, tamen obiicienda memento.* [You should be more careful in reproaching people for these things.]⁶³

VIRGINIO: Explain yourself.

PIERO: During the Sack of Rome there was a Captain Orteca who took your son as his prisoner.

GHERARDO: *(Aside)* Uh oh, here comes the cock-and-bull.

PIERO: This captain had two soldier allies, and he decided to trick those guys by sending Fabrizio and me on to Siena in secret. Later, though, he began to reflect upon the good men of Siena, how they respect the law and principles of fairness, how they are friends of our city and men of honor, and consequently how they would set the boy free. So he had him moved from Siena to one of the castles belonging to the governor of Piombino.⁶⁴ And all the while, *per usque millies* [countless times over] we had to write for the ransom money set at a thousand ducats.

VIRGINIO: Figliuol mio! Straziavanlo, almanco?

PEDANTE: Non certo; ma il trattavan da gentiluomo.

GHERARDO: Io sto con la morte alla bocca.

PEDANTE: Non avemmo mai risposta di lettere che noi mandassemo.

GHERARDO: Tu intendi. Che sí che ti cavarà di man qualche scudo.

VIRGINIO: Segue.

PEDANTE: Or, essendoci condotti col campo spagnuolo in Corregia, fu questo capitano ammazzato; e la corte prese la sua robba e noi ha liberati.

VIRGINIO: E dov'è il mio figliuolo?

PEDANTE: Piú presso che non credete.

VIRGINIO: È forse in Modana?

PEDANTE: Se mi promettete il beveraggio, quia omnis labor optat praemium, io vel dirò.

GHERARDO: Or questa è la cosa, truffatore!

PEDANTE: Voi avete il torto. Truffatore io? Absit.

VIRGINIO: Prometto ciò che voi volete. Dove è?

PEDANTE: Nell'ostaria del "Matto".

GHERARDO: La cosa è fatta: i mille fiorini son giocati. Ma che mi fa a me? Pur ch'i' abbi lei, mi basta. Io son ricco d'avanzo.

VIRGINIO: Andiamo, maestro, ch'io non credo veder quell'ora ch'io 'l vegghi, ch'io l'abbracci, ch'io 'l baci e lo pigli in collo.

PEDANTE: Padrone, oh quanto mutatur ab illo! E' non è piú fanciullo da pigliare in collo. Voi non lo conoscereste. Gli è fatto grande. E so certo che non riconoscerà voi,

The Deceived

VIRGINIO: My suffering child. Did they torture him too?

PIERO: No no, he was cared for as a gentleman.

GHERARDO: *(Aside)* I can figure out what he'll say next.

PIERO: And from all those letters, not a single answer.

GHERARDO: *(Aside to Virginio)* You can see he's after your money.

VIRGINIO: *(To Piero)* Go on.

PIERO: Then we were taken along with the Spanish troops to Correggia,[65] and there he got himself killed, so the courts took over his possessions, and we were released.

VIRGINIO: Then where's my boy?

PIERO: Closer than you might think.

VIRGINIO: In Modena?

PIERO: You have to promise me a reward before I'll tell you, because *quia omnis labor optat praemium* [every effort deserves a reward].

GHERARDO: A cheat in the end — just look at what he's after.

PIERO: *(To Gherardo)* A cheat? There you're wrong. *Absit* [I'm far from it]!

VIRGINIO: Whatever you want, I promise. Just tell me where he is.

PIERO: At the Jester Inn.

GHERARDO: *(Aside)* What the hell! A thousand ducats gambled and lost. See if I care. Just to get her is enough, even more wealth than I need.

VIRGINIO: Then off we go, Scholar–Tutor. I never thought I'd live to see him, hug him, kiss and fasten him in my arms.

PIERO: Ah, but Master, *quanto mutatus ab illo* [how changed he is from what he was].[66] He's not a kid anymore like you'd hold in your arms. You'll hardly know him, he's grown up so much. And you've changed too, so he may

cosí sète mutato! Praeterea avete questa barba, che prima non la portavate; e, s'io non vi sentivo parlare, non vi arei mai conosciuto. Che è di Lelia?

VIRGINIO: Bene. Gli è fatta grande e grossa.

GHERARDO: Come grossa"? Se gli è cotesto, tientela; ch'io, per me, non la voglio.

VIRGINIO: Oh! oh! Io dico che gli è fatta già una donna. O maestro, io non v'ho ancor baciato.

PEDANTE: Padrone, io non dico per vantarmi; ma io ho fatto per il vostro figliuolo... so ben io. E n'ho avuta cagione; ch'io non lo richiesi mai di cosa che subito egli non s'inchinasse a farla.

VIRGINIO: Come ha imparato?

PEDANTE: Non ha perduto il tempo a fatto, ut licuit per varios casus, per tot discrimina rerum.

VIRGINIO: Chiamatelo un poco fuore; e non gli dite niente. Vo' veder se mi conosce.

PEDANTE: Egli era uscito dell'ostaria poco fa. Veggiamo se gli è tornato.

Scena terza

PEDANTE, STRAGUALCIA, VIRGINIO e GHERARDO.

PEDANTE: Stragualcia! o Stragualcia! È tornato Fabrizio?

STRAGUALCIA: Non anco.

PEDANTE: Vien qua. Fa' motto al padron vecchio. Questo è messer Virginio.

STRAGUALCIA: Èvvi passata la còllora?

PEDANTE: Non sai ch'io non tengo mai còllora con te?

STRAGUALCIA: Fate bene.

PEDANTE: Or da' qua la mano al padre di Fabrizio.

The Deceived

not recognize you either. *Praeterea* [What's more] that beard you have is completely new. Without hearing your voice, I wouldn't have known you. And Lelia, how's she doing?

VIRGINIO: Um, all grown up and filled out now.

GHERARDO: Filled out? What's that supposed to mean, pregnant? If that's it, she's still all yours. I'm having nothing of that.

VIRGINIO: No, not at all. I mean she's a woman now. And you, my Scholar, let me embrace you at last. *(Hugs and kisses him on each cheek.)*

PIERO: I'm not boasting, Master, but I've managed a lot for your son, I can assure you. There was never a thing I requested that he didn't perform immediately.

VIRGINIO: And his studies?

PIERO: Not a moment lost, *ut licuit per varios casus, per tot discrimina rerum* [doing everything possible under the dangerous circumstances].[67]

VIRGINIO: Go fetch him, but don't explain a thing. I'm curious to see if he knows me.

PIERO: He left the inn a short time ago. Let's see if he's back.

Scene 3

PIERO, STRAGUALCIA, VIRGINIO, *and* GHERARDO.

PIERO: Hey Stragualcia! Stragualcia! Is Fabrizio back yet?

STRAGUALCIA: No, not yet.

PIERO: I want you to come over here and say hello to my old boss. This is Master Virginio.

STRAGUALCIA: *(To Piero)* You still mad at me?

PIERO: You should know I never stay mad at you.

STRAGUALCIA: Thank goodness.

PIERO: So shake the hand of Fabrizio's father.

STRAGUALCIA: Porgetemela voi.

PEDANTE: Non dico a me; dico a questo gentiluomo.

STRAGUALCIA: È questo il padre del nostro padrone?

PEDANTE: Sí, è.

STRAGUALCIA: O padron magnifico, a tempo veniste per pagar l'oste. Ben gionto.

PEDANTE: Costui è stato un buon servitore a vostro figliuolo.

STRAGUALCIA: Volete forse dir ch'io non gli son piú?

PEDANTE: No.

VIRGINIO: Che tu sia benedetto, figliuol mio! Pensa ch'io ho da ristorar tutti quelli che gli han fatto buona compagnia.

STRAGUALCIA: Voi mi potete ristorar con poca cosa.

VIRGINIO: Dimanda.

STRAGUALCIA: Acconciatemi per garzon con questo oste che è il miglior compagno del mondo e 'l meglio fornito e 'l piú savio e quel che meglio intende il bisogno del forestiero che oste che mai io vedesse. Io, per me, non credo che sia altro paradiso al mondo.

GHERARDO: Gli ha nome di tener molto bene.

VIRGINIO: Hai tu fatto colazione?

STRAGUALCIA: Un poco.

VIRGINIO: Che hai mangiato?

STRAGUALCIA: Un par di starne, sei tordi, un cappone, un poca di vitella; e bevuto due boccali solamente.

VIRGINIO: Frulla, dàgli ciò che vuole; e lascia pagare a me.

PEDANTE: Or che vuoi?

STRAGUALCIA: Vi bacio las manos. A questo modo son fatti i padroni, maestro! Messer Pietro, voi sète troppo misero e volete ogni cosa per voi. Sapete da quanti v'è stato detto. Frulla, porta un poco da bere a questi gentiluomini.

The Deceived

STRAGUALCIA: *(To Piero)* Give me your hand first.

PIERO: No, no, not to me. To this man here.

STRAGUALCIA: The real father of our master?

PIERO: As I said.

STRAGUALCIA: *(Shaking hands with Virginio)* O munificent patron, pleased to meet you, and welcome. You're here just in time to settle up with the innkeeper.

PIERO: This man took really good care of your son.

STRAGUALCIA: You hinting that I won't in the future?

PIERO: No.

VIRGINIO: Good man, I welcome you. Rewards are in order for all of you who remained his close companions.

STRAGUALCIA: There's one little reward I'd gladly accept.

VIRGINIO: And what would that be?

STRAGUALCIA: A job with this innkeeper. He's the finest chap alive, and smart, with the best stock of goods I've ever seen. He knows better than anyone what a traveler needs. For me, there's no other paradise on earth.

GHERARDO: He's got a great reputation.

VIRGINIO: So, have you had anything to eat?

STRAGUALCIA: Not much.

VIRGINIO: What've you had?

STRAGUALCIA: Well, two partridges, six song birds, one neutered cock, a wee chunk of veal, and a mere two flasks of the grape.

VIRGINIO: Let him have whatever he wants, Frulla, and pass me the reckoning.

PIERO: You happy now?

STRAGUALCIA: I kiss *las manos*. Such are all good bosses. You, Mister Teacher, you're just a skinflint. You keep everything for yourself. So many people tell you that. Mister Frulla, fetch good drink for these gentlemen.

PEDANTE: Non bisogna, no.

STRAGUALCIA: So che voi berete. Pagarò io. Che credete che sia? Due animelle, una fetta di salsiccione... Volete? Maestro, bevete voi ancora.

PEDANTE: Per far teco la pace, son contento.

STRAGUALCIA: Oh! gli è buono! Padrone, voi avete da voler bene al maestro che vuol meglio al vostro figliuolo che agli occhi suoi.

VIRGINIO: Dio gli facci di bene.

STRAGUALCIA: Tocca prima a voi e poi a Dio. Bevete, gentiluomo.

GHERARDO: Non accade.

STRAGUALCIA: Per gentilezza, entrate drento, tanto che Fabrizio torni; e, poi che la cena è in ordine, cenaremo qui, questa sera.

PEDANTE: Questo non è forse male.

GHERARDO: Io vi lasciarò, ché ho un poco di facenda a casa.

VIRGINIO: Abbi cura che colei non si parta.

GHERARDO: Non ci vo per altro.

VIRGINIO: Gli è tua; fanne a tuo modo; per me, te ne do licenzia.

GHERARDO: In fine, e' non si possono aver tutti i contenti. Pazienzia! Ma, s'i' veggo bene, questa è Lelia che sarà uscita fuora. Quella da poco della fantesca l'arà lasciata fuggire.

Scena quarta

LELIA *da ragazzo*, CLEMENZIA *balia e* GHERARDO.

LELIA: Parti, Clemenzia, che la Fortuna si tolga giuoco del fatto mio?

CLEMEZIA: Dàtene pace e lascia fare a me, ché trovarò qualche modo da contentarti. Va', cavati questi panni, ché tu non sia veduta cosí.

PIERO: None for me, thanks.

STRAGUALCIA: Sure, you'll have a drink. I'm buying. It won't break the bank. Have some cured meat, a slice of this or that sausage. Go on Mister Teacher, have a drink on me.

PIERO: All right, just to make things up.

STRAGUALCIA: *(To Virginio)* He's a good man, Master. He's loved your son more than his own eyeballs and deserves your regard for it.

VIRGINIO: May God provide for him.

STRAGUALCIA: You first, then God will take over. — And you, good man, have more wine.

GHERARDO: Well, just a sip.

STRAGUALCIA: Please come in till Fabrizio gets back, and then we can all dine here tonight, since everything is already cooked.

PIERO: Brilliant suggestion.

GHERARDO: I'm afraid I'll have to leave you. There's a little something to attend to at the house.

VIRGINIO: Take care she doesn't slip past you.

GHERARDO: Just the reason I'm on my way home.

VIRGINIO: She'll be yours now for sure. Just manage everything as you see best. You have my full blessing.

GHERARDO: *(To himself)* Just keep calm, because when all's said and done, you can't have everything. Hey, that's Lelia who's come out, if my eyes aren't lying. Did that dumb maidservant turn her lose?

Scene 4

LELIA *in male disguise,* CLEMEZIA, *and* GHERARDO.

LELIA: So Clemenzia, aren't I just the plaything of Fortune?

CLEMEZIA: Trust me in this, and don't worry. I'll come up with something to make it all work. But you should get out of those clothes before you're seen in them.

GHERARDO: Io la vo' pur salutare e intender com'egli è fuggita. Dio ti contenti e te, Lelia, sposa mia dolce. Chi t'ha aperto l'uscio? La fantesca, eh? A me piace ben che tu sia venuta a casa della tua balia; ma l'esser veduta in questo abito è poco onore e a te e a me.

LELIA: Oh sventurata! Costui m'ha conosciuta. Con chi parlate voi? Che Lelia! Io non son Lelia.

GHERARDO: Oh! Poco fa, che noi t'inserrammo con Isabella mia figliuola, tuo padre ed io, non confessasti tu d'esser Lelia? e, poi, credi ch'io non ti conosca, moglie mia? Va' cavati questi panni.

LELIA: Tanto v'aiti Dio, io arei voglia di marito!

CLEMEZIA: Vanne in casa, Gherardo mio. Tutte le donne fan delle citolezze, chi in un modo e chi in un altro. E sappi che poche e forse niuna ve n'è che non scapuzzi qualche volta. Pure, son cose da tenerle segrete.

GHERARDO: Per me, non se ne saprà mai nulla. Ma come è fuggita di casa mia, che l'avevo serrata con Isabella?

CLEMEZIA: Chi? costei?

GHERARDO: Costei.

CLEMEZIA: Tu t'inganni, ché non s'è mai oggi partita da me: e, per giambo, s'era testé messi questi panni, come fan le fanciulle; e dicevami ch'io mirasse se stava bene.

GHERARDO: Tu mi vuoi far travedere. Dico che noi la inserrammo in casa con Isabella.

CLEMEZIA: Donde venite voi adesso?

GHERARDO: Dall'ostaria del "Matto", che v'andai con Virginio.

CLEMEZIA: Beveste?

GHERARDO: Un trattarello.

The Deceived

GHERARDO: *(Aside)* I have to talk to her and find out how she got out. *(To Lelia and Clemenzia)* God bring you joy, Clemenzia, and to my charming bride Lelia as well. Who opened the door for you? I'm betting it's Pasquella. But you did well to go to your nursemaid's house, even though being caught out in this get-up won't do much for your honor or for mine.

LELIA: *(Aside)* Unlucky me! He knows who I am. — Who are you talking to? You think I'm Lelia? Well, I'm not.

GHERARDO: Well, a little while ago when your father and I locked you up with Isabella, didn't you confess that you were Lelia? You think I don't know my own wife? Go get yourself out of those clothes.

LELIA: May God help you, me looking for a husband!

CLEMEZIA: You too, dear Gherardo. You should go back to your house. All women enjoy pranking, some in this way, others in that. Take it from me, there aren't many women, maybe none, who don't do strange things now and again. But it's best just to keep these things under wraps.

GHERARDO: Count on me to keep it a secret. But how on earth did she sneak out of the house after I shut her in with Isabella?

CLEMEZIA: She? She who?

GHERARDO: She, there.

CLEMEZIA: You're cockeyed. She hasn't left my side the entire day. She was just fooling around putting these clothes on and asking me how she looks. That's how young girls are!

GHERARDO: You're kidding me, aren't you? I repeat: I locked her in at my place with Isabella.

CLEMEZIA: So where are you coming from now? *(Lelia goes inside.)*

GHERARDO: I've been with Virginio at the Jester Inn.

CLEMEZIA: Drinking I suppose?

GHERARDO: Barely a sip.

CLEMEZIA: Or andate a dormire, ché voi n'avete bisogno.

GHERARDO: Fammi veder un poco Lelia prima ch'io mi parti; ch'io gli vo' dare una buona nuova.

CLEMEZIA: Che nuova?

GHERARDO: Gli è tornato suo fratello sano e salvo e che 'l padre l'aspetta all'ostaria.

CLEMEZIA: Chi? Fabrizio?

GHERARDO: Fabrizio.

CLEMEZIA: S'io 'l credessi, ti darei un bacio.

GHERARDO: Sí che la gioia è bella! Famel piú presto dare a Lelia.

CLEMEZIA: Io vo' correre a dirglielo.

GHERARDO: Ed io a darne un follo a quella sciagurata che l'ha lasciata partire.

Scena quinta

PASQUELLA *fante, sola.*

Uh trista a me! Io ho avuta sí fatta la paura ch'io son uscita fuor di casa. E so che, s'io non vi dicessi di che, donne mie, voi nol sapreste. A voi lo vo' dire; e non a questi uominacci che se ne farebben le belle risa. Que' due vecchi pecoroni dicevan pur che quel giovinetto era donna; e rinserroronlo in camera con Isabella mia padrona; e a me dieder la chiave. Io vòlsi entrar dentro e veder quel che facevano: e trovai che s'abbraciavano e si baciavano insieme. Io ebbi voglia di chiarirmi se era o maschio o femina. Avendolo la padrona disteso in sul letto, e chiamandomi ch'io l'aiutasse mentre ch'ella gli teneva le mani, egli si lasciava vincere. Lo sciolsi dinanzi: e, a un tratto, mi sentii percuotere non so che cosa in su le mani; né cognobbi se gli era un pestaglio

CLEMEZIA: Well, go sleep it off, I say, because that's what you need.

GHERARDO: Let me say a word to Lelia before I take off. I've got some good news for her.

CLEMEZIA: About what?

GHERARDO: Her brother's back hale and hearty, and her father's at the inn waiting for him.

CLEMEZIA: You mean Fabrizio?

GHERARDO: Fabrizio.

CLEMEZIA: Prove that true and you get a kiss.

GHERARDO: Happiness is a wonderful thing. But spare me the kiss. I'll give it to Lelia instead.

CLEMEZIA: I'm running right in to let her know.

GHERARDO: I'm heading straight off to pay back the numbskull who let her get away.

Scene 5

PASQUELLA, *alone*.

PASQUELLA: Heavenly days, I've taken such a fright that I bolted right out of the house. — Ladies, you'll never believe what's been going on, so let me tell you. And this is not for you smutty-brained men, who'll just start laughing. You know those two old dotards were as sure as all get out that the guy was a girl — the one they locked up in the bedroom with my mistress, Isabella, before giving me the key. I was keen to get inside to see what they were up to, and there they were hugging and smooching. Well then I had to find out if this was a male or a female. Missy had this thing pinned down on the bed by its hands and was calling me for some help. It wasn't doing anything to stop her from winning, so I got its clothes open in the front and just like that something hit my hand — something like a big pestle,

o una carota o pur quell'altra cosa. Ma, sia quel che si vuole, e' non è cosa che abbia sentita la grandine. Come io la viddi cosí fatta, fugge, sorelle, e serra l'uscio! E so che, per me, non ve tornarei sola; e, se qualcuna di voi non mel crede e voglia chiarirsene, io gli prestarò la chiave. Ma ecco Giglio. Io vo' vedere s'io posso far tanto ch'io gli cavi di man quella corona e uccellarlo; perché si tengon tanto accorti, questi spagnuoli, che non si credon ch'altri si truovi al mondo che loro che tanto ne sappi.

Scena sesta

GIGLIO *spagnuolo e* PASQUELLA *fante.*

GIGLIO: Aglià sta Pasquella. Ya penso que le paresca que muccio tardasse, per arta gana que tiene de ser con migo. Ya sape, la malditta, quanto valen los spagnuolos en las cosas dellas mugeres. Oh come se holgan de nos otros estas puttas italianas!

PASQUELLA: Io ho già pensato in che modo ho a fare a farlo star forte. Lascia pur fare a me.

GIGLIO: Esta male aventurada lavandera sí se piensa ch'io gli desse el rosario. Renniego dell'imperador se io non quiero qu'ella hurti tanto à suo amo que me compri calzas y giubbon y camisas, de dos in dos. Holgaromme yo con ella à mio plazer y despues tommaré à mio rosario sin dezir nada; que ya me pienso que ya non s'accorda d'ello.

PASQUELLA: Se mi lascia una volta in mano quella corona, se la vede mai piú, cavami gli occhi. E, se mi dirà niente, gli farò fare un sí fatto spauracchio dal mio Spela che mai non n'ebbe un sí fatto.

GIGLIO: Oh que benditta sia quella bien aventurada madre que vi fezio e criò tan hermosa, tan bien criada, tan verdadera! Ya penso que me speravate.

you know, like a stick. It was in fine fettle whatever it was. And as soon as I could see the size of the thing, I'm telling you ladies, I bolted and locked the door after myself. And I've got no immediate plans for going back in there, not alone anyway. And if you ladies don't believe me and want an eyeful for yourself, here's the key. Ah, here's Giglio coming in. I've got to get my hands on that rosary and make him look like an idiot. Spaniards like him are so full of themselves they can't imagine anyone else in the world as wily as they are.

Scene 6

GIGLIO *and* PASQUELLA.

GIGLIO: *(Aside)* There's Pasquella. I bet she thinks I'm so late getting here just because she's craving so much to stay with me. Dumb wench, she knows how great we Spaniards are with women. These Italian broads, boy, do they go crazy for us.

PASQUELLA: *(Aside)* I know how I'll cheat this bozo. Just watch me.

GIGLIO: *(Aside)* This no-name scullery maid thinks she's getting my rosary. Well, damn the emperor if I don't get her so loved up that she steals enough from her master to buy me socks by the dozens, shirts, and tunics. I'll make her do all my pleasures and then dump her and head off, rosary in hand. She's probably forgotten about it, anyway.

PASQUELLA: *(Aside)* All I need is one grab at that rosary and for him it's a goner, or you can extract my eyeballs. Then if he whines about it, Spela can lambaste him like he's never gotten it before.

GIGLIO: O my beauty. Blessed is the mother who bore you, so shapely and so faithful. I'm certain you were waiting for me.

PASQUELLA: Mira che dolci paroline che gli hanno! T'ho aspettato in su questo uscio piú d'una mezza ora, per veder se tu ci passavi; ché 'l mio padrone non era in casa e aremmo avuto tempo di stare insieme un pezzo.

GIGLIO: Rencrescime, per Dios, che ho tenuto que fazer. Mas entriamo.

PASQUELLA: Ho paura che 'l padron non torni, ché ha un pezzo che andò fuora. Ma tu ti debbi esser scordata la corona, eh?

GIGLIO: Non, madonna; que à qui sta.

PASQUELLA: Mostra. Oh! Tu volevi fare acconciare il fiocco. Perché non l'hai fatto?

GIGLIO: Io le farò acconciar otra volta: y, per dezir la verdade, io non me ne so accordado.

PASQUELLA: Oh! È segno che tu facevi un gran conto di me, feminaccio che tu sei! Mi vien voglia...

GIGLIO: Non vi corruzate, madonna, con vostro figliuolo; que ben sapite que non tengo otra amiga que vos.

PASQUELLA: Son stata molto a cògliarti in bugia! Poco fa tu dicesti che n'avevi due, delle gentildonne, per amiche.

GIGLIO: Io las ho lasciatas per à voi, que non voglio io otra que voi. Non m'intendite?

PASQUELLA: Or bene sta. Mostrami un poco se questa corona è rosario. La mi par molto lunga.

GIGLIO: Non so, io, quanti siano.

PASQUELLA: È segno che la dici spesso: nol debbi tu forse sapere il paternostro. Eh! Dàgli un po' qua, ch'io gli conti.

GIGLIO: Tommala; mas vamo dentro en casa.

PASQUELLA: Sai? Guarda che tu non sia veduto entrare.

GIGLIO: A qui non sta ninguno.

The Deceived

PASQUELLA: *(Aside)* Spouting his usual crap! — I've been hanging out by the door here for at least half an hour to see if you'd come by. The boss is away so we had our golden opportunity to meet in the middle.

GIGLIO: Damn pity that other matters came up to keep me away. So let's go inside right now.

PASQUELLA: No, my master's due back soon because he went off quite a while ago. But you haven't forgotten the rosary have you?

GIGLIO: No, my lady, it's on me somewhere.

PASQUELLA: Let's see it. Ah, but you were going to have the box repaired. How come you didn't?

GIGLIO: I can do it later on. To tell you the truth, I forgot all about it.

PASQUELLA: Just shows how much you were thinking about me, you skirt chaser. You know what I aim....

GIGLIO: Dear lady, don't get upset with your own dear boy. You're my only sweetheart, you know that.

PASQUELLA: It doesn't take long to catch you in a fib. Just a bit ago you were boasting about your two lady friends.

GIGLIO: Ah, but I dumped them both for you. It's just you alone I want. Can't I make you understand?

PASQUELLA: Fine. But what about all those beads? Is that a real rosary? It looks pretty long for one.

GIGLIO: Who knows how many beads there are?

PASQUELLA: I can see you're not using it much. I bet you can't even say your Paternoster. Here, let me have it for a second, and I'll count them.

GIGLIO: Sure, here. But let's go in the house.

PASQUELLA: You think we should? Have a good look around to see if anyone could spot you coming in.

GIGLIO: I don't see anyone.

PASQUELLA: Entriamo. Uh trista a me! Le mie galline son tutte qui. Fermati, Giglio, un poco costí; ché, se fuggissero, non le giugnerei oggi.

GIGLIO: Facite presto.

PASQUELLA: Chino, chino, belline, belline, belline, iscio, iscio! Che ve rompiate il collo! Che sí che se ne fuggirà qualcuna? Para, para ben, Giglio.

GIGLIO: Donde stan estos pollos? Aqui non veo ni gallos ni gallinas.

PASQUELLA: Non gli vedi? Eccoli qui. Levati; lasciami un poco serrare l'uscio, tanto ch'io ce gli rimetta.

GIGLIO: Oh! Voi inserrate col fierro. Oh! Este porqué?

PASQUELLA: Perch'io non vorrei che questi polli l'aprisseno.

GIGLIO: Fazite presto, ché algun non vienga y desturbe nostra fazienda.

PASQUELLA: Venga pur chi vuole, ché qua dentro non è per intrare.

GIGLIO: Oh que malditta seas, vieia putta! Dizetemi: por que non aprite?

PASQUELLA: Giglio, sai, ben mio? Io vo' prima dir tutta questa corona. Tu pòi andartene, per istasera. E' non mi ricordavo ch'io ho anco a dire una orazione che non la soglio mai lasciare.

GIGLIO: Que trepparie son este? que corona? que orazion es esta?

PASQUELLA: Che orazione? vuoi ch'io te la insegni? Sai? È buona a dire. "Fantasima, fantasima, che dí e notte vai, se a coda ritta ci venisti, a coda ritta te n'andrai. Tristi con tristi, in mal'ora ci venisti e me coglier ci credesti e 'ngannato ci remanesti. Amen".

The Deceived

PASQUELLA: Good then, let's.... *(Opens the door)* No wait, heavens, my hens are all right here. Wait up, Giglio. No, stand over there. If they get out, we'll be all day chasing them.

GIGLIO: Well, hurry then.

PASQUELLA: All right, chickies, sweet little chickies, go back, go back. Shoo. Shoo. You can break your little necks for all I care. Oh no, they're getting out, some of them. Do something! Catch them, Giglio!

GIGLIO: I don't see a damned one, hens, cocks, where are they?

PASQUELLA: Don't you see 'em? Over here. Step back a bit so I can close the door and get them caged up where they should be.

GIGLIO: What are you doing in there? Did you just lock the door?

PASQUELLA: *(From inside)* Yep, the roosters won't be able to open it.

GIGLIO: Open right now before someone happens along to mess everything up.

PASQUELLA: Let them happen along because nothing's opening up around here.

GIGLIO: *(Aside)* Dang blast her, the bitch. — So how come you aren't going to open up?

PASQUELLA: Dearest Giglio, it's going to take me quite a while to go through a rosary this long, so you can go away for the evening. Oh, and I almost forgot that other prayer I have to say.

GIGLIO: Nonsense and piffle. Prayer and rosary?

PASQUELLA: Yes, prayer. I can teach it to you if you want. It's a really good one: "Phantom, phantom, wandering through all day all night, coming at me bolt upright. Then bolt upright you'll take your leave, as well as take your evil sprite. Possess me now you might have thought, but you're deceived, by a very long shot. Amen."[68]

GIGLIO: Io no intendo à esta vostra orazione. Se non volite aprire, renditemi mio rosario, que io me irò con Dios. Voto allos santos martilogios que esta vieia alcahueta, disdicciada, vellacca ingagnommi. Madonna Pasquella, aprite; presto, per vostra vida.

PASQUELLA: "Che fa lo mio amor ch'egli non viene? L'amor d'un'altra donna me lo tiene". Meschina a me!

GIGLIO: E que! Non faze, donna Pasquella, que à qui sta sperando que gli apriate.

PASQUELLA: "Non ti posso servir, signor mio caro". Oimè!

GIGLIO: Aze musiga esta male avventurada. Ya non se accuerda que à qui sto. Daré colpo in esta puerta, voto à Dios. Tic, tac, tic, toc.

PASQUELLA: Chi è là?

GIGLIO: Vostro figliuolo.

PASQUELLA: Che volete? Il padron non è in casa. Bisogna che si gli dica niente?

GIGLIO: Una parabla.

PASQUELLA: Aspetate, ché non può stare a venire.

GIGLIO: Aprite, que aspettarò drento. Partióse. Do renniego de todo el mondo, se non bruso toda esta posada, se non mi rende mio rosario. Tic, tic, toc.

PASQUELLA: Olà! Ch'è da esser? Voi avete una poca discrezione, perdonatemi. Chi voi sète? Oh! Par che voi vogliate spezzar questa porta.

GIGLIO: Voto à Dios e a santa Letania che anco la brusciarò, se non mi rendide mio rosario.

PASQUELLA: Cercatevene pure altrove; ché in su l'orto non ce ne abbiam, de' rosai.

GIGLIO: Non dico se non mis paternostros.

GIGLIO: That doesn't make any sense. If you're not opening the door, I'll be off, but not without my rosary. *(Aside)* By all the martyrs good and bad, if this yammering witch has set me up. — Lady Pasquella, if you want to go on living, you'd better open this door.

PASQUELLA: *(In song)* "Why is my beloved not here yet? Another love is keeping him." Oimè!

GIGLIO: Listen, Lady Pasquella, stop saying that. I'm right here waiting to enter.

PASQUELLA: *(Still singing)* "Lordling mine, I can't be yours," alas.

GIGLIO: *(Aside)* Damned female and her bloody songs. She's already forgotten I'm out here. Well for God's sake I'll have to knock. *(Knock, knock)*

PASQUELLA: Who's there?

GIGLIO: Your boy.

PASQUELLA: What do you want? The master's not at home right now. Have you a message for him?

GIGLIO: A very brief one.

PASQUELLA: Just hold on. He'll be along any moment.

GIGLIO: I'd prefer to wait inside. Can you please open the door? *(Aside)* She better fork over that rosary, or damn the world if I don't burn the whole place to the ground. *(Knock, knock, knock)*

PASQUELLA: Coming! Who's out there? Could you take it a bit easier? I'm sorry, but do I know you? Hey there, what are you trying to do, bust the door?

GIGLIO: Bust it or burn it down by God and Saint Scythian if you don't hand over the rosary.

PASQUELLA: Check somewhere else. No rosemary in our garden this year.

GIGLIO: All I do is say my Paternosters.

PASQUELLA: Che n'ho io a fare, se voi non dite se non i vostri paternostri? Vorreste forse ch'io diventasse una marrana come voi e imparasse a dirgli ancor io?

GIGLIO: Oh reniego de la putta, vellacca! Aun me dizeis marrano?

PASQUELLA: Sai? Se tu non ti levi d'intorno a l'uscio, ti bagnarò.

GIGLIO: Ecciade l'agua; el fuogo porrò io a esta puerta. Malditta sea! Todo me ha mollado, esta putta, vellacca, viegia alcahueta, male aventurada! Oh reniego de todos los frailes!

PASQUELLA: Bagna'vi? Non me ne avviddi. Ma ecco il padrone. Se volete niente, domandatelo a lui e non mi rompete piú il capo.

GIGLIO: Se à qui me truova esto vieio, mil palos non mi mancan. Meior es de fuir.

Scena settima

GHERARDO *e* PASQUELLA.

GHERARDO: Che facevi tu, intorno a l'uscio, di quello spagnuolo? Che hai tu da far con lui?

PASQUELLA: Domandava non so che rosaio. Io, per me, non l'ho mai inteso.

GHERARDO: Oh! Tu hai fatto ben quel ch'io ti dissi! Ho cosí voglia di romperti l'ossa.

PASQUELLA: Perché?

GHERARDO: Perché hai lasciato partir Lelia? Non ti diss'io che tu non gli aprisse?

PASQUELLA: Quando partí? non è ella in camera?

GHERARDO: È il malan che Dio ti dia.

PASQUELLA: So che la v'è, io.

The Deceived

PASQUELLA: What's it got to do with me if you say your Paternosters? Do you want me to become a Marrano like you and learn to recite them myself?[69]

GIGLIO: *(Aside)* So now she calls me a Marrano! Damn the slut and slanderer.

PASQUELLA: Know what? If you don't buzz off you're going to get soaked.

GIGLIO: Throw the water. I'm about to incinerate this door. *(She dumps the water.)* Damnation, I'm drowned by this craven whore of a witch, the old vixen! Damn all the friars.

PASQUELLA: O sorry, did I get you wet? I didn't see you out there. Ah, and there's the master, so now you can deal with him and leave me alone.

GIGLIO: If the old buzzard finds me here, I might get thrashed. I'd better skedaddle.

Scene 7

GHERARDO *and* PASQUELLA.

GHERARDO: What's with that Spaniard here at our door? What's going on with him?

PASQUELLA: Oh, something about rosemary and a garden, but I wasn't paying much attention.

GHERARDO: So you went ahead and did exactly what I thought you would, and now I'm going to break your neck.

PASQUELLA: What for?

GHERARDO: For letting Lelia get away. Didn't I expressly order you not to?

PASQUELLA: Why are you saying "get away"? She's right here in the bedroom, isn't she?

GHERARDO: Blazing malediction on you.

PASQUELLA: She's in there. I'm darned sure of that.

GHERARDO: So che la non v'è; ché l'ho lasciata in casa di Clemenzia sua balia.

PASQUELLA: Non l'ho io testé lasciata in camara, in ginocchio, che infilzavano i paternostri?

GHERARDO: Forse è tornata prima di me.

PASQUELLA: Dico che non s'è partita, ch'io sappi. La camara è pur stata serrata.

GHERARDO: Dov'è la chiave?

PASQUELLA: Eccola.

GHERARDO: Dammela: ché, se non v'è, ti vo' rompere l'ossa.

PASQUELLA: E, se la v'è, daretemene una camiscia?

GHERARDO: Son contento.

PASQUELLA: Lasciate aprire a me.

GHERARDO: No; voglio aprir io: tu trovaresti qualche scusa.

PASQUELLA: Oh! Io ho la gran paura che non gli truovi a' ferri. Pure, ha un pezzo ch'io gli lasciai.

Scena ottava

FLAMMINIO, PASQUELLA e GHERARDO.

FLAMMINIO: Pasquella, quant'è che 'l mio Fabio non fu da voi?

PASQUELLA: Perché?

FLAMMINIO: Perché gli è un traditore; e io lo gastigarò. E, poi ch'Isabella ha lasciato me per lui, se l'arà come merita. Oh che bella lode d'una gentildonna par sua, innamorarsi d'un ragazzo!

PASQUELLA: Uh! Non dite cotesto, ché le carezze ch'ella gli fa gli le fa per amor vostro.

The Deceived

GHERARDO: And I know she's not, because I was with her a minute ago at Clemenzia's place.

PASQUELLA: Yeah, well last time I saw her she was on her knees with Isabella reciting a bunch of Paternosters.

GHERARDO: Maybe she's beaten me back home.

PASQUELLA: I'm telling you she never left. The room's still locked and always has been.

GHERARDO: What happened to the key?

PASQUELLA: It's right here.

GHERARDO: Pass it over, and if she's not in there, you'd better watch your neck bone.

PASQUELLA: And if she's in there, do I get a new blouse out of the deal?

GHERARDO: Sure, why not?

PASQUELLA: Here, I'll open the door.

GHERARDO: Nah, I'll do it myself. You'd just make excuses.

PASQUELLA: Oh boy, if he barges in on them still making nooky, but that was a while ago.

Scene 8

FLAMMINIO, PASQUELLA *and* GHERARDO.

FLAMMINIO: Say, Pasquella, how long's it been since Fabio left?

PASQUELLA: Why?

FLAMMINIO: He's a traitor, that's why, and I'm out to get him. Isabella's dumped me for him and she's getting what's coming to her, too. Nice thing this is, for a girl of the nobility to fall in with a lackey.

PASQUELLA: Don't get all hot and bothered about it. So she gave him some hugs. Just signs of how much she really loves you.

FLAMMINIO: Digli che ancora, un dí, se ne pentirà. A lui, com'io lo truovo (i' porto questo coltello in mano a posta), gli vo' tagliar le labbra, l'orecchie e cavargli un occhio; e metter ogni cosa in un piatto; e poi mandarglielo a donar. Vo' che la si sfami di baciarlo.

PASQUELLA: Eh sí! Mentre che 'l cane abbaia, il lupo si pasce.

FLAMMINIO: Tu il vedrai.

GHERARDO: Oimè! A questo modo son giontato io? a questo modo, eh? Misero a me! Quel traditor di Virginio, traditoraccio! M'ha pure scorto per un montone. Che farò io?

PASQUELLA: Che avete, padrone?

GHERARDO: Che ho, ah? Chi è colui che è con mia figliuola?

PASQUELLA: Oh! Nol sapete voi? non è la cítola di Virginio?

GHERARDO: Cítola, eh? Cítola, che farà fare a mia figliuola de' cítoli, dolente a me!

PASQUELLA: Eh! non dite coteste parolacce! Che cos'è? non è Lelia?

GHERARDO: Dico che gli è un maschio.

PASQUELLA: Eh, non è vero! Che ne sapete voi?

GHERARDO: L'ho veduto con questi occhi.

PASQUELLA: Come?

GHERARDO: Adosso alla mia figliuola, trist'a me!

PASQUELLA: Eh! che dovevano scherzare!

GHERARDO: È ben che scherzavano.

PASQUELLA: Avete veduto che sia maschio?

GHERARDO: Sí, dico: ché, aprendo l'uscio a un tratto, egli s'era spogliato in giubbone e non ebbe tempo a coprirsi.

The Deceived

FLAMMINIO: Well, tell her that she'll regret it someday. And as for him, see this knife here in my hand? Just let him know that I'm about to slice off his lips, sever his ears, and gouge out an eye to serve to the lady on a trencher. Then she can kiss him all she wants.

PASQUELLA: *(Aside)* How the world turns. "While the dogs bark, the wolf fills its paunch."

FLAMMINIO: You'll see. *(Exits in a huff)*

GHERARDO: *(Enters in anger)* For the love of God, is this the way things turn out? Everything's come to an end and I'm screwed. Virginio, that double-crosser, that sneaky bastard, making a jerk out of me. My God, there must be something to do.

PASQUELLA: What's the matter, sir?

GHERARDO: What's the matter? Who's that guy in there with my daughter?

PASQUELLA: You don't know yet? Isn't she Virginio's sweet girl child?

GHERARDO: If that's a girl child, it's one that will set my girl child up with one of her own. This is bloody wretched.

PASQUELLA: No, don't talk like that. You say it's not Lelia?

GHERARDO: Like I said, it's all masculine.

PASQUELLA: I can hardly believe that. You've got to be wrong.

GHERARDO: I've got my own eyes to see with.

PASQUELLA: What's he doing there?

GHERARDO: Lying on top of my daughter for a start.

PASQUELLA: They're just kids horsing around.

GHERARDO: Didn't look like horsing around to me.

PASQUELLA: You sure about all this?

GHERARDO: Here's how it was. I open up the door, quick like that, and he's there with just a shirt on, and no time to cover his bum.

PASQUELLA: Vedeste voi ogni cosa? Eh! Mirate che gli è femina.

GHERARDO: Io dico che gli è maschio e bastarebbe a far due maschi.

PASQUELLA: Che dice Isabella?

GHERARDO: Che vuo' tu ch'ella dica? Svergognato a me!

PASQUELLA: Ché non lasciate andar or quel giovine? Che ne volete fare?

GHERARDO: Che ne vo' fare? Accusarlo al governatore; e farollo gastigare.

PASQUELLA: O forse fuggirà.

GHERARDO: E io l'ho rinserrato drento. Ma ecco Virginio. Apponto non volevo altro.

Scena nona

PEDANTE, VIRGINIO e GHERARDO.

PEDANTE: Io mi maraviglio, per certo, che già non sia tornato a l'ostaria; e non so che me ne dire.

VIRGINIO: Aveva arme?

PEDANTE: Credo de sí.

VIRGINIO: Costui sarà stato preso: ché abbiamo un podestà che scorticarebbe li cimici.

PEDANTE: Io non credo però che a' forestieri si faccia queste scortesie.

GHERARDO: Addio, Virginio. Questo è atto da uomo da bene? questa è cosa convenevole a uno amico? questo è il parentado che volevi far con esso me? chi t'hai pensato di gabbare? credi ch'io sia per comportarla? Mi vien voglia...

VIRGINIO: Di che cosa ti lamenti di me, Gherardo? che t'ho io fatto? Io non cercai mai di far parentado teco. Tu me

The Deceived

PASQUELLA: Are you sure you saw things right? It still could have been a girl.

GHERARDO: It was a male, all right, with gear enough for two.

PASQUELLA: And Isabella, what'd she say?

GHERARDO: What do you think she'd say? To me, nothing but impudence.

PASQUELLA: So what are you going to do with him? Maybe you should just turn him out.

GHERARDO: I've got other plans. I'm hauling him before the magistrates to have him sentenced.

PASQUELLA: Unless he gets away.

GHERARDO: Not possible. I locked him in again. Ah, there's Virginio, the very man I'm gunning for.

Scene 9

PIERO, VIRGINIO, *and* GHERARDO.

PIERO: I'm amazed he's not back at the inn by now. I'm at a loss for words.

VIRGINIO: Did he have his weapon?

PIERO: As far as I know.

VIRGINIO: Well, maybe he's been arrested for that. And our chief magistrate can skin a bug.

PIERO: They wouldn't give a foreigner such a bad time.

GHERARDO: *(Entering)* Hey there, Virginio, greetings. You're hardly the gentleman I took you for. Why would you do this to a friend? It's not the way to become any kin of mine. Who did you figure you're messing with, anyway? Or that I wouldn't care? Well, here's what's coming to....

VIRGINIO: Why are you up in arms with me, Gherardo? What have I done? It wasn't my idea to become your kin. It's

n'hai rotto il capo uno anno. Ora, se non ti piace, non vada avanti.

GHERARDO: Anco hai ardimento di rispondere, come s'io fusse un beccone? Traditoraccio, giontatore, barro, mariuolo! Ma il governatore saprà ogni cosa.

VIRGINIO: Gherardo, coteste parole non pertengono a un par tuo e massimamente con me.

GHERARDO: Anco non vuol ch'io mi lamenti, questo tristo! Sei diventato superbo perché hai ritrovato tuo figliuolo, eh?

VIRGINIO: Tristo se' tu.

GHERARDO: Oh Dio! Perché non son giovine com'io era? ch'io ne farei pezzi, del fatto tuo.

VIRGINIO: Puossi intender quel che tu vuoi dire o no?

GHERARDO: Sfacciato!

VIRGINIO: Io ho troppo pazienzia.

GHERARDO: Ladro!

VIRGINIO: Falsario!

GHERARDO: Menti per la gola. Aspetta!

VIRGINIO: Aspetto.

PEDANTE: Ah gentiluomo! Che pazzia è questa?

GHERARDO: Non mi tenete.

PEDANTE: E voi, messer, mettetevi la veste.

VIRGINIO: Con chi si pensa avere a fare? Rendemi la mia figliuola.

GHERARDO: Scannarò te e lei.

The Deceived

you who's been going on about it for over a year. So if you're changing thoughts in the matter, we can drop the whole thing.

GHERARDO: That takes real gumption to make out I'm the offender. You're just a slithering cheat, a swindler, a blackguard, and a conman. Wait'll the courts get through with you.

VIRGINIO: What a way to talk to me, Gherardo. It's unbecoming in a man of your class.

GHERARDO: I can't even tell things as they are to this wicked geezer. All high and mighty because your son's back, is that it?

VIRGINIO: Talk about wicked.

GHERARDO: Crap! If I were in my prime again, you'd be ribbons.

VIRGINIO: Any way of being filled in on what the hell you're talking about?

GHERARDO: Insolence!

VIRGINIO: I have too much patience.

GHERARDO: Thief!

VIRGINIO: Counterfeiter.

GHERARDO: You lie through your teeth. And where are you going?

VIRGINIO: I'm not going anywhere.

PIERO: *(Intercedes as Gherardo grows more threatening)* Hey, my friend, don't go berserk.

GHERARDO: Unhand me.

PIERO: You should get back into your jacket, sir.

VIRGINIO: Have you forgotten who I am? I'll have my daughter back.

GHERARDO: You'll both have your throats slashed. *(Exits back into his house)*

PEDANTE: Che cosa ha da far questo gentiluomo con esso voi?

VIRGINIO: Non so, io; se non che, poco fa, gli messi Lelia mia figliuola in casa, ché la voleva per moglie. Ora voi vedete. E temo non gli facci dispiacere.

PEDANTE: Ah, ah, gentiluomo! Non si vuole con l'arme! Con l'arme?

GHERARDO: Lasciatemi!

PEDANTE: Che differenzia è la vostra?

GHERARDO: Questo traditore m'ha disfatto.

PEDANTE: Come?

GHERARDO: S'io non lo taglio a pezzi, s'io non lo squarto con questa ronca...

PEDANTE: Ditemi, di grazia, come la cosa sta.

GHERARDO: Entriamo in casa, poi che il traditore s'è fuggito, ch'io vi contarò ogni cosa. Non sète voi il maestro di suo figliuolo, che veniste a l'ostaria con noi?

PEDANTE: Sí, sono.

GHERARDO: Entrate.

PEDANTE: Sopra la fede vostra?

GHERARDO: Oh sí!

ATTO QUINTO

Scena prima

VIRGINIO, STRAGUALCIA, SCATIZZA, GHERARDO *e* PEDANTE.

VIRGINIO: Venite con me quanti voi sète. Stragualcia, vien tu ancora.

The Deceived

PIERO: What's set this man off against you?

VIRGINIO: I haven't got a clue. He wanted Lelia over at his place, intending to marry her, so we took her there. Maybe that's got something to do with it. And now look how things have turned out. I'm frankly afraid for her safety.

PIERO: *(Gherardo reappears brandishing a pike.)* Whoa, my good man. We'll not have any weapons drawn. Let's have no weapons.

GHERARDO: Don't get in my way.

PIERO: What's going on here?

GHERARDO: This buzzard has wrecked my life.

PIERO: In what way?

GHERARDO: I'm going to shred him to bits. With this pike I'll quarter him and.... *(Virginio exits in haste.)*

PIERO: For God's sake, what's all this about?

GHERARDO: Now that the scoundrel has fled, we can go inside, and I'll tell you. After all, you're his son's tutor. You were with us at the inn, right?

PIERO: I was.

GHERARDO: Well then, come inside.

PIERO: Do you pledge my safety?

GHERARDO: On my word, trust me.

Act 5

Scene 1

VIRGINIO, *dressed in mail with a shield,* STRAGUALCIA, SCATIZZA, GHERARDO, PIERO, *and* FABRIZIO.

VIRGINIO: Everybody, come along with me. That means you, Stragualcia.

STRAGUALCIA: Con l'arme o senza? Io non ho arme.

VIRGINIO: Tolle costí, in casa dell'oste, qualche arme.

SCATIZZA: Padrone, con targone bisognarebbe una lancia.

VIRGINIO: Non mi curo piú di lancia. Mi basta questo.

SCATIZZA: Questa rotella sarebbe piú galante per voi, essendo in giubbone.

VIRGINIO: No; questa copre meglio. Oh! Par che questo montone m'abbia trovato a furare. Ho paura che 'l non abbia ammazzata quella povera figliuola.

STRAGUALCIA: Questa è buona arme, padrone. Io lo voglio infilzare con questo spedone come un beccafico.

SCATIZZA: Oh! Che vuoi tu far dell'arrosto?

STRAGUALCIA: Son pratico in campo; e so che, la prima cosa, bisogna far provision di vettovaglia.

SCATIZZA: Oh! Cotesto fiasco perché?

STRAGUALCIA: Per rinfrescare i soldati, se alla prima battaglia fusser ributtati indrieto.

SCATIZZA: Questo mi piace; ché ei avverrà.

STRAGUALCIA: Volete che, insieme insieme, infilzi il vecchio e la figliuola, i famegli, la casa e tutti come fegatelli? Al vecchio caccierò lo spedone in culo e faroglielo uscir per gli occhi; gli altri tutti a traverso come tordi.

VIRGINIO: La casa è aperta. Costoro aran fatto qualche imboscata.

STRAGUALCIA: Imboscata? Mal va. Io ho piú paura del legname che delle spade. Ma ecco il maestro che esce fuora.

PEDANTE: Lasciate fare a me, ch'io vi do la cosa per acconcia, messer Gherardo.

STRAGUALCIA: With or without weapons, because I haven't got any.

VIRGINIO: Go into the inn and get some.

SCATIZZA: Know something, master. Looking at that big shield of yours, you need a lance too.

VIRGINIO: I don't need one. This is enough gear already.

SCATIZZA: Here, this smaller round shield would look more chivalric, now that you're into your doublet.

VIRGINIO: No, I've got more protection with this. Now for this booby who thinks I'm trying to cheat him. He may have already killed my poor girl.

STRAGUALCIA: *(Returning from the inn)* This here's the perfect weapon, boss. With this spit I can run him through like a woodcock.

SCATIZZA: Sure, but what's the roast for?

STRAGUALCIA: I'm familiar with the field-camp. First thing you look after is the commissariat.

SCATIZZA: What's the wine for, then?

STRAGUALCIA: If we lose the first sally, we refresh the forces.

SCATIZZA: Good plan considering the likelihood.

STRAGUALCIA: So running them all through, is that what you're after? The old guy, the daughter, servants, the whole flock of them, like a bunch of chicken livers on a roasting fire? The old man up the arse and out his eyes, and the others lined up like thrushes, side-by-side?

VIRGINIO: Now the door's open. You think they're up to some kind of trick?

STRAGUALCIA: Trick, stick, switch, and here comes the schoolmaster. A wooden stick scares me worse than swords.

PIERO: *(Talking to Gherardo, still inside the inn)* Let me take care of this. — I'll cut a peace deal for you, Mister Gherardo.

STRAGUALCIA: Guardatevi, padrone: ché questo maestro si potrebbe essere ribellato e accordato coi nimici; ché pochi si trovan de' suo' pari che tenghino il fermo. Volete ch'io cominci a infilzarlo e ch'io dica "e uno"?

PEDANTE: Messer Virginio, padrone, perché queste arme?

STRAGUALCIA: Ah! ah! Non tel dissi io?

VIRGINIO: Che è della mia figliuola? Díemela, ch'io la vo' menare a casa mia. E voi avete trovato Fabrizio?

PEDANTE: Sí, ho.

VIRGINIO: Dov'è?

PEDANTE: Qui dentro, che ha tolto una bellissima moglie, se ne sète contento.

VIRGINIO: Moglie, eh? e chi?

STRAGUALCIA: Molto presto! Ricco, ricco!

PEDANTE: Questa bella e gentil figliuola di Gherardo.

VIRGINIO: Oh! Gherardo, testé, mi voleva amazzare.

PEDANTE: Rem omnem a principio audies. Entriamo in casa, ché saprete il tutto. Messer Gherardo, venite fuora.

GHERARDO: O Virginio, il piú strano caso che fusse mai al mondo! Entra.

STRAGUALCIA: Infilzolo? Ma gli è carne da tinello.

GHERARDO: Fa' metter giú queste arme, ché gli è cosa da ridere.

VIRGINIO: Follo sicuramente?

PEDANTE: Sicuramente, sopra di me.

VIRGINIO: Orsú! Andate a casa, voi altri, e ponete giú l'armi e portatemi la mia veste.

STRAGUALCIA: Check that out, boss. It's the Tutor, and it looks like he's turned coat and sided with the enemy. No loyalty to depend on from the likes of him. I could start with him, you know, run him through and shout, "first man down."

PIERO: Master Virginio, what's all this armor for?

STRAGUALCIA: So there, I told you so.

VIRGINIO: What's become of my daughter? I want her back now. She should be taken home. And has Fabrizio been found?

PIERO: He has.

VIRGINIO: So where is he?

PIERO: Inside. And he's found a handsome bride for himself, if you'll give your blessing.

VIRGINIO: A wife? Who could that possibly be?

STRAGUALCIA: *(Aside)* That was fast work. Riches, riches!

PIERO: Gherardo's daughter, so lovely and so demure.

VIRGINIO: Ho ho. Would that be the same Gherardo who's out to assassinate me?

PIERO: *Rem omnem a principio audies.* Come on inside and get the whole story. Messer Gherardo, you can come out now.

GHERARDO: Well, well, Virginio, come in and hear the weirdest story ever.

STRAGUALCIA: *(Aside)* I could still put him on the spit, but his meat's not worth the roasting.

GHERARDO: Tell them to drop their weapons. They look ludicrous.

VIRGINIO: Do you think I really should?

PIERO: You can trust him, I give you my word.

VIRGINIO: So be it. Back home everyone. Depose your arms and bring me my coat.

PEDANTE: Fabrizio, viene a conoscer tuo padre.

VIRGINIO: Oh! Questa non è Lelia?

PEDANTE: No; questo è Fabrizio.

VIRGINIO: O figliuol mio!

FABRIZIO: O padre, tanto da me desiderato!

VIRGINIO: Figliuol mio, quanto t'ho pianto!

GHERARDO: In casa, in casa, ché tu sappia il tutto. E piú ti dico, che tua figliuola è in casa di Clemenzia sua balia.

VIRGINIO: O Dio, quante grazie ti rendo!

Scena seconda

CRIVELLO, FLAMMINIO e CLEMENZIA *balia*.

CRIVELLO: Io l'ho veduto in casa di Clemenzia balia con questi occhi e udito con questi orecchi.

FLAMMINIO: Guarda che fusse Fabio.

CRIVELLO: Credete ch'io nol conoscesse?

FLAMMINIO: Andiam là. S'io 'l truovo...

CRIVELLO: Voi guastarete ogni cosa. Abbiate pazienzia fino ch'egli esca fuore.

FLAMMINIO: E' nol farebbe Iddio ch'io avessi piú pazienzia.

CRIVELLO: Voi guastarete la torta.

FLAMMINIO: Io mi guasti. Tic, toc, toc.

CLEMEZIA: Chi è?

FLAMMINIO: Un tuo amico. Viene un poco giú.

CLEMEZIA: Oh! Che volete, messer Flamminio?

FLAMMINIO: Apre, ché tel dirò.

CLEMEZIA: Aspettate, ch'io scendo.

FLAMMINIO: Com'ell'ha aperto l'uscio, entra dentro; e mira se

The Deceived

PIERO: Come out, Fabrizio, and salute your father. *(The boy appears.)*

VIRGINIO: But this is Lelia, no?

PIERO: No, this is Fabrizio.

VIRGINIO: O, my dearest son!

FABRIZIO: O, my father, how long I've been looking for you.

VIRGINIO: My dear, dear boy, how long I've wept for you.

GHERARDO: Well, enter, enter, and hear everything that's happened. And I might add that Lelia is safe with her nursemaid, Clemenzia, at her place.

VIRGINIO: To God on high goes all the praise.

Scene 2

CRIVELLO, FLAMMINIO, *and* CLEMEZIA.

CRIVELLO: These eyes took sight of him and these ears took sound of him in Clemenzia's house.

FLAMMINIO: We're talking Fabio, right?

CRIVELLO: Don't I know him when I see and hear?

FLAMMINIO: Let's go, and if I find him....

CRIVELLO: You'll mess up everything. Hold on a bit till he comes out.

FLAMMINIO: That's more patience than God's got to give.

CRIVELLO: You'll rain on the party.

FLAMMINIO: Then let it pour, even on me too. *(Loudly, knock, knock, knock)*

CLEMEZIA: Who's there?

FLAMMINIO: Your friend. Come on down. Answer the door.

CLEMEZIA: Goodness! Mister Flamminio. What can I do for you?

FLAMMINIO: Open up and I'll inform you.

vi è; e chiamami.

CRIVELLO: Lasciate fare a me.

CLEMEZIA: Che dite, signor Flamminio?

FLAMMINIO: Che fai, in casa, del mio ragazzo?

CLEMEZIA: Che ragazzo? E tu dove entri, prosuntuoso? vuoi intrare in casa mia per forza?

FLAMMINIO: Clemenzia, al corpo della sagrata, intemerata, pura, se tu non mel rendi...

CLEMEZIA: Che volete ch'io vi renda?

FLAMMINIO: Il mio ragazzo che s'è fuggito in casa tua.

CLEMEZIA: In casa mia non vi è servidor nissun vostro; ma sí bene una serva.

FLAMMINIO: Clemenzia, e' non è tempo da muine. Tu mi sei stata sempre amica, ed io a te; tu m'hai fatti de' piaceri, ed io a te. Or questa è cosa che troppo importa.

CLEMEZIA: Qualche furia d'amor sarà questa. Orsú, Flamminio! Lasciatevi un poco passar la collera.

FLAMMINIO: Io dico, rendemi Fabio.

CLEMEZIA: Vel renderò.

FLAMMINIO: Basta. Fallo venir giú.

CLEMEZIA: Oh! Non tanta furia, per mia fé! ché, s'io fussi giovane e ch'io vi piacessi, non m'impacciarei mai con voi. E che è di Isabella?

FLAMMINIO: Io vorrei che la fosse squartata.

CLEMEZIA: Eh! Voi non dite da vero.

FLAMMINIO: S'io non dico da vero? Ti so dir che la m'ha chiarito!

CLEMEZIA: E sí! A voi giovinacci sta bene ogni male, ché sète piú ingrati del mondo.

CLEMEZIA: Wait till I can get down there.[70]

FLAMMINIO: *(To Crivello)* When the door opens, bolt inside, and if he's there, call me.

CRIVELLO: I can handle it.

CLEMEZIA: So what's this all about, Mister Flamminio?

FLAMMINIO: Why's my servant lad inside your house?

CLEMEZIA: No servant lads here. — And you, Crivello, you little scamp, where do you think you're going? You figure you can just barge in?

FLAMMINIO: By God's holy flesh, Clemenzia, if you don't produce....

CLEMEZIA: Produce what?

FLAMMINIO: My boy. You're hiding him in there.

CLEMEZIA: Maidservant, maybe. Boyservant, no.

FLAMMINIO: Not the right time for joshing, Clemenzia. You're a long-time friend. We've helped each other a lot. This is an important matter.

CLEMEZIA: Love mania. That must be it. You've got to calm yourself, Flamminio. Calm, calm yourself.

FLAMMINIO: I repeat, I want Fabio back.

CLEMEZIA: Then he'll be right out.

FLAMMINIO: That's all I'm after. Just send him down.

CLEMEZIA: God in the skies, calm yourself. You know what? If I...if I were young and you fancied me, I wouldn't give you a second glance. So then, what about Isabella?

FLAMMINIO: I could mince her into bits.

CLEMEZIA: Come on, you're kidding.

FLAMMINIO: You think I'm kidding? She's made things plain as day to me, I can tell you that.

CLEMEZIA: Not surprised. Frisky bullocks like you need some checking now and again, because of all the world's creatures, you're the least grateful.

FLAMMINIO: Questo non dir per me: ch'ogni altro vizio mi si potrebbe forse provare; ma questo dell'essere ingrato, no, ché piú mi dispiace che ad uom che viva.

CLEMEZIA: Io non lo dico per voi. Ma è stata in questa terra una giovane che, accorgendosi d'esser mirata da un cavaliere par vostro modanese, s'invaghí tanto di lui che la non vedeva piú qua né piú là che quanto era longo.

FLAMMINIO: Beato lui! felice lui! Questo non potrò già dir io.

CLEMEZIA: Accadde che 'l padre mandò questa povera giovane innamorata fuor di Modena. E pianse, nel partir, tanto che fu maraviglia, temendo ch'egli non si scordasse di lei. Il qual, subito, ne riprese un'altra, come se la prima mai non avesse veduta.

FLAMMINIO: Io dico che costui non può esser cavaliere; anzi, è un traditore.

CLEMEZIA: Ascolta: c'è peggio. Tornando, ivi a pochi mesi, la giovane e trovando che 'l suo amante amava altri e da quella tale egli era poco amato, per fargli servizio, abbandonò la casa, suo padre e pose in pericolo l'onore; e, vestita da famiglio, s'acconciò con quel suo amante per servitore.

FLAMMINIO: È accaduto in Modena questo caso?

CLEMEZIA: E voi conoscete l'uno e l'altro.

FLAMMINIO: Io vorrei piú presto esser questo aventurato amante che esser signor di Milano.

CLEMEZIA: E che piú? Questo suo amante, non la conoscendo, l'adoperò per mezzana tra quella sua innamorata e lui; e questa poveretta, per fargli piacere, s'arrecò a fare ogni cosa.

FLAMMINIO: Oh virtuosa donna! oh fermo amore! cosa veramente da porre in esempio a' secoli che verranno! Perché non è avvenuto a me un tal caso?

CLEMEZIA: Eh! In ogni modo, voi non lasciareste Isabella.

The Deceived

FLAMMINIO: How can you say that? Anything else, but ungrateful, never. No one hates ingratitude more than I do.

CLEMEZIA: Here's a story, and it's not about you. Once there was a maiden living here in Modena who was beloved by a gentleman — a man of your social stature — and the girl fell for him head over heels and lost touch with everything else.

FLAMMINIO: Lucky chap. He must have been elated, which I can't say for myself right now.

CLEMEZIA: But then the girl's father sent the poor besotted thing away from the city, despite her infatuation. It was amazing to see her tears, fearful as she was of being forgotten. Yet that's what he did — took another sweetheart — as though she'd never existed.

FLAMMINIO: That's no gentleman, I say. He's worse than a renegade.

CLEMEZIA: But that's not the end. After a few months, the maiden returned and found her lover chasing after a girl who didn't love him. So she dressed herself up as a page, left her father and, to the peril of her honor, took a servant's position in her beloved's household.

FLAMMINIO: Here in Modena, this happened?

CLEMEZIA: Not only that, but you knew them both.

FLAMMINIO: To be this beloved, I'd trade away the lordship of Milan.

CLEMEZIA: You want to hear what happened next? This man she loved never caught on, but turned her into a messenger to his new sweetheart. So to please him, the poor thing did all his bidding.

FLAMMINIO: How wonderfully good, how faithful this girl is. Her love is a model for future times. Why couldn't I have been so lucky?

CLEMEZIA: So you say, but you couldn't give up Isabella for that!

FLAMMINIO: Io lasciarei, quasi che non t'ho detto Cristo, per una tale. E pregoti, Clemenzia, che tu mi facci conoscer chi è costei.

CLEMEZIA: Son contenta. Ma io voglio che voi mi diciate prima, sopra alla fede vostra e da gentiluomo, se tal caso fusse avvenuto a voi, quello che voi fareste a quella povera giovane e se voi la cacciareste, quando voi sapesse quello che la v'ha fatto, se l'uccidereste o se la giudicareste degna di qualche premio.

FLAMMINIO: Io ti giuro, per la virtú di quel sole che tu vedi in cielo, e ch'io non possa mai comparire dove sien gentiluomini e cavalieri par miei, s'io non togliesse prima per moglie questa tale, ancor che fusse brutta, ancor che la fusse povera, ancor che la non fusse nobile, che la figliuola del duca di Ferrara.

CLEMEZIA: Questa è una gran cosa. E cosí mi giurate?

FLAMMINIO: Cosí ti giuro; e cosí farei.

CLEMEZIA: Tu sia testimonio.

CRIVELLO: Io ho inteso; e so ch'egli il farebbe.

CLEMEZIA: Ora io ti vo' far conoscer chi è questa donna e chi è quel cavaliere. Fabio! o Fabio! Vien giú al signor tuo che ti domanda.

FLAMMINIO: Che ti par, Crivello? Parti ch'io amazzi questo traditore o no? Egli è pure un buon servitore.

CRIVELLO: Oh! Io mi maravigliavo ben, io! Sarà pur vero quello ch'io mi pensavo. Orsú! Perdonategli: che volete fare? In ogni modo, questa chiappola d'Isabella non vi volse mai bene.

FLAMMINIO: Tu dici il vero.

The Deceived

FLAMMINIO: I could give up Christ Himself for a girl like that — almost. So Clemenzia, who is this girl?

CLEMEZIA: I'll tell you, but first you have to tell me, on the sworn oath of a gentleman, how you'd react to such a maiden if this had happened to you? Once you found out what she'd done, would you kick her out? Or kill her outright? Or would you find her worthy of reward?

FLAMMINIO: I swear by the sun's golden rays in the heavens I'd have her for my wife upon pain of eternal exile from the company of knights and gentlemen. However hideous she might be, however poor or low, I would take her above the Duke of Ferrara's daughter.

CLEMEZIA: Quite the oath, that. You'd honor it as stated?

FLAMMINIO: I've pronounced it and I'd keep it.

CLEMEZIA: *(To Crivello)* You're my witness.

CRIVELLO: I heard him speak and I vouch for his word.

CLEMEZIA: Then it's time to present you to this girl and her gentleman.[71] Fabio, hello, Fabio. Come down here. Your master's here for you.

FLAMMINIO: So what do you make out of all this, Crivello? Should I butcher the little tramp? He's a good servant, after all.

CRIVELLO: I was wondering, I was, and what I thought must be true. Might as well forgive him. Not much else to do about it. As for that Isabella, the hussy never loved you from the start.

FLAMMINIO: Too true, I'm afraid.

The Intronati of Siena

Scena terza

PASQUELLA, CLEMENZIA, FLAMMINIO, LELIA *da femina e* CRIVELLO.

PASQUELLA: Lasciate fare a me: ché gli dirò quanto me avete detto, ché ho inteso.

CLEMEZIA: Questo è, messer Flamminio, il vostro Fabio. Miratel bene: conoscetelo? Voi vi maravigliate? E questa medesima è quella sí fedele e sí costante innamorata giovane di chi v'ho detto. Guardatela bene, se la riconoscete o no. Voi sète ammutito, Flamminio? Oh! Che vuol dire? E voi sète quel che sí poco apprezza l'amor della donna sua. E questo è la verità. Non pensate d'essere ingannato. Conoscete se io vi dico il vero. Ora attenetemi la promessa o ch'io vi chiamarò in steccato per mancatore.

FLAMMINIO: Io non credo che fusse mai al mondo il piú bello inganno di questo. È possibile ch'io sia stato sí cieco ch'io non l'abbi mai conosciuta?

CRIVELLO: Chi è stato piú cieco di me che ho voluto mille volte chiarirmene? Che maladetto sia! Oh! Ch'io son stato il bel da poco!

PASQUELLA: Clemenzia, dice Virginio che tu venga adesso adesso a casa nostra perché gli ha dato moglie a Fabrizio suo figliuolo che è tornato oggi; e bisogna che tu vada a casa per metterla in ordine, ché tu sai che non vi sono altre donne.

CLEMEZIA: Come moglie? E chi gli ha data?

PASQUELLA: Isabella, figliuola di Gherardo mio padrone.

FLAMMINIO: Chi? Isabella di Gherardo Foiani tuo padrone o pure un'altra?

PASQUELLA: Un'altra? Dico lei. Flamminio, sapete bene che porco pigro non mangia mai pera marce.

The Deceived

Scene 3

PASQUELLA, CLEMEZIA, FLAMMINIO, LELIA, *back in women's clothes, and* CRIVELLO.

PASQUELLA: *(To someone inside Gherardo's house)* Let me take care of that. I'll let him know what you said and what I've managed to find out.

CLEMEZIA: *(Lelia appears at Clemenzia's door)*[72] See this boy, Mister Flamminio? It's your Fabio. Have a good look at him. You see who he is? Anything surprising? This girl before you is that very maiden I told you about — the one so faithful and true. Look closely. Do you recognize her? You're awfully quiet, Flamminio. What's that all about? You're the very one who scorned her love. It's no trick. Admit it's the truth. You're just one more of the deceived. The truth is as plain as can be. So what about your promise, or shall I haul you before the tribune as an oath breaker?

FLAMMINIO: I can't imagine a more accomplished deception. How could I have been so blind? It never once dawned on me who she was.

CRIVELLO: Me too, blind as they come. I meant to check this out for myself a hundred times, damn me, and I didn't — what a fool.

PASQUELLA: Oh, Clemenzia. Virginio told me to send you right back to our house as soon as possible because Fabrizio — this son of his who just got back today — he's already married off. And since he's got no other womenfolk about the place, he needs you to get things ready.

CLEMEZIA: He got him a wife? Who on earth?

PASQUELLA: It's Gherardo's girl, Isabella.

FLAMMINIO: Your master, Gherardo Foiani? His daughter Isabella, or another one?

PASQUELLA: Another one? No, it's her. Like they say, Flamminio, "A lazy pig never eats rotten apples."[73]

FLAMMINIO: È certo?

PASQUELLA: Certissimo. Io son stata presente a ogni cosa; io gli ho veduto dare l'anello, abbracciarsi, baciarsi insieme e farsi una gran festa. E, prima che gli desse l'anello, la padrona gli aveva dato... so ben io.

FLAMMINIO: Quanto ha che questo fu?

PASQUELLA: Adesso, adesso, adesso. Poi mi mandorno, correndo, a dirlo a Clemenzia e a chiamarla.

CLEMEZIA: Digli, Pasquella, ch'io starò poco poco a venire. Va'.

LELIA: O Dio, quanto bene insieme mi dài! Io muoio d'allegrezza.

PASQUELLA: Sta' poco, ché io ancora ho tanto da fare che guai a me! Voglio ire adesso a comprare certi lisci. Oh! Io m'ero scordata di domandarti se Lelia è qui in casa tua; ché Gherardo gli ha detto di sí.

CLEMEZIA: Ben sai che la v'è. Vuol forse maritarla a quel vecchio messer Fantasima di tuo padrone? che si doverebbe vergognare.

PASQUELLA: Tu non conosci bene il mio padrone: ché, se tu sapesse come gli è fiero, non diresti cosí, eh!

CLEMEZIA: Sí, sí; credotelo: tu 'l debbi aver provato.

PASQUELLA: Come tu hai fatto il tuo. Orsú! Io vo.

FLAMMINIO: A Gherardo la vuol maritare?

Clemenzia. Sí, trista a me! Vedi se questa povera giovane è sventurata.

FLAMMINIO: Tanto avesse egli vita quanto l'averà mai. In fine, Clemenzia, io credo che questa sia certamente volontà di Dio che abbia avuto pietà di questa virtuosa giovane e dell'anima mia; ch'ella non vada in perdizione. E

The Deceived

FLAMMINIO: Are you dead out certain?

PASQUELLA: Dead out, because I was there for the whole business, watching when he gave her the ring, when they hugged, when they kissed, and when they celebrated. And even before the ring business, she let him...nevermind, I'm dead out certain.

FLAMMINIO: How long ago was all this going on?

PASQUELLA: Right now, it's happening now. They just sent me here on the double to fetch Clemenzia.

CLEMEZIA: You can return right away. Tell them I'll be there in a minute.

LELIA: *(Aside)* Thanks be to You, O Lord, for working everything out. I'm so ecstatic I could die.

PASQUELLA: Don't be too long about it. I'm going in all directions trying to get everything done. I need some cosmetics from the shop. Right, and I forgot to find out if Lelia's at your place, because Gherardo still wants to marry her.

CLEMEZIA: Of course she's here. You know that. Can you really imagine her married off to that ghostly master of yours? Has he got no shame?

PASQUELLA: You don't know my master like I do. He can be quite the man. You bad mouth him out of ignorance.

CLEMEZIA: No, I quite believe you. I can't imagine you haven't tried him out for yourself.

PASQUELLA: Sure, just like you've tested your own master. But listen, I've got to go.

FLAMMINIO: She's going to be hitched to Gherardo?

CLEMEZIA: So it would seem, to my utter grief. Ill-fated thing, this poor girl.

FLAMMINIO: May he live long enough never to have her! You know what I deeply believe, Clemenzia? That this is the will of God — that His mercy has been granted upon this virtuous maiden and upon my own soul that

però, madonna Lelia, quando voi ve ne contentiate, io non voglio altra moglie che voi; e promettovi, a fé di cavaliere, che, non avendo voi, non son mai per pigliar altra.

LELIA: Flamminio, voi mi sète signore e ben sapete, quel ch'io ho fatto, per quel ch'io l'ho fatto; ch'io non ho avuto mai altro desiderio che questo.

FLAMMINIO: Ben l'avete mostrato. E perdonatemi, se qualche dispiacere v'ho io fatto, non conoscendovi, perch'io ne son pentitissimo e accorgomi dell'error mio.

LELIA: Non potreste voi, signor Flamminio, aver fatta mai cosa che a me non fusse contento.

FLAMMINIO: Clemenzia, io non voglio aspettare altro tempo, ché qualche disgrazia non m'intorbidasse questa ventura. Io la vo' sposare adesso, se gli è contenta.

LELIA: Contentissima.

CRIVELLO: Oh ringraziato sia Dio! E voi, padrone, signor Flamminio, sète contento? E avertite ch'io son notaio; e, se nol credete, eccovi il privilegio.

FLAMMINIO: Tanto contento quanto di cosa ch'io facesse già mai.

CRIVELLO: Sposatevi e poi colcatevi a vostra posta. Oh! Io non v'ho detto che voi la baciate, io.

Clemenzia. Or sapete che mi par che ci sia da fare? Che ve ne intriate in casa mia, in tanto ch'io andarò a fare intendere il tutto a Virginio e darò la mala notte a Gherardo.

FLAMMINIO: Va', di grazia; e contalo ancora a Isabella.

it not end up in perdition. So I say to you, my dearest Lelia, if you agree, I want no other wife but you. By my knighthood, I vow if you won't have me, I'll never take another.

LELIA: You are my lord, Flamminio. Surely you understand now why I acted as I did. This was my only desire.

FLAMMINIO: You've proven all that to perfection. My full apologies if, in failing to know you, I've brought you unhappiness. I'm chagrined by my error and feel the regret.

LELIA: Never could you do something, my Flamminio, that would bring me unhappiness.

FLAMMINIO: Then let's not wait another moment, Clemenzia, risking yet more misfortunes that might threaten this good fortune. If my lady is willing, I wish to marry her right now.

LELIA: I couldn't be more willing.

CRIVELLO: Thanks be to God. What about you, my Lord Flamminio? You're willing too? You never knew that I have an official diploma for this, and if you have any doubts, I happen to have it on me. See I'm a notary.[74]

FLAMMINIO: I'm willing as can be. I've never done anything as great as this in my whole life.

CRIVELLO: Then take each other's hand in marriage and off you go to bed. Hey, I didn't tell you to kiss her yet.

CLEMEZIA: So here's what I propose now. The two of you remain here at my place while I go fill in Virginio on all the news and consign Gherardo to a miserable night.

FLAMMINIO: Good, and don't forget to tell Isabella.

Scena quarta

PASQUELLA e GIGLIO *spagnuolo*.

GIGLIO: Por vida del rey, que esta es la vellacca di Pasquella que se burlò de mí y urtommi mis quentas per enganno. Oh como me huelgo de topalla!

PASQUELLA: Maladetto sia questo appoioso! Ben mi s'è dato testé tra' piei, che possi egli rompere il collo con quanti ne venne mai di Spagna! Che scusa trovarò ora?

GIGLIO: Signora Pasquella!

PASQUELLA: La cosa va bene. Io son già fatta signora.

GIGLIO: Vos me haveis burlado y mi tolleste mio rosario e non fazieste lo que me teniades promettido.

PASQUELLA: Zi! zi! zi! Sta' queto, sta' queto.

GIGLIO: Por que? es ninguno à qui que nos oda?

PASQUELLA: Zi! zi! zi!

GIGLIO: Io non veo à qui ninguno. Non m'engagnarete otra volta. Que dezite voi?

PASQUELLA: Tu mi vòi rovinare.

GIGLIO: Tu mi vòi ingagnare.

PASQUELLA: Va' via, lasciami stare adesso; ché ti parlarò otra volta.

GIGLIO: Renditeme mio rosario y despues parlate lo que volite, que non quiero que podiate dezir que m'engagnaste.

PASQUELLA: Tel darò. Credi ch'io l'abbi qui? Tu credi forse ch'io ne facci una grande stima? Mi mancarà delle corone, s'io ne vorrò!

GIGLIO: Por que m'enseraste de fuore y despues aziades musigas y diezieste non so que "Fantasmas, fantasmas" y non so que orazion y non so que traplas?

PASQUELLA: Di' piano. Tu mi vuoi rovinare. Ti dirò ogni cosa.

The Deceived

Scene 4

PASQUELLA *and* GIGLIO.

GIGLIO: *(Aside)* God's bones, it's that blasted Pasquella who tricked me and made off with my stuff. Am I ever glad to meet up with her!

PASQUELLA: *(Aside)* Not this pain up the royal, again. Just when I don't need him in my way. He and all his Spanish buddies can break their necks for all of me. So how do I get out of this one?

GIGLIO: Ah, milady Pasquella!

PASQUELLA: *(Aside)* Off to a good start. I'm already a lady.

GIGLIO: You've made off with my rosary by deceit, and you haven't kept your promise.

PASQUELLA: Hush, hush! Quiet! Quiet!

GIGLIO: How come? Is someone listening in?

PASQUELLA: Just hush, be totally silent.

GIGLIO: But there's no one here. You're not going to trick me again, so what's on your mind?

PASQUELLA: My reputation's on the line.

GIGLIO: You're having me on.

PASQUELLA: You've got to leave. Don't bother me now. I'll get back to you later.

GIGLIO: I just want my rosary. Then we can talk whenever. I just can't let you brag about tricking me.

PASQUELLA: Of course I'll give it to you. But do you suppose I have it on me now? You think it matters that much to me? There's no end to the rosaries I can have.

GIGLIO: So why lock the door on me, and do that singing, and reciting "Phantom, phantom" and all those other prayers and crap?

PASQUELLA: You have to shush. You could ruin my life. I'll explain.

GIGLIO: Que cosa? Que nol dezite?

PASQUELLA: Tírate piú in qua in questo canto, ché la padrona non vegga.

GIGLIO: Burlatime otra volta o no?

PASQUELLA: Ben sai ch'io ti burlo. Son forse avvezza a burlare, eh? Vero, eh?

GIGLIO: Hor dezite presto: que es esto?

PASQUELLA: Sai? Quando noi parlavamo insieme, Isabella, la mia padrona, era venuta giú pian piano e stava nascosta accanto a me e sentiva ogni cosa. Quando io volsi cacciare i polli, ella se n'andò in camera e da un buco stava a vedere quel che noi facevamo. Io, che me ne accorsi, feci vista di non l'aver veduta e d'averti voluto ingannare; tanto ch'io gli mostrai que' paternostri. Ella me gli tolse e, credendo che io t'avessi giontato, se ne rise e se gli messe al braccio. Ma io glie li torrò stasera e renderottegli, se tu non me gli vuoi aver dati.

GIGLIO: Y es verdade todo esto? Cata che non m'enganni.

PASQUELLA: Giglio mio, se non è vero, ch'io non ti possa piú mai vedere. Credi ch'io non abbi cara la tua amicizia? Ma voi spagnuoli non credete in Cristo, non che in altro.

GIGLIO: Hora, que non fazite quello que era concertado entra nos?

PASQUELLA: La mia padrona è maritata; e questa sera faciam le nozze; e ho da far tanto ch'io non posso attendere. Aspetta a un'altra volta. Uh come son rincrescevoli!

GIGLIO: Alla magnana, ah? Domattina, digo. Non es à si?

The Deceived

GIGLIO: Explain? Go on and tell me.

PASQUELLA: Come over this way, into the alcove, so my mistress can't see you.

GIGLIO: This is another trick of yours.

PASQUELLA: What makes you so sure? You take me for a deceiver? Is that all you can think of me?

GIGLIO: Just get it out fast, whatever you have to say.

PASQUELLA: Pay attention now. Remember when we were talking? Isabella came down and ever so silently hid herself near me, well within earshot of what we were saying. As I tried to shoo in my chickens, she went over to a room with a hole in the wall where she could see everything we were doing. But I caught on and pretended I didn't know she was there. I had to make out like I was deceiving you. After you'd left, I showed her the rosary. She was convinced that I'd conned you, took it away from me, started to laugh, and twisted it around her arm. But don't worry. If you don't want me to keep it, I'll get it off her tonight and return it.

GIGLIO: Really? You sure? Because you'd better not be lying to me.

PASQUELLA: If it's not the truth, may I never lay eyes on you again, my dearest Giglio. You think I don't prize our friendship? It's like you Spaniards. You don't believe in a thing, not even Christ.

GIGLIO: So let's do it now, what we agreed to earlier.

PASQUELLA: Oh, not right now. I can't because my mistress just got married, and tonight there'll be the festivities. What a lot of things I've got to get done. Just hang on for a bit longer. *(Aside)* Ugh, these Spaniards! What a botheration.

GIGLIO: Then how about tomorrow? Tomorrow morning. Agreed?

PASQUELLA: Lascia fare a me; ché mi ricorderò di te, quando sarà tempo; non dubitare. Uh! uh! uh! uhimene!

GIGLIO: Voto à Dios que te daré escuccilladas per la cara, se otra veze m'engannes.

Scena quinta

CITTINA *figliuola di Clemenzia balia, sola.*

Io non so che stripiccio sia drento a questa camara terrena. Io sento la lettiera fare un rimenio, un tentennare che pare che qualche spirito la dimeni. Uhimene! Io ho paura, io. Oh! Io sento uno che par si lamenti; e dice piano: "Aimè! non cosí forte". Oh! Io sento un che dice: "Vita mia, ben mio, speranza mia, moglie mia cara". Oh! Non posso intendere il resto: mi vien voglia di bussare. Oh! Dice uno: "Aspettami". Si debbono voler partire. Odi l'altro che dice: "Fa' presto tu ancora". Che sí che rompon quel letto? Uh! uh! uh! Come si rimena a fretta a fretta! In buona fica, ch'io lo voglio ire a dire alla mamma.

Scena sesta

ISABELLA, FABRIZIO e CLEMENZIA *balia.*

ISABELLA: Io credevo del certo che voi fusse un servitor di un cavalier di questa terra che tanto vi s'assomiglia che non può esser che non sia vostro fratello.

FABRIZIO: Altri sono stati oggi che m'hanno còlto in iscambio: tanto ch'io dubitavo quasi che l'oste non m'avesse scambiato.

ISABELLA: Ecco Clemenzia, la vostra balia, che vi debbe venire a far motto.

CLEMEZIA: Non può esser che non sia questo, ché par tutto Lelia. O Fabrizio, figliuol mio, che tu sia il ben tornato: che è di te?

The Deceived

PASQUELLA: Let me handle it. When the time is right, you'll be in my thoughts. Not to worry. *(Aside)* Pew, pew, pew, he's downright revolting. *(Exit)*

GIGLIO: You deceive me one more time and I vow to God I'll mess up your face.

Scene 5

CITTINA, *daughter of Clemenzia the nursemaid, alone.*

CITTINA: What a funny noise coming out of the room downstairs. The bed in there is thumping away like some ghost got into it. My gosh, this is really scary. Now there's this voice in a soft moan, warning, "Yes, yes, oh, not so hard!" And now, O my God, the other voice is saying, "My life, my bliss, my only hope, my dearest sweetie wife." Oh, and now I can't make out the rest. Maybe I should knock. Oh! One of them's saying "Hold up for me." They must be going somewhere. Now it's the other one saying, "No, no, you come too." I think they're about to break the bed. Oh, wow, the mattress is bouncing like crazy. By blessed Saint Cuntbert,[75] I'd better go tell mother.

Scene 6

ISABELLA, FABRIZIO, *and* CLEMEZIA.

ISABELLA: I mistook you for a servant to one of our knights. You resemble him so much you must be his brother.

FABRIZIO: Other people have made the same mistake today. Even the inn-keeper looked baffled.

ISABELLA: Here comes your nursemaid, Clemenzia. She'll certainly want to chat with you.

CLEMEZIA: *(Aside)* That's got to be him. He's Lelia's spitting image. — O Fabrizio, my beloved child, so good to see you home. How are things with you?

FABRIZIO: Bene, balia mia cara. Che è di Lelia?

CLEMEZIA: Bene, bene. Ma entriamo in casa, ché ho da parlare a longo con tutti voi.

Scena settima

VIRGINIO *e* CLEMENZIA.

VIRGINIO: Io ho tanta allegrezza d'aver trovato mio figliuolo ch'io son contento d'ogni cosa.

CLEMEZIA: Tutta è stata volontà di Dio. È stato pur meglio cosí che averla maritata a quel canna-vana di Gherardo. Ma lasciatemi intrar dento, ch'io vegga come la cosa sta: ch'io lasciai gli sposi molto stretti; e son soli. Venite, venite. Ogni cosa va bene.

Scena ottava

STRAGUALCIA *a li spettatori.*

Spettatori, non aspettate che costoro eschin piú fuore perché, di longa, faremmo la favola longhissima. Se volete venire a cena con esso noi, v'aspetto al "Matto". E portate denari, perché non v'è chi espedisca gratis. Ma, se non volete venire (che mi par di no), restativi e godete. E voi, Intronati, fate segno d'allegrezza.

■ ■ ■

The Deceived

FABRIZIO: Couldn't be better my dear nanny. How about Lelia?

CLEMEZIA: Fine, fine. But shall we go inside? There are so many things I have to tell you all.

Scene 7

VIRGINIO, CLEMEZIA, *and* STRAGUALCIA.

VIRGINIO: Now that my son's home, I'm not only happy, but satisfied with everything that's happened.

CLEMEZIA: All according to God's will. No question it's a better outcome than if you'd married your daughter to that dilapidated Gherardo. But I'm anxious to get back inside so I can keep up with everything that's going on. I've just left our bride and groom alone in a close cuddle. *(Enters and calls back)* — You can come in. Everything's fine in here. *(Virginio enters. Stragualcia remains.)*

Scene 8

STRAGUALCIA *and the Audience.*

STRAGUALCIA: All you in the audience, there's no sense waiting for them to come back out here, because this long story will get even longer if you do. But if you want to come to dinner with us, you'll find me over at the Jester. And don't forget your money, because nobody's paying for you. And if you don't feel like joining in, which seems to be the case, be happy and joyful anyway. And those of you in the Intronati's entourage, feel free to clap your hands.

■   ■   ■

Notes

The Italian text is based on the text in *Il teatro italiano*. Vol. 2, *La commedia del Cinquecento,* ed. Guido Davico Bonino (Turin: Einaudi, 1977), 87–183.

1. The speaker of the prologue refers to the entertainment presented by the Intronati on January 6, 1532, a little over a month before the performance of the present play. It was called *The Sacrifice*, in which each member of the Academy went up to an altar to burn some love relic and recite a poem renouncing love. This is more fully described in the Introduction, pp. xix–xx. The Prologue will establish the connection between the two plays, the second serving as an apology for the first and as a token of invitation to renew relations between the sexes in every sense of the term.

2. This kind of talk needs no glossing, but it does signal the degree to which the entire work is a kind of phallic celebration. Servants will get erections while watching others kissing and different intruders will witness the imposing dimensions of Fabrizio's masculinity ready for action while mistaking him for Lelia.

3. Theater historians could ask for a more ample description, but they can at least be certain that the play was acted among stage props undoubtedly representing a section of the city of Modena with all the houses and inns requisite to the action.

4. The word is "zucca," and amusingly the pumpkin was not only an allusion to the head, but an Intronati emblem in the form of a salt container with two crossed pestles placed on top.

5. The Fontebecci is one of the oldest fountains in the region, presumably dating to Roman times. It is far outside the city to the west at a crossroads leading from Florence to Rome and from Siena to Volterra.

6. When the army of the Holy Roman Empire defeated the French with whom Pope Clement VII had taken sides, 34,000 Imperial troops forced their commanders to let them sack the Vatican and the city of Rome to replace their long-overdue salaries. Along with the 6,000 Spaniards and 14,000 Germans, many Italians were involved, one division among them led by Cardinal Pompeo Colonna. Along the way, several other

cities were sacked, and the troops were joined by hundreds of bandits and thugs looking to enjoy the easy pickings. Within a day of their arrival on May 5, 1527, they had breached the walls of the city and began the bloodshed by executing 1000 of the Vatican guards. No parts of the city were spared from looting, including churches and palaces. The rape and theft continued for some eight months and left the city in shambles. The pope was compelled to pay an inordinately high ransom for his life as well as cede several papal territories. By the end, an egregious failure of leadership had been exposed on both sides, some 6,000 to 12,000 of the city's 55,000 citizens had been murdered, and the marauders themselves, when nothing was left to loot, began to starve for lack of food and perish from diseases contracted from the unburied corpses and the plague.

7. A modest sum for the occasion, perhaps, but ten gold scudi was the amount of an average annual income.

8. The Ghisilieri or Ghisleri were an old Bolognese family. The Cavalier da Casio, in all likelihood, is Girolamo Casio de' Pandolfi (1464–1533), a Bolognese merchant well-known at the time for his verses.

9. A convent of cloistered nuns named for San Crescenzio is more of the Intronati's phallic humor, for no Italian can miss the pun on *crescere* meaning to swell or become erect. Sister Amabile bears a name with rather more secular than sacred connotations, and when a manservant goes there looking for Lelia, the nuns solicit his sexual services quite openly.

10. The Tuscan poet is Giovanni Boccaccio in reference to the Preface to Day 4 in the *Decameron*. There he contradicts his critics by asserting that, in spite of his advancing years, he was still sexually potent.

11. The "dogs" were the Spanish soldiers, participants in the sack of Rome, who had taken Lelia prisoner, and who may have abused her — that point is never made clear.

12. Friars of the Convent of St. Francis. Apparently they were suspiciously friendly with the women — a contextual supposition. The establishment in mind, if it is in Modena, must be the church of San Francesco on the SW quarter of the city nearing the walls with its attached monastery. The church was begun in 1244 and completed in 1445, but it was entirely restructured in 1535, only three years after the play's first performance. The only point of interest with regard to the play

	has to do with its social history in the early sixteenth century, and the extent to which the friars were visited by citizens' wives.
13.	Twelfth Night is over and done, so the eve of the Befana has also passed. The Befana (the name perhaps derived from a mispronunciation of Epifania) is an old woman or witch figure who wanders the earth on the eve of Epiphany or Twelfth Night (Jan. 5) giving gifts to children. The custom is strongest in Rome and central Italy, and she is associated with several ancient legends. It is also Virginio's way of calling Clemenzia an old hag whose day for omens and muttering is over.
14.	Clemenzia has a very close relationship to Virginio and his family given that she was nursemaid to both his children, that is, she suckled them as infants, and there are fairly explicit indicators that she knew her boss intimately on occasion as well. She is protective of Lelia in a maternal way, and a separate scene is created for Fabrizio's reunion with her at the end of the play.
15.	Carlini are coins of small value.
16.	The name translates as Brother Onion and is doubtless a reference to Frate Cipolla in Boccaccio's *Decameron*, Day 4, Story 10.
17.	Count Guido Rangone, 1485–1539, served as a condottiere for differing political factions, thereby exposing those aligned with him to the political repercussions of those choices, whether on the imperial or the papal side. His family was Modenese where they had their palazzo near the Grand Canal, also mentioned in the play.
18.	The Carandini were a noble family based in Modena, allied with the papal party.
19.	Mirandola is a small town in the province of Modena some 20 miles to the northeast.
20.	Sister Amabile de'Cortesi has made her vows to a cloistered order. Hence the irony of her name signifying something like Sister Courtly Charm or Sister Cheerful Courtesy.
21.	This is the modern town of Rovarino in the province of Modena.
22.	She would plant a set of horns on his head, the sign of a cuckold — a man cheated on by his wife.

23. Spela is talking figuratively about Gherardo's ability to fulfil his wife's sexual needs in terms of depositing big or little coins into her purse.
24. Spela refashions Gherardo's behavior as outright lovesickness, provoking him to accuse his servant of treating him like Calendrino, the bubby character in four of Boccaccio's stories in the *Decameron* in which he is made the butt of his friends' jokes because of his gullibility.
25. See Virgil, *Eclogue* 10.l.69.
26. The Bazohara or Bazzovara Gate, which no longer stands, was once the southwestern entry to the city. It led to the piazza on the south side of the cathedral. (The Franciscan church discussed in note 10 was nearby.)
27. Spella, who is a low-lifer, offers a few malapropisms as he hunts for such literary terms as epistle, sonnets, and rhymes.
28. Bartolomeo Colleoni, 1400–1476, was a celebrated condottiere, best known for his long service to Venice. In the piazza outside the church of San Giovanni and Paolo there is a huge equestrian statue in his honor. Fathers who put their daughters in convents are deceived like the "great men" of Colleoni's time because they also placed their daughters in convents rather than let them run loose in the city.
29. Earlier translators might have left this in Italian, while modern editors are proud to show their worldly sophistication. If pressed clothing is the body in a double mangle, then it's a threesome. So says Guido Davico Bonino in his edition of *Gl'Ingannati*, in *Il teatro italiano, II*, "La commedia del Cinquecento" (Turin: Einaudi, 1977), 2:87–183, at 116, n. 11, in reference to *La Betia* V.343–46, or Ruzante. You cannot put it past the Intronati.
30. The Maremma, a rural region in southwestern Tuscany, epitomized rusticity and a lack of urbanity. References to it in Boccaccio expose the provincialism of the speaker, as in IV.2 and VI.6. It was swampy and malarial, and often used as a place of exile. But it did have wild horses, bred over time to become the Maremmano. This is a large and muscular animal, used for draft work in the past, but is today the horse of choice of the Italian Mounted Police.
31. See n. 19 above.
32. The gold scudo of 1532 was rather close in value to the florin or the Venetian ducat. Ten scudi was an average annual income at

that time. Hence, a thousand of them wished upon anyone was simply hyperbolical gratuitousness.

33. "Che! Son gentildonne, forse, di casa porcina, eh?" (What? They must be very fine ladies — maybe even from the House of Sows?) The casa porcina would be a house of ill repute, making syphilis or related diseases the risk mentioned by Giglio.

34. The famous image of Santa Maria of Montserrat is housed in the Benedictine monastery church on the mountain of that name near Barcelona, in Catalonia, Spain. It is a twelfth-century Romanesque statue of the Virgin (said to be much older) seated with the Christ child on her lap and the orb of the world in her right hand. Remarkably, she is black, and the statue once carried the inscription "Negra sum sed formosa" (I am black but beautiful). The image was and remains a much frequented pilgrimage destination.

35. Asafetida is a resinous gum used in medicines and herbal remedies, noted for its fetid smell of ammonia.

36. This slight detail actually establishes the time of the play's performance as the last day of Carnival in 1532, which would have been February 12.

37. This is his male leg, of course, and the original says "ready to vomit." The Intronati have these signs of virility on their minds, so every allusion counts.

38. The reference is to the bell tower in Siena called The Torre del Mangia (Tower of the Eater). The name is a reference to the first bell ringer, whose nickname was "Mangiaguadagni," meaning "he who eats all the profits." But the hyperbolical size comparison is to the tower itself, which was the second tallest in all of Italy at 102 meters. It stands next to the Palazzo Pubblico where the play was first performed.

39. The Rangoni Palace was located on the Grand Canal and once belonged to the Fogliani family. The honored guests at various times received there include Lorenzo de' Medici, Pope Leo X when he was still a cardinal, Cardinal Bibbiena, and the French king, Francis I. The cathedral of Modena, dedicated to the Assumption of the Virgin and the patron of the city, Saint Geminianus (buried in the crypt), was consecrated in 1184. The architecture was the work of Lanfranco, while the magnificent sculptures and reliefs on the exterior were designed by his contemporary, Wiligelmo. The church, with its famous

bell tower, stands at the very center of the city adjacent to the Piazza Grande.

40. The proverb means: "So you think you're the cat's pyjamas," or "hot stuff." But the origin of the Modenese proverb comes from a nude female bas relief once placed over the door of the cathedral displaying the genital region as though "strutting her wares." She is now in the Museum of the Opera of the Cathedral. But while the proverb is one thing, she is, in fact, a pagan fertility figure: a woman seated with her legs apart and her hands positioned to emphasize her sex as a pre-Christian symbol of fecundity, motherhood, and the continuity of life for her entire community. See Bonino, *Gl'Ingannati*, 136, n. 2.

41. To lead a bear to Modena was an ancient proverb applicable to anyone so foolish as to engage in an enterprise that could only bring harm or injury.

42. Cantalicius is Giovanni Battista Valentini, who was born in Cantalice, c.1450, and died in Rome in 1515. He was a grammarian and humanist, who taught extensively throughout Tuscany and lived for a time after 1476 in Siena where he wrote his *Rheatina: pro defensione senensius*. He was named bishop by Julius II in 1503.

43. This quotation has been traced by Nerida Newbegin to Terence's play, *Eunuch*, l.519: "My mind's been on my saucepans for ages."

44. The trivella is a drill which, according to legend, was used to find water by Modena's first settlers.

45. The play's sightseers are in the vicinity of the cathedral, which would associate the quip about a large phallic shadow with the famous belltower, the Ghirlandina, to which the Modenese assigned universal magnificence. This leaning monster was named for the balustrades at the top of the octagonal Gothic cusp, which crowns the five-story Romanesque base. The tower was completed in 1319, standing at just over 86 meters. That it had an appeal to the phallic imagination, whether male or female, is potentially perplexing. But if such a popular notion existed among the "mad" folk of Modena in the sixteenth century, it must be honored. Historical validation, however, is pending. Ironically, during the renovations to the tower early in this century, the structure actually was enveloped in a huge and costly painted cover around the scaffolding. It got its sheath almost five centuries later.

Notes

46. The names of the inns are the Jester, with an allusion to the Joker on the playing card, and the Mirror, with a possible allusion to Cato and the need for self-knowledge. They have not been historically identified, although they may have been suggested by two historical inns, the Pellegrino and the Tre Re situated on the Contrada dei Tre Re in Modena.

47. This Socratic sentence was included in the *Distica Catonis,* a collection of moral maxims wrongly attributed to Cato the Elder.

48. All these unflattering regional stereotypes with their matching inns would have raised considerable laughter. All manner of Italians were welcomed at the Mirror and Jester, although the Neapolitans might stay at the Amore. That the Florentines, who were not well disposed towards the Sienese after the return of the Medici to power in 1529, lodged at the Jester Inn surely carried political overtones. But xenophobia sets in when it comes to the Germans, who stay at the Swine, and the Spanish who stay at the Crook. The Sienese are said to be so like the Modenese, namely crazy, that they never stay at inns, but enjoy the hospitality of the locals.

49. Alfonso Piccolomini, captain of the people of Siena and formerly a general in the army of Charles V.

50. By inference from the original *rampino,* meaning a grappling-hook, used by Spanish marauders or pirates to fasten onto and board captured vessels.

51. The sympathy between these two citizenries suggests that the madness of the Modenese must apply equally to the Sienese.

52. Pedants, at least those in the traditions of comedy, were generally associated with pederasty. Stragualcia uses the pedant's love for boys to settle the choice of an inn. The Pedant's response shows no resistance to such an assessment, here, but the two of them will argue violently over the matter later on. Pederasty was also a serious crime.

53. This comic name might be translated into English as Sister Gossipy Tattle-Tale.

54. By way of clarification, the old men take Fabrizio for Lelia, and to hear that she has once more been in the camp of the Spanish soldiers, as she was following the Sack of Rome, they're convinced beyond all doubt that she has been sexually violated,

and that what's done is final, making her ruined and virtually unmarriageable.

55. This is Francesco Maria Molza, a poet who was born in Modena in 1489 and died there in 1544 (of syphilis). The account he gives of a woman who mistook herself for a clay pot and was fearful of being broken no doubt originated in the medical literature on the diseases of the imagination and of melancholy. Case studies of patients tell of just such amazing delusions and the tricks used by physicians to shock them out of their pathological obsessions. Molza was a man with near delusions of his own in going off to Rome to cultivate amorous obsessions with the women of the city to inspire his muse. His decadent pursuits became legendary. This is the same Molza to whom one modern scholar attributed the authorship of this play, but the theory is not widely espoused. See the Introduction, xviii.

56. The brothers of Melchizedek are the followers of this mystical king and priest, the first to be so named in the Book of Genesis. This priestly line became important to Christians because Jesus was said to be "a priest in the order of Melchizedek" (Hebrews 7.13–17). But the doctrine remains esoteric, even for Christians, giving the name overtones of things ancient and secretive.

57. Penelope is the loyal and devoted wife of Odysseus who resisted suitors for some twenty years while waiting for his return, weaving and unweaving her tapestries. Her story is told in Homer's *Odyssey*.

58. This is brutal talk, because it is an allusion to the Pedant's proclivity for sodomy, which was, in many jurisdictions, punishable by burning.

59. The nobility of the Maremma is entirely ironic insofar as the area is known as an empty and underpopulated area of pampas, malarial swamps, and dullard rustics. Boccaccio, in *Decameron* 4.2, will use the backward and impoverished Maremma to epitomize the entire world.

60. Of "cuius masculini," the Pedant points out merely that it is bad Latin and can hardly be glossed, but it carries overtones, again, of the Pedant's questionable manliness and sexual tastes. It is used as an insult, and they are getting nastier.

61. Petrarch, *Canzoniere* 7.10.

Notes

62. Horace, *Epistles* 2.1.116: "Blacksmiths do what blacksmiths do."
63. Virgil, *Eclogues* 3.7. Damoetas is speaking to Menalcas, warning him that reproaching other people should be done with great care. The Pedant uses the quotation to tell Gherardo not to treat him with such suspicion.
64. Jacopo V of Appiano, lord of the state of Piombino, a commune on the Tuscan coast near Livorno.
65. The modern Correggio, a small town in the province of Reggio Emilia.
66. Virgil, *Aeneid* 2.274–75.
67. Virgil, *Aeneid* 1.204.
68. The "Phantom" prayer is from Boccaccio's *Decameron* (7.1). A wife, with her lover at the door knocking, convinces her husband that it's a phantom or bogeyman, and then improvises her prayer to make her husband think she's expelling a ghost when, in fact, she's telling her lover through the door to go away. Pasquella modifies it to tell Giglio at the door that if he came with an erected spirit, he's going away with one, too — more of the play's phallic humor.
69. A Marrano is a converted Jew who continues to practice Judaism in secret. In Spain and Portugal, such people were closely scrutinized by the Inquisition. Hence, calling a pureblooded Spaniard by this name would be a serious insult. Were Giglio a conversos, he would have had to learn all the rites and prayers of the Roman Catholic Church.
70. This exchange provides a modest hint that the stage setting offered more than a backdrop. Clemenzia replies from an upstairs window before offering to come down, suggesting some form of constructed house property — a house with at least two floors and a door enabling entries and exits.
71. This is a subtle moment. For Clemenzia, Fabio is called down as the girl in her story. But Flamminio takes the call for Fabio at face value, thus delaying the discovery of Lelia until he actually sees her beneath the mask and realizes how deceived he had been all along.
72. Here is another clue about the stage set. Virginio stated earlier that Lelia couldn't be taken back to his house in her enraged state without being seen by the whole city and hence should be taken to Gherardo's, whereas here, Clemenzia's house is close enough to Gherardo's to be within speaking distance.

73. "A lazy pig never eats rotten apples" is proverbial: A wise person always brings his or her business to a successful conclusion, presumably in reference here to Isabella, who grabbed a good thing when it came her way without putting any effort into it. Proverbs always require an appropriate "mapping" upon the intended subject, and the subtle reader might want to explore alternate mappings of the pig and the apples in this context.

74. What an unexpected convenience for the play, that a servant like Crivello should also be a notary and have his diploma in his pocket! But however unlikely, he is as good a witness as any to confirm the vows of two lovers and thereby authorize the plighted troth that constitutes a marriage. Legally, a notary is not required.

75. The original wordplay is on "in buona fede" (in good faith) mispronounced as "fica," creating a malapropism by replacing faith with twot or cunt — accidently by the speaker, but quite intentionally by the Intronati.

■ ■ ■

Renaissance and Modern Plays from Itaica Press

Aminta by Torquato Tasso. Translated & edited by Charles Jernigan & Irene Marchegiani Jones. Dual-language edition.

The Scruffy Scoundrels (Gli Straccioni), by Annibal Caro. Translated & edited by Donald Beecher & Massimo Ciavolella. Dual-language edition.

Phyllis of Scyros (Filli di Sciro) by Guidubaldo Bonarelli. Edited & translated by Nicolas J. Perella. Dual-language edition.

Six Characters in Search of an Author (Sei personaggi in cerca d'autore) by Luigi Pirandello. A new translation by Martha Witt & Mary Ann Frese Witt.

Henry IV (Enrico IV) by Luigi Pirandello. A new translation by Martha Witt & Mary Ann Frese Witt

Watching the Moon and Other Plays by Massimo Bontempelli. Translated by Patricia Gaborik. Includes *Watching the Moon (La guardia alla luna)*, *Stormcloud (Nembo)*, and *Cinderella (Cenerentola)*.

■   ■   ■

*This Book Was Completed on 9 December 2017
At Italica Press, New York. It Is
Set in Adobe Garamond
And Printed on
Acid-Free
Paper.*

■

www.ingramcontent.com/pod-product-compliance
Lightning Source LLC
Chambersburg PA
CBHW022054160426
43198CB00008B/230